D1488251

The Misunderstood Mission of Jean Nicolet

THE MISUNDERSTOOD MISSION
OF JEAN NICOLET

Uncovering the Story of the 1634 Journey

PATRICK J. JUNG

WISCONSIN HISTORICAL SOCIETY PRESS

Published by the Wisconsin Historical Society Press
Publishers since 1855

The Wisconsin Historical Society helps people connect to the past by collecting, pre-serving, and sharing stories. Founded in 1846, the Society is one of the nation's finest historical institutions.
Join the Wisconsin Historical Society: wisconsinhistory.org/membership

Photographs identified with WHI or WHS are from the Society's collections; address requests to reproduce these photos to the Visual Materials Archivist at the Wisconsin Historical Society, 816 State Street, Madison, WI 53706.

The silhouettes on the front cover are based on statues of Samuel de Champlain and Jean Nicolet located in Plattsburg, New York, and Red Banks, Wisconsin, respectively. On the front flap is *The Landfall of Jean Nicolet*, WHI Image ID 1870.

Printed in Canada
Cover design by TG Design
Typesetting by Integrated Composition Systems
22   21   20   19   18   1   2   3   4   5

Library of Congress Cataloging-in-Publication Data
Names: Jung, Patrick J., 1963– author.
Title: The misunderstood mission of Jean Nicolet : uncovering the story of the 1634 journey / Patrick J. Jung.
Description: Madison WI : Wisconsin Historical Society Press, [2018] | Includes bibliographical references and index. |
Identifiers: LCCN 2018011945 (print) | LCCN 2018013590 (e-book) |
    ISBN 9780870208805 (e-book) | ISBN 9780870208799 (hardcover : alk. paper)
Subjects: LCSH: Nicollet, Jean, 1598–1642. | Canada—History—To 1763 (New France) | Champlain, Samuel de, 1574–1635 | Wisconsin—Discovery and exploration. | Explorers—France—Biography.
Classification: LCC F1030.15 (e-book) | LCC F1030.15.J86 2018 (print) |
    DDC 910.92—dc23
LC record available at https://lccn.loc.gov/2018011945

♾ The paper used in this publication meets the minimum requirements of the American National Standard for Information Sciences—Permanence of Paper for Printed Library Materials, ANSI Z39.48–1992.

For Nancy Oestreich Lurie,
whose excellence as a scholar made this story possible.

CONTENTS

New France in the age of Champlain and Nicolet. MAP BY RICK REGAZZI

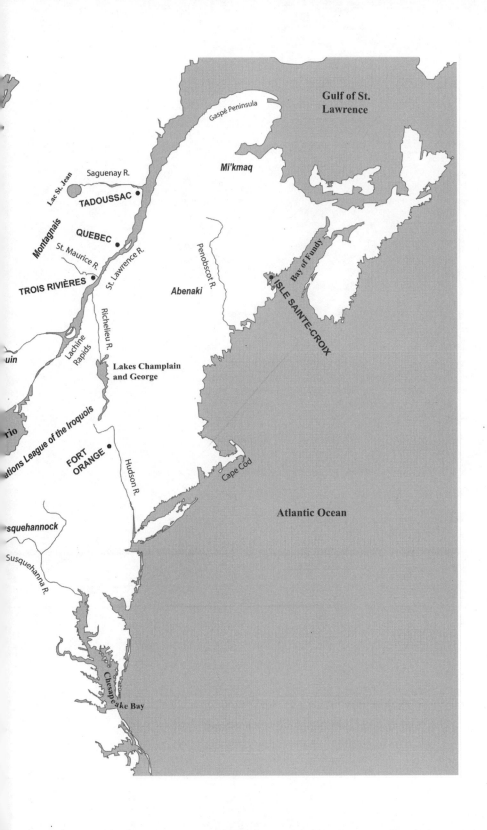

Introduction

The story of Jean Nicolet figures heavily into the early history of Wisconsin. For many years, Wisconsin schoolchildren learned the story of how, in 1634, Nicolet arrived at Green Bay believing he had discovered the Northwest Passage, the elusive waterway through North America that would provide Europeans with a route to Asia and the riches of the Kingdom of Cathay, or China. According to this oft-told chronicle, Nicolet was one in a long line of explorers who, since the time of Christopher Columbus, had risked life and limb in pursuit of this sublime dream. After traveling hundreds of miles by canoe across Lakes Huron and Michigan, Nicolet donned a richly embroidered Chinese robe for the occasion of his arrival, but, of course, he did not meet the powerful mandarins who represented the Ming emperor. He met American Indians, particularly the Puans (also known as the Winnebagos), one of the groups that constituted Wisconsin's aboriginal inhabitants, and Natives who, in Nicolet's eyes, probably did not seem very different from those with whom he lived on the eastern shores of Lake Huron. Nicolet demonstrated the might of his pistols. The Indians who assembled by the thousands honored him with great feasts of roasted beaver. He was disappointed, perhaps even crestfallen, when he realized that he had not reached the fabled wealth of the Far East.

This narrative is almost always accompanied by visual images—paintings in particular—that depict Nicolet as appearing a bit foolish for believing he had made landfall in China when, in fact, he was only in present-day Wisconsin. I had seen these images and read this story in the social studies book I possessed as a child when, during the 1973–1974 school year, I attended the fourth grade at 81st Street School in Milwaukee. Later I learned—as an academic historian passing from young adulthood into middle age and after many years of research into the history of Indian–white relations in the Great Lakes region—that much of this story, from beginning to end, is patently false. I also learned the true story is richer, more interesting, and more complicated than that which historians have presented over the past one hundred fifty years.

Nicolet told the story of his journey several times before his death in 1642 and perceived it to be one of the highlights of his career in the colony of New France, which in Nicolet's time consisted of little more than the small settlement at Quebec and a trade network and missionary stations that stretched northward into the Canadian Shield and westward into Lake Huron. The Jesuit missionaries to whom he related the account of his expedition documented its principal events. However, in the annual publications known as the *Relations* that recounted their activities in North America, the Jesuit missionaries did not provide as much detail concerning Nicolet's journey as the modern researcher would desire. These vague, often ambiguous texts have been the principal culprits that have allowed earlier Nicolet scholars to insert any number of factual errors, poorly supported conclusions, and even outright fabrications into their analyses. Nevertheless, the historical record contains enough information to discern the purpose of Nicolet's mission and the context in which it occurred. In addition, the itinerary, route, and significant events of the journey can be determined through a meticulous reading of the extant sources. Reconstructing the particulars of Nicolet's mission is largely an academic exercise but one that scholars have generally botched over the past century and a half.

As I conducted my research, I discovered earlier historians as well as scholars up to the present day have consistently described Nicolet primarily as an explorer; this is incorrect. His expedition to Green Bay was, in one sense, a voyage of discovery, as he was the first Frenchman to visit the region. Yet, it was the only such voyage Nicolet undertook. In his career prior to and after his 1634 voyage, he had served in other capacities. After arriving in New France in 1619, Nicolet worked as an interpreter between the various tribes and the French trading companies with which the Indians exchanged peltries for goods of European manufacture. He also traded with the Indians on his own account and later assisted the Jesuit missionaries as a lay evangelist. Of great importance was his role as a diplomat to the Indian nations per the orders of Samuel de Champlain, the commander of the colony, and Champlain's successor, Charles Huault de Montmagny. Nicolet had participated in no journeys of exploration before 1634. The same was true of his career after his 1634 voyage and up to his death, a period during which he served as an interpreter at Trois-Rivières in Quebec.

Most significantly, his voyage to Green Bay was a diplomatic mission, not a voyage of discovery. I learned, contrary to established belief, Nicolet was not seeking a water route to China, nor was his principal duty the acquisition of geographical information about the Great Lakes. His primary mission—in fact, his only objective—was to negotiate peace between New France's Indian allies and the Puans at Green Bay. Any other duties he performed were subordinated to this overarching task. Thus, Nicolet was not really a great explorer; he was, on the other hand, a great diplomat to the Indians during his years of service in New France.

Presenting this interpretation of Nicolet's journey first requires examining his superior, Samuel de Champlain. In fact, I present more information about Champlain than I do about Nicolet. This emphasis is unavoidable and necessary. A much larger amount of documentation exists about Champlain than about his subordinate, and, most important, we cannot fully understand Nicolet as a historical figure unless we first examine Champlain. Much of what Nicolet did as an ambassador to the Indians, particularly his 1634 diplomatic mission to the Puans, seems at first glance to be ill defined and unknowable because of the paucity of sources. On the other hand, Champlain's well-documented career offers important insights into Nicolet. Much of what Champlain did as an explorer and colonial administrator charged with maintaining relations with the Indian societies of New France—the actions he took and the methods he employed—were strikingly similar to those performed by Nicolet during the course of his journey to Green Bay. Champlain was particularly concerned with the threat posed by the Five Nations League of the Iroquois to those tribes allied with the French. His efforts to subdue the Iroquois, either through diplomacy or force of arms, bear a strong resemblance to those of Nicolet with the Puans. Thus, Champlain's story provides a window that illuminates the ambiguous sources concerning his protégé. Such an examination of the life and career of Samuel de Champlain has been sorely lacking in earlier studies of Jean Nicolet. This oversight, in my view, has been detrimental to our understanding of both men.

I also examine the history of the search for the Northwest Passage, another subject that has been either absent or insufficiently addressed in other works. Doing so achieves another goal I have for this book, namely, to put Nicolet's story into a transnational context. Transnational history examines the multifaceted connections between discrete cultural and political entities over space and time, be they empires, nation-states, or tribal communities. Transnational history, according to one scholar, "may be defined as the study of movements and forces that cut across national boundaries."[1] Certainly, the search for the Northwest Passage fits this definition, as it was a centuries-long, supranational project by the Spanish, Portuguese, Italians, English, French, Dutch, and later the Canadians and Americans to bridge the earth's vast geographical distances and create a more tightly knit global community.

Champlain searched for the Northwest Passage early in his career but later turned his attention to creating strong commercial, political, and diplomatic ties with the Indian tribes of northeastern North America. The complex alliances and intense rivalries the various tribal societies developed with not only the European colonizers but also other Native communities were, in the truest sense, transnational phenomena in their own right. As Allan Greer, a preeminent scholar of early French North America, has observed, New France during the era of Jean Nicolet was "a dynamic zone of contact and colonization; it was an expansive colonial system, constructed jointly by French and Native peoples."[2] This jointly constructed zone defined Jean Nicolet's career; his diplomatic mission to the Puans also sought to shape it. Nicolet may not have been searching for the Northwest Passage, but his life in New France was a product of many of the same forces that had brought about this vast undertaking; these forces brought Europeans and the Indians of North America into contact before and after his life in the colony of New France. Just as we must first understand Samuel de Champlain to illuminate the career of Jean Nicolet, we must also discern the complex world in which Nicolet lived: a world created mutually by the French and Indians in the Great Lakes region.

Finally, Nicolet's mission occurred during a critical period. At the time of his journey, the English had only recently restored New France to the French after a three-year occupation from 1629 to 1632. The

Iroquois, who since the earliest days of the colony had posed a threat to the French and their Indian allies, became a more serious peril in the early 1630s. The Puans, although a great distance from the western frontiers of New France, became yet another force with which the French had to reckon. Earlier historians, as mentioned, have often fixated on Champlain's desire to find the Northwest Passage. However, by the time of Nicolet's journey, Champlain almost certainly doubted such a route could be found through the Great Lakes. Additionally, Champlain had much greater concerns in 1634, particularly securing the colony and its Native allies from attacks by powerful Indian enemies to the south and west: the Iroquois and Puans, respectively. Simply stated, Champlain did not have the luxury in 1634 to send Nicolet on a journey to find a waterway he no longer believed existed via the Great Lakes. Thus, if we want to understand Jean Nicolet's expedition, it is crucial we examine the evolution of Champlain's thought concerning the geography of North America, his shift from seeking the Northwest Passage to building a stable trade network with the Native communities, and his closely related goal of securing New France after the restoration of the colony in 1632.

—‖—

The genesis of this book lay in the research and writing of another work on Jean Nicolet that I published several years ago with the late Dr. Nancy Oestreich Lurie, formerly an anthropologist at the Milwaukee Public Museum and a prodigious scholar. I would be remiss if I did not emphatically state that much of the new information concerning Jean Nicolet was largely the product of Nancy's many years of patient and copious research not only into the semi-mythical historical figure of Nicolet but also into the history and culture of the Ho-Chunk Indians, the descendants of the Puans. Much of what we wrote reflected Nancy's research into the ethnographic and archaeological data concerning the Ho-Chunks and their Puans ancestors.[3] While we presented some of the new material I had discovered about Samuel de Champlain, constraints forced us to tell much of that story in an abbreviated manner.

In addition to examining the importance of Champlain's influence upon the 1634 voyage, I have sought to relate the saga of Nicolet in a narrative form that appeals to the general reader. This is not the first attempt to write such history; in 1881, Consul W. Butterfield undertook a similar project when he published *History of the Discovery of the Northwest by Jean Nicolet in 1634*. However, Butterfield was one of the many early chroniclers who either repeated spurious conclusions or put forth their own fanciful suppositions that had no basis in fact. For example, Butterfield asserted Nicolet's principal purpose in making his 1634 journey was "solving the problem of a near route to China" and, expecting that "a party of mandarins would soon greet him," Nicolet wore "a large garment of Chinese damask."[4] Nicolet and Champlain were not so geographically naive as to suppose a water route to the Pacific Ocean existed by way of the Great Lakes; nor did Nicolet wear a Chinese robe, as Butterfield and others supposed, in preparation for meeting the ambassadors of the Ming emperor. These were just two of the many factual blunders later researchers had uncritically repeated to the point they became rock-solid dogmas. Not surprisingly, these errors even found their way into murals and paintings, historical markers, and elementary school social studies textbooks (including the book I used as a child in the fourth grade).[5]

When I started writing this book, I wanted to avoid detailed examinations of other scholars' work and instead produce a smooth-flowing, chronological narrative. As I continued to write, I realized the impossibility of completely omitting such analyses, given the limited primary source material and the need to discuss how best to interpret it. Nevertheless, I have endeavored to limit such examinations to a minimum. I believe I have crafted the graceful narrative I originally sought, although the reader will notice those sections where I stop and examine the various arguments previous scholars have proffered about Jean Nicolet and the Native communities with which he made contact. The historical record simply has too many gaps to do otherwise. Trying to present this story as though it were based on unassailable facts would be misleading. I have endeavored to present my critiques of earlier historical interpretations in an easily discernible manner that will allow the reader to see how past scholars have mishandled the various sources that record Nicolet's story. Eliminating wrong answers in historical research is equally as important as presenting correct conclusions. I hope the reader will not see these digressions as cumbersome interruptions but instead as interesting interludes that make the remainder of the narrative more informative and enjoyable.

Correcting previous errors concerning Nicolet does not strip away the mystique surrounding him. In fact, Nicolet's story becomes even more intriguing when we realize he did not seek a passage to China through the Great Lakes but nevertheless spent one to two months traveling by canoe into the interior of North America to regions never before seen by a European. The physical stamina, immense courage, and sheer tenacity such a feat required are in themselves important components of a compelling narrative. Furthermore, Nicolet went westward to meet a powerful tribe with a fearsome reputation to conclude a treaty of peace. He had no guarantee he would succeed in this endeavor, and he must have known he might not survive or return to the colony of New France. The danger and uncertainty he faced in carrying out his mission, and the fact he succeeded despite the odds, make for a more awe-inspiring story than do fictional accounts of Chinese robes and water routes to China via Lake Michigan. For these reasons, Nicolet deserves a more accurate picture painted of his colorful career as an interpreter and diplomat in the service of his king and commander in the vast region of North America known in his time as Nouvelle France.

—I⊢—

A discussion of terminology is in order. The Indian tribes of North America have been known by a bewildering array of names produced by an equally rich number of languages. The French called the ancestors of Wisconsin's contemporary Ho-Chunk people *Puans* (sometimes spelled *Puants*), or "Stinkards," which was a rough translation of the Algonquian term *Ounipigou*. This translates as "People of the Stinking Water" and is rendered into English as Winnebago. These terms had nothing to do with their hygiene but originated from the fact the Puans lived near the malodorous waters of Green Bay. In most historical sources, both the Puans of Nicolet's day and their later Ho-Chunk progeny are called the Winnebagos. However, we have no idea what the Puans called themselves. The French Jesuit Pierre-François-Xavier de Charlevoix, in 1721, was the first person known to use the word *Ho-Chunk*, which is an anglicized version of *Hocank* or *Hotcangara*. In their own tongue, which is part of the Chiwere-Siouan language group, Ho-Chunk means "People of the Big Voice" and signifies that other Chiwere-Siouan speakers, such as the Iowa,

Missouria, and Oto tribes, claim descent from the Ho-Chunks. However, this term likely came into use long after Nicolet's 1634 visit, so it would be ahistorical and anachronistic to call the people of his time the Ho-Chunks. The Puans suffered a calamitous decline in population after a destructive war with the Illinois Confederacy in the 1640s. The Ho-Chunks who arose from the remnants of the earlier Puans society had, in many ways, a significantly different culture. The Puans of Nicolet's time likely were matrilineal and reckoned descent and inheritance through the female line. They also lived in densely populated, sedentary villages. The later Ho-Chunks, emerging as they did with the advent of the French fur trade in the western Great Lakes, lived in smaller, more mobile villages based on patrilineal descent where clan affiliation was inherited through the male line.[6] Given these facts, it would be inaccurate to call the people whom Nicolet visited either the Ho-Chunks or the Winnebagos. Thus, the term used throughout this text for the Ho-Chunks' ancestors is *Puans* unless quoting from a source that uses an alternative appellation.

In many cases, references are made in the text to the later Ho-Chunk people, particularly when discussing their oral traditions that refer to the earlier Puans. Today, the descendants of the Puans who reside in Wisconsin use the name Ho-Chunk, while their kin who moved to Nebraska during the nineteenth century continue to use the name Winnebago. This serves to illustrate to the reader the complexity of this issue and the fact that historians have no simple solutions to the problem of what name to use for the people whom Nicolet met at Green Bay in 1634. In fact, this is the first written work that uses *Puans* to refer to the early seventeenth-century ancestors of today's Ho-Chunk and Winnebago people in Wisconsin and Nebraska respectively. It is hoped future scholars will continue to employ this convention for the sake of accuracy.

Other Indian societies are referred to by their most common historical names and include the Ottawas, Hurons, and Menominees. In all cases, the singular form of a tribal name is used when discussing individuals or when using the word as an adjective. Following contemporary convention, the plural form is used when discussing more than one member of a tribe. In the case of the Montagnais, Iroquois, and Puans (all of whose names are of French derivation), the same word is used for both the singular and plural. Also following current practice, *Algonquin* refers to the Indians who lived in the Ottawa River valley in Nicolet's time, while *Algonquian* refers to those tribes, including the Algonquins, that spoke languages and dialects of the Algonquian language family. *Iroquois* refers to those tribes that belonged to the Five Nations League of the Iroquois. Also in accordance with current convention, the Indians Jacques Cartier encountered in the 1530s and 1540s who were linguistically related to the tribes of the Five Nations League are referred to as the St. Lawrence Iroquoians. *Iroquoian*, on the other hand, refers to tribes that spoke related languages and dialects within the Iroquoian language family, such as those of the Five Nations League, the St. Lawrence Iroquoians, the Hurons, the Petuns, and the Neutrals.[7]

A final discussion also is in order. Members of the general public may be surprised by the often violent practices of the early seventeenth-century French and the Native peoples in northeastern North America with whom they made contact. While historians, cultural anthropologists, and archaeologists have long known about these customs, such traditions may seem strange and even disturbing to the average reader. Both cultures, for example, practiced public torture and execution, although their reasons for doing so differed significantly. Examinations of these cultural conventions are included in this text not for gratuitous shock value; instead, they illustrate the great dissimilarities between our world and that which existed four centuries ago. It was a world seemingly more brutal than our own, although the people of that world would undoubtedly find much of what we consider acceptable in the twenty-first century to be inscrutable and even scandalous. Thus, we must suspend judgment when examining historical cultures, whether they were European or American Indian. Moreover, discerning the historical figure known as Jean Nicolet requires that we fully understand his world and his time. Doing so reveals a sublime tapestry that evokes various emotions in the contemporary reader: admiration, amazement, astonishment, and sometimes alarm. By understanding these historic cultures, we achieve a greater appreciation for the past and a more accurate knowledge concerning the generations that preceded our own. In the process, we also come to a better awareness of ourselves and the world in which we live.

1

The Search for the Northwest Passage

1524–1602

We know little about the early life of Jean Nicolet de Belleborne (also spelled Nicollet). He was born in Normandy, probably at Cherbourg, in 1598. His father, Thomas, was a royal postal courier between Cherbourg and Paris. His mother was Marguerite de Lamer, although some sources list her name as Marie. Their son must have received a superior education for his day because he was literate and able to write. Jean Nicolet arrived in the North American colony of New France in 1619, although one Jesuit biographer mistakenly recorded the year as 1618. Evidence for the later date comes from a bill of sale that records Nicolet's presence at a transaction where he sold a parcel of land in Hainneville near Cherbourg in May 1619. The fact the family had land to sell provides further evidence of his social station, for Nicolet and his family were members of France's burgeoning and socially conscious bourgeoisie, or middle class; his father claimed the status of bourgeois in at least one document. Unlike the nobility, whose status depended upon birth, the bourgeoisie gained its status through education and employment as artisans and merchants in the emerging capitalist economy. The legal profession and government service (as in Thomas's case) also provided paths to bourgeois status, and Jean Nicolet thoroughly absorbed his father's values. He had two brothers, Gilles and Pierre, who spent time in Canada during their brother's residence there. Documents in France provide the names of two other brothers and two sisters. He may have had more siblings, but the records suffer many gaps.[1]

While we know only the sketchiest details about Nicolet's life in France, more information is available regarding his activities in New France thanks to the writings of two missionaries who documented the principal events of his career. However, even here we have just the barest scraps of information recorded by the Jesuit priests Paul Le Jeune and Barthélemy Vimont, both of whose narratives yield only eight printed pages about Nicolet. Scattered references to Nicolet also appear in the writings of other Jesuits.[2] Le Jeune's and Vimont's narratives, particularly those passages that describe Nicolet's journey, are often so vague it is seemingly impossible to discern with any degree of certainty the route he traveled, his final destination, the tribal affiliations of the Indians he met, or what he did during the course of his visit. Therefore, it should not surprise the contemporary reader that debate continues to rage among historians, anthropologists, and archaeologists over the basic facts of Nicolet's 1634 mission.[3] Nevertheless, with patience, we can penetrate the veil of almost four centuries that shrouds our understanding of Jean Nicolet.

Lifting this veil requires examining both the forces that brought the French to North America and the Indian societies with which they made contact. The French were relative latecomers to Europe's Age of Exploration. Bartolomé Dias rounded the southern tip of Africa in 1488 and paved the way for another Portuguese explorer, Vasco da Gama, to reach India in 1498. Christopher Columbus, sailing between 1492 and 1504, hoped to bypass Portugal's circum-Africa route by sailing westward from Europe to secure Asia's riches for Spain. While he died thinking he had reached the East Indies, Columbus had, instead, brought knowledge of the West Indies and Central and South America to Europe and secured for the Spanish their initial claims to these vast domains. The French had little choice but to explore northward of the lands claimed by Spain and in doing so confirmed the existence of yet another continent, North America, which they hoped would offer some passage to the Pacific Ocean and the rich trade with Asia. In the process of searching for this Northwest Passage, the French encountered Native societies with which they developed relationships that ranged from alliance to war. Like their Spanish

counterparts, the French realized the Americas possessed natural resources that would allow them to amass great wealth until such a passage
could be found.[4] The resident Indian tribes, on the other hand, had their
own complex societies as well as alliances and rivalries that predated the
arrival of the French. North America provided the French many potential
opportunities; their presence on the continent afforded Native societies
both prospects and perils.

The idea of the Northwest Passage emerged in part from the fact
Europeans had mapped the contours of South America earlier than its
hemispheric counterpart. Many Europeans in the sixteenth century understood North America to be small, dispersed islands, and some denied
its very existence into the 1530s. Spanish explorers slowly developed an
understanding of the coastal areas of the Gulf of Mexico from the Yucatan
Peninsula to Florida by 1520. The French king François I decided France
should enter the fray lest it be denied its share of the theoretically lucrative but as-yet undeveloped Asian trade by sailing west. In 1523, he commissioned Giovanni da Verrazzano of Florence to locate a passage to Asia
north of the Spanish possessions. In January 1524, Verrazzano sighted
Cape Fear, North Carolina, and mistook the expanse of water beyond the
long, narrow islands he encountered to be the Pacific Ocean. The fact that
Vasco Núñez de Balboa had crossed the Panama Isthmus in 1513 and
became the first European to set his eyes upon the Pacific by traveling
westward undoubtedly influenced Verrazzano's thinking. In fact, what
Verrazzano saw was Pamlico Sound beyond North Carolina's Outer
Banks. He continued his investigation of the coast up through New
England and north to Nova Scotia. In the process, Verrazzano filled in
the gaps of Europeans' geographical knowledge of what lay between
Newfoundland (explored earlier for the English by John Cabot) and the
Spanish and Portuguese domains that stretched from Florida to the
Straits of Magellan. His most significant contribution was affirming
North America was a separate continent and not connected to Asia re-
gardless of Cabot's claims to the contrary. While some stubborn cartog-
raphers would continue, for the next two hundred years, to depict North
America and northeastern Asia as a contiguous landmass, the best geo-
graphic minds of the age knew better.[5] These minds later included Samuel
de Champlain.

Verrazzano tried to convince his king that colonizing these new lands would be a fruitful venture, but François I was more interested in making war against the Habsburg monarch Charles V, ruler of the Holy Roman Empire and king of Spain. This turned out to be a rather poor decision; it derailed any immediate exploration and resulted in François I becoming Charles V's prisoner in 1525. François I was eventually freed, and by 1534, he was ready to commission another voyage. Verrazzano's failure to find a water passage through North America had significant consequences for future French exploration. His successor, Jacques Cartier of St. Malo, would search for the Northwest Passage farther north of where Verrazzano had gone, following the path of Cabot and many French, Breton, and Basque fishermen who plied the waters off the shores of Labrador and Newfoundland. He would find a great body of water that expanded westward into the continent, and while it would not provide a passage to Asia, the St. Lawrence River bestowed upon future generations of Frenchmen a veritable highway deep into the interior of North America.[6]

François I met Cartier in 1532, the same year Pope Clement VII's niece, Catherine de' Medici, married the king's son, the future King Henri II. The marriage proved fortuitous, for François I managed to convince his new papal in-law to issue an edict in 1533 that modified an earlier instrument (issued by the pro-Spanish pope and Borgia family member Alexander VI in 1493) that divided the New World between Spain and Portugal. Clement VII declared this earlier edict now applied only to lands hitherto discovered and excluded those not yet explored. With this act, France had the sanction required to compete with her rivals in the dual arenas of North American exploration and settlement. Cartier led this new effort. According to his commission, Cartier was to seek a passage to China and, hopefully, find precious metals and gems. Cartier had two ships of about sixty tons burden and sixty-one men each. After a journey of twenty days, his small fleet made landfall at Cape Bonavista on Newfoundland on May 10, 1534. From there, he sailed north and passed through the Strait of Belle Isle between Labrador and Newfoundland. He then explored the southern shore of the Gulf of St. Lawrence at Gaspé and later sailed north toward Anticosti Island, which stands as a sentinel at the entrance to the great bay. Cartier likened the barren, rocky coast of southern Labrador to the Land of Cain, referring to Cain's place of exile after killing his brother, according to the Bible story. That he was not the first European to see that coastline became evident when he and his crew unexpectedly met a large fishing vessel out of La Rochelle. Another unmistakable sign of earlier European visitors became manifest when Cartier sailed south to Chaleur Bay and saw Mi'kmaq Indians holding peltries at the end of sticks: a common gesture indicating a desire to trade furs for goods of European manufacture.[7]

At Gaspé Bay, Cartier met a fishing party of St. Lawrence Iroquoians from a village called Stadacona that lay farther to the southwest on the St. Lawrence River. Cartier and his men mingled with the Natives and traded metal items for fish and furs. Cartier made an important alliance with Stadacona's chief, Donnacona, who accompanied the party. Donnacona protested when Cartier erected a thirty-foot-high wooden cross with the inscription *Vive le roy de France* ("Long live the King of France") and also included a carved panel with three fleur-de-lis, the symbol of the French monarchy. Donnacona sensed the French were staking a claim to the land where he rightly exercised authority. Cartier assuaged Donnacona's fears by offering gifts to show his benign intent. In fact, Cartier's charms were such he was able to convince Donnacona to let his two teenage sons, Domagaya and Taignoagny, accompany him to France. These young men, Cartier hoped, would be able to act as interpreters for another voyage he was already formulating. Donnacona, on the other hand, believed he had made a powerful ally who would be useful in the world of Laurentian tribal politics.[8]

In July 1534, thirty canoes of Stadaconans bade their young countrymen farewell. Cartier sailed northeastward toward Anticosti Island, which he mistakenly believed was connected to the southern shore of the Gulf of St. Lawrence; he thus failed to find the St. Lawrence River. He probably would have discovered the great river after exploring the northern coast of Anticosti and pushing farther west, for he rightly concluded the island did not connect with the northern shore of the gulf, but bad weather forced the tiny fleet to begin its return. Cartier and his men arrived back in St. Malo in early September. His sponsors were obviously satisfied with his results; Cartier received another commission and three ships with supplies adequate for a fifteen-month journey. His flagship, *La Grande Hermine*, was about twice the size of his earlier vessels. He departed St. Malo on May 19, 1535, and immediately headed for the northern shore of the gulf. On August 10, the Feast of St. Lawrence, he took refuge in a small harbor he called *La baye sainct Laurins*, which would lend its name to the St. Lawrence River and the Gulf of St. Lawrence. He corrected his earlier mistake and learned that Anticosti was, indeed, an island and not a peninsula. His Native guides proved useful and informed Cartier the great river continued to narrow as he pushed westward. Cartier noted, "Our Indians told us that this was the beginning of the Saguenay . . . and that thence came the copper they call *caignetdazé*. . . . The two Indians assured us that this was the way to the mouth of the great river Hochelaga [the St. Lawrence River], and the route towards Canada."[9]

His interpreters' tales of Saguenay fired Cartier's imagination; he saw it as another Mexico or Peru and himself as a French Cortes or Pizarro. In addition to these great riches, he imagined Hochelaga to be the very gateway to Asia. He would more than simply fulfill the charges outlined in his commission; he would be the greatest explorer and conqueror of his day. By September 1, 1535, he anchored at the mouth of the Saguenay River near the site of what later became the trading post of Tadoussac. He tarried only a day before proceeding westward; his voyage up the Saguenay River to the mystical kingdom of the same name would wait. Six days later, Cartier arrived at the Island of Orleans, where, he believed, "the province and territory of Canada begins."[10] The French later learned the word *Canada*, spelled variously as *Cannata* or *Kanata*, was simply an Iroquoian word for "village" or "settlement" that his interpreters used when referring to their village of Stadacona. Cartier, on the other hand, used it to describe the region surrounding Stadacona at present-day Quebec. As with his use of the term *St. Lawrence*, succeeding generations adopted it as a label for the entire country. He again met with Donnacona, who talked with his two sons, whom he had not seen in a year. Despite the initial friendly reception, the intricacies of regional tribal politics soon poisoned the well of Franco-Indian relations. Domagaya and Taignoagny balked at accompanying Cartier farther up the St. Lawrence to Hochelaga, for the chief there had long sought to dominate Donnacona and his people. Donnacona wanted to monopolize his relationship with the French to gain leverage in this political struggle.[11]

Cartier proceeded to Hochelaga without his Indian guides. He took his smallest vessel through the many rapids and used his longboats to negotiate the final three-day journey to the Island of Montreal. There he spied the village of Hochelaga: a more substantial settlement than Stadacona and palisaded as well. Hochelaga stood near a hill Cartier named Mount Royal, or Montreal in French. From this precipice, Cartier spied either the Lachine Rapids or another set of rapids, the Sault-au-Récollet. Cartier also realized, and had earlier learned from his interpreters, that the St. Lawrence became increasingly fresh as one pushed west. Both bits of news appeared to be unwelcome evidence the St. Lawrence River might not provide the much-hoped-for Northwest Passage. However, Cartier brightened when the Indians of Hochelaga pointed to his silver whistle chain and gilt-copper dagger handle and noted where he could find more: Saguenay! This was now the second time he had heard about this mysterious kingdom and its seemingly limitless wealth. He also learned another great river, the Ottawa, flowed toward Saguenay. Cartier was undoubtedly confused because the Indians of Hochelaga insisted Saguenay lay to the west, and not the northwest via the Saguenay River, as the Stadaconans had noted.[12]

He returned to Stadacona where his men had built a fort for the winter; it was now mid-October and too late to sail back to France. It would be a miserable winter for Cartier and his men, all but ten of whom succumbed to scurvy; twenty-five ultimately died. The rest survived only when one of Cartier's interpreters demonstrated how to cure the disease with a concoction made from the bark and leaves of the white cedar tree. Donnacona continued to regale Cartier with tales of Saguenay and insisted both the Saguenay and Ottawa Rivers provided access to the wealth of this kingdom. It is difficult to know what exactly the Stadaconans referred to when they told Cartier stories of Saguenay. The Hochelagans almost certainly spoke of Lake Superior, which, when one included a journey through Lake Huron and the St. Mary's River, was accessed via the Ottawa River route. Moreover, Lake Superior was an important source of copper for the Indians of the Great Lakes region and part of a vast trade network that, even before the arrival of the French, stretched from Hudson Bay, through the Great Lakes, and into the St. Lawrence Valley. On the other hand, the Stadaconans, particularly Donnacona, told

Cartier the Kingdom of Saguenay possessed "immense quantities of gold, rubies, and other rich things, and that the men there are white as in France and go clothed in woolens." Amazingly, Donnacona also claimed to have visited another country where "the people, possessing no anus, never eat nor digest, but simply make water [urine] through the penis." Yet another North American people, according to Donnacona, were pygmies with only one leg.[13]

It is not clear whether Cartier misconstrued the information he received from the Stadaconans or whether they intentionally misled him. The Hochelagans seemed only to refer to Lake Superior and its rich copper when they talked of Saguenay; Donnacona's claims appeared quite a bit more hyperbolic. His sons probably had not mastered the French language during their year in Cartier's service, and their failure to communicate their intended information accurately is a distinct possibility. Samuel de Champlain experienced a similar difficulty in communication roughly seventy years later. The other likelihood was that the Stadaconans, Donnacona in particular, intentionally fed Cartier lies. Donnacona was embroiled in political disputes with other local chieftains; he may have seen an alliance with the French as strengthening his position politically. Thus, he may simply have told Cartier what he thought the Frenchman wanted to hear. Conversely, Donnacona may have wanted to be rid of these presumptuous interlopers who seemingly sought to claim his country. Certainly, Cartier was determined to be France's first conquistador in the Spanish mold. Cartier decided François I needed to hear the wondrous tales of Saguenay firsthand, so he and his men seized Donnacona, his sons, and seven other Stadaconans and returned with them to France. The loss of so many crewmembers over the winter required him to abandon one of his ships, *La Petite Hermine*. He sailed for France in May 1536 and arrived back at St. Malo after a fourteen-month absence in July 1536.[14]

Upon his return, Cartier trotted out Donnacona to substantiate the reports he had made to King François I. The St. Lawrence River, Cartier insisted, might provide a water route to Asia. The description of the Kingdom of Saguenay piqued François I's interest. He hoped the treasures of this mysterious domain would provide France with the kinds of riches Spain extracted from Mexico and Peru, and the kind of wealth Portugal amassed from the spice trade with Asia and the slave trade in Africa. Indeed, Saguenay appeared to be a kind of cornucopia that would ensure France had the wealth needed to maintain its great power status. Donnacona sensed François I's interest in various agricultural products and added clove, nutmeg, pepper, oranges, and pomegranates to the list of Saguenay's resources. Indeed, the tales of Donnacona and Cartier's description of the St. Lawrence guaranteed another journey would be in the offing. However, war between François I and Charles V from 1536 until 1538 delayed preparations for Cartier's third expedition. During this interlude, Cartier developed an extensive wish list that included six ships with crews, forty musketeers, thirty carpenters, and smaller numbers of blacksmiths, tailors, cobblers, and other craftsmen. His inclusion of jewelers and metallurgists indicate he hoped to find the precious metals and gems of Saguenay. Clearly, he planned to found a colony, with François I's support. In his commission to Cartier, François I mentioned Asia only in passing and the discovery of a water route to the Far East not at all.[15]

Much to his chagrin, Cartier soon found his authority usurped by a royal favorite, Jean-François de La Rocque, sieur de Roberval, who received a commission that placed him in overall command of the expedition with orders to establish a colony in the New World. The king also charged Roberval with converting the Indians to Roman Catholicism, a curious order because Roberval was a Protestant. In fact, he had never even been to sea and was decidedly unqualified to lead such a venture. Why François I appointed him remains a mystery. But the king's decision to make the voyage, in part, a missionary endeavor was clearly done to placate the new pope, Paul III. The move was designed to counter Charles V's aggressive lobbying of the pope to declare the New World the sole domain of Spain and Portugal. In fact, both Charles V and his brother-in-law, King João III of Portugal, suspected this new French expedition's main purpose was to plunder Spanish and Portuguese possessions in the Americas.[16]

By the spring of 1541, Cartier had assembled a fleet of five vessels packed with livestock and men and women who were rounded up from local jails to be colonists. Because Roberval had additional preparations to make, he gave Cartier permission to leave without him. Cartier arrived at Stadacona in August 1541 and informed the new chief, Agona, that Donnacona had passed away. As for the other Indians, Cartier lied and said they were now great lords who had decided to remain in France. In reality, they had all died except for a young girl, whom Cartier had not brought back. The narrative of Cartier's third voyage is quite brief and lacking many details, but it states the initial warm welcome extended to the French by the Stadaconans was "all dissimulation," and later events confirmed the underlying tension he had detected.[17] Cartier established his settlement about nine miles upstream from Stadacona at present-day Cap Rouge. Cap Rouge at one time was referred to as Cap aux Diamants (Cape of Diamonds), providing strong evidence for why Cartier chose this location. The limestone appeared to be full of diamonds and gold ore, just the riches he coveted. Yet the apparent diamonds turned out to be nothing more than quartz and mica, and the metallic mineral was simply iron pyrites, better known as fool's gold. For many years afterward, his countrymen referred to acts of deception or dishonesty with the analogy "as false as Canadian diamonds."[18]

As the colonists and crew busied themselves with building fortifications at their new settlement, named Charlesbourg-Royal, Cartier in September 1541 took several longboats and men and organized a reconnaissance expedition toward Hochelaga as part of his larger goal of finding the Kingdom of Saguenay. His experiment of taking two Indians, Domagaya and Taignoagny, and training them as interpreters had produced dubious results. On the way to Hochelaga, he visited a friendly chief at a village called Achelacy and left two young French boys who would learn the language of the St. Lawrence Iroquoians. Thus began the long tradition by the French of producing loyal interpreters among their own population; Jean Nicolet would later serve in this capacity. Cartier managed to negotiate the Lachine Rapids by portaging, but he went no farther. He procured four young guides from a nearby village called Tutonaguy. His Indian guides used sticks to make a crude map that indicated another great rapids, roughly sixty miles upstream; this was the Long Sault, known today as the International Rapids. Curiously, Cartier could have avoided the Long Sault by ascending the Ottawa River. He knew about this river but did not attempt to reach the land of Saguenay via this route, possibly intending to examine it later or deciding that the apparently rich deposits of gold and diamonds downstream were a more worthwhile endeavor. Either way, he returned to Charlesbourg-Royal.[19]

With his return, Cartier's narrative of his third voyage abruptly ends; other sources provide only small bits of evidence for what followed. The winter of 1541–1542 was not easy. While scurvy did not carry off many souls, persistent Indian attacks did. The sources do not indicate what prompted the attacks, but thirty-five settlers died from what appears to have been a prolonged siege. Roberval had not arrived, and without the additional manpower required to reinforce Charlesbourg-Royal, Cartier and his settlers decided to abandon the settlement in June 1542. Cartier probably assuaged any feelings of failure with the belief he possessed eleven barrels of gold, a basket full of diamonds, and seven barrels of silver. These buoyed his spirits until, upon his return, he learned he possessed nothing but worthless rocks. On the way home, he met Roberval's fleet of three vessels anchored in the harbor at what is today St. John's, Newfoundland. The need to secure additional funding had delayed Roberval's departure. Cartier related his troubles to Roberval, who ordered him to return to Canada. Cartier wanted nothing further to do with the venture; he and his fleet stole away in the middle of the night. Roberval continued on his own, but without Cartier's crew and colonists; more important, without Cartier's knowledge, Roberval was doomed to fail.[20]

Roberval's experience was, in many ways, similar to that of Cartier. He established his settlement in the same spot as Cartier, although Roberval renamed it France-Roy. Because he brought along artillery and other weapons, his settlement was stronger and did not suffer from Indian attacks. The new settlement probably had about 150 persons, about 50 of whom died of scurvy during the winter. Obviously, Cartier did not inform Roberval of the curative properties of white cedar during their brief meeting. Those who survived subsisted on meager rations and suffered under Roberval's severe, Protestant discipline. By June 1543, as the river thawed and the first signs of spring arrived, Roberval, like Cartier, began his own search for the Kingdom of Saguenay. Roberval, also like Cartier, pushed upstream on the St. Lawrence. Another party under his pilot, Jean Alfonse, sailed eastward and ascended the Saguenay River. Alfonse, upon seeing the river broaden after a few miles, seemed convinced it was the long-sought-after waterway to the Pacific and, hopefully, *la mer du Cattay*, or the Sea of China. Of course, the Saguenay does not lead to the Pacific, and had he gone farther, the sight of the Chicoutimi Rapids would have dispossessed Alfonse of the notion of the river providing any kind of easy access. Roberval, like Cartier, turned back after reaching the Lachine Rapids when one of his boats wrecked, causing eight men to drown. Discouraged, Roberval and his people soon abandoned their settlement and arrived back in France in September 1543.[21]

With this sad, anticlimactic denouement, the curtain came down upon the first phase of French settlement in North America. However, Cartier's voyages and Roberval's valiant efforts were but the first act in this drama; the curtain would rise again, but not until six decades passed. Several factors vitiated France's commitment to North American exploration, not the least of which was the religious turmoil between Catholics and Protestants (most of whom were Calvinists, known in France as Huguenots) that embroiled the country. Roberval was killed during the course of a religious riot in 1560 after leaving a meeting with fellow Calvinists. Henri II, who ascended the French throne upon the death of François I in 1547, had no interest in furthering the cause of North American exploration. During the interregnum that separated the eras of Cartier and Champlain, the French did not completely abandon the New World. French fishermen and whalers continued to harvest the riches of the sea off the coasts of northeastern North America and in the Gulf of St. Lawrence.[22]

The French also secured bundles of furs through trade with the Indians, and these peltries kept the dream of French exploration and colonization alive. The French entry into the fur trade was an unintentional product of weakness on the high seas, particularly vis-à-vis the English, who dominated the better fishing grounds and drove the French deeper into the Gulf of St. Lawrence by about 1580. Here, furs received through trade with the Native communities were so plentiful that by about 1600, the fur trade became a separate and autonomous commercial activity. Merchants who sought furs as a primary commodity organized several private ventures. In 1583, Étienne Bellenger sailed to Nova Scotia with the intention of establishing a permanent trading post that would grow into a colony, but he found so many furs he abandoned his plans and returned to France to sell his peltries at a handsome profit. Two of Cartier's nephews received the first fur trade monopoly from the king in 1588, although they appear to have done nothing with it. Nevertheless, for the next fifty years afterward, the French crown granted such favors to those individuals willing to form trading companies that became the principal means by which exploration and settlement were realized in French North America. Bellenger's success encouraged Troilus de La Roche de Mesgouez to organize a similar venture. He had tried and failed to do so in 1578 and again in 1584. The Wars of Religion delayed his efforts until 1598, when King Henri IV granted him exclusive rights to the French fur trade in North America and forbade other merchants from participating.[23]

However, La Roche's choice of sites could not have been worse. He left about sixty convicts and beggars on Sable Island roughly ninety miles off the coast of present-day Nova Scotia in 1598. He was unable to recruit any free French persons to volunteer for the long, dangerous journey to such a distant and desolate place. The island's main natural resource was a herd of wild cattle descended from bovines left by an earlier Portuguese expedition. A supply ship visited once per year to deliver supplies and collect whatever furs the colonists had harvested during the course of hunting cattle, wolves, foxes, and seals. Not surprisingly, this project, too, was unsuccessful. A supply ship failed to arrive in 1602, and in 1603, eleven miserable survivors returned to France. Most of the others had apparently succumbed to famine or violence at the hands of their fellow colonists.[24]

A more serious effort was made by Pierre Chauvin, sieur de Tonnetuit. With the assistance of François Gravé, sieur du Pont, a man who later played a role in the explorations of Samuel de Champlain, Chauvin organized an expedition in 1600 to Tadoussac, a Montagnais village at the confluence of the Saguenay and St. Lawrence Rivers where European fishermen and whalers had long stopped to trade with the Indians. Chauvin and a group of colonists (which included Pierre Dugua, sieur de Mons, another person who played an important role in Champlain's career) built a habitation at Tadoussac in the spring of 1600. Chauvin's commission required him to bring fifty colonists annually over the course of ten years. However, that autumn, he departed for France with a cargo of furs and left a mere sixteen men behind in a crude log hut; only five survived the winter. The survivors most likely returned with the next ship that arrived in spring of 1601. When this vessel departed that autumn, it left no French colonists behind. Trade at Tadoussac continued but only as a summertime activity. Chauvin's colonists, like those of Cartier and Roberval, had little desire to endure the harsh Canadian winters. Chauvin learned, as did other Frenchmen who secured fur trade monopolies, that settling colonists was an expensive enterprise that gouged into one's profits. Chauvin's third and final trade voyage, which almost certainly possessed no colonists, departed Tadoussac in October 1602; the next year, Champlain would explore the St. Lawrence River and begin the next phase of French history in North America.[25]

The colonizing activities of Bellenger, La Roche, and Chauvin failed in establishing trading posts or long-term settlements, but they were at least limited financial successes that ensured contact between France and North America never completely ended. Roberval's 1541 commission was the first document by which France declared its possession of territory in North America, and Cartier's voyages provided the French with a claim to the northeastern portion of the continent that, while tenuously held, even into the era of Champlain, legitimated the activities of French fishermen, whalers, and merchants. While the French seemingly lost interest in finding the Northwest Passage after Cartier's voyages (and Cartier seems to have lost interest himself by his third voyage), it would be more accurate to say this larger project was postponed until Champlain was able to continue what his predecessor from St. Malo had initiated seven decades earlier. The French learned during this hiatus that, while Canada lacked gold and diamonds, it possessed other riches such as fish, whale oil, and especially furs. These would suffice until such a passage could be found, and Cartier's published works kept alive the idea that such a waterway might exist. Of course, his explorations of the Gulf of St. Lawrence and the St. Lawrence River revolutionized Europeans' understanding of North America. The eastern coast, from Labrador to the Yucatan Peninsula, had slowly emerged from almost half a century of European exploration, and Cartier's voyages had largely filled in the remaining gaps of knowledge concerning the northeastern corner of the continent.[26]

Cartier's explorations also altered mapmakers' understanding of North America, which had important implications for Champlain as well as his subordinate, Jean Nicolet. The Flemish cartographer Gerard Mercator, using Cartier's writings, illustrated the St. Lawrence River and two of its tributaries: the Ottawa and Saguenay Rivers. Cartier learned from the St. Lawrence Iroquoians that one could travel up the Ottawa River and find a large freshwater lake. Mercator published a map in 1569 that provided the first crude cartographic depiction of the Great Lakes, which was largely obscured by a vignette. In 1587, he published a more revealing map that showed the probable route of the Ottawa River through the mythical land of Saguenay. At the head of this river was a large, fresh-water lake that emptied into a yet-to-be-discovered northern sea. In a sense, Mercator came remarkably close to understanding the true geography of North America, for, as the French later learned, it is possible to go up the Ottawa River, make a portage, and enter Georgian Bay of Lake Huron. Mercator also developed a nascent idea concerning Hudson Bay, although in his day, knowledge of such a saltwater body was purely speculative. Nevertheless, Mercator's freshwater lake emptied into a hypothetical northern sea linked to both the Atlantic and Pacific Oceans. Other cartographers followed his lead, and by the late 1500s, many maps of North America included these same elements. Mercator called this freshwater body *Mare dulce*, or the Freshwater Sea. The French mapmaker André Thévet labeled it *Lac de Conibaz* (Lake Conibas), a name derived from a St. Lawrence Iroquoian word that, according to Cartier, described the mollusk shells found there. While it is unknown whether Champlain ever saw Mercator's or Thévet's maps, there is no doubt he later inherited this geographical theory of North America.[27]

By the time Champlain began his explorations, the ethnic constitution of the St. Lawrence River valley had shifted. During Cartier's voyages, the St. Lawrence Iroquoians populated the St. Lawrence Valley. They most likely spoke the same language, or at least mutually intelligible dialects, and shared many cultural practices that made them distinct from neighboring Iroquoian tribes. Archaeological and ethnohistorical evidence suggests four distinct tribes or discrete community networks of St. Lawrence Iroquoians resided along the length of the St. Lawrence River from present-day Quebec to the eastern end of Lake Ontario. The rivalry between Stadacona's chief, Donnacona, and his counterpart at Hochelaga presents evidence these communities did not comprise a single polity. When Champlain arrived in 1603, the residents of Stadacona were gone; the new inhabitants were the Algonquian-speaking Montagnais, also known as the Innu. The village that Cartier's

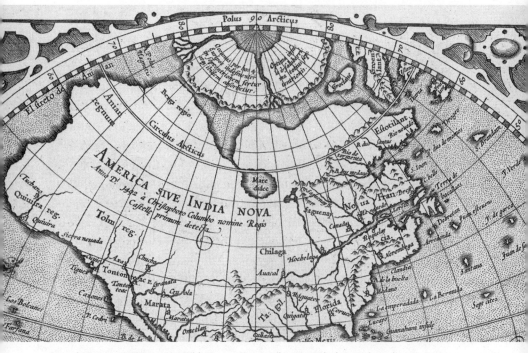

Gerard Mercator's 1587 map, *Orbis Terrae Compendiosa Descriptio*, was based on Jacques Cartier's explorations. Mercator was the first cartographer to depict Lake Huron (labeled *Mare dulce* on the map), the first mapmaker to illustrate the route to Lake Huron via the Ottawa River, and the first to link the lake to a hypothetical northern sea that provided access to the Pacific Ocean. Other mapmakers followed Mercator's lead, and Champlain inherited this early theory of North American geography from them. COURTESY OF THE JOHN CARTER BROWN LIBRARY AT BROWN UNIVERSITY

St. Lawrence Iroquoians called Stadacona was, in 1603, called by the Algonquian name Kébéc, or Quebec, as Champlain wrote it, which meant "narrows" and referred to the narrowing of the St. Lawrence River at that point. The village of Hochelaga at present-day Montreal had been abandoned and possibly conquered and destroyed. Intertribal warfare was almost certainly one cause of these demographic changes, but it remains unknown what ultimately happened to the residents of Stadacona and Hochelaga. The current theory is that their more powerful Iroquoian neighbors either annihilated or absorbed them.[28]

The region between Quebec and Montreal was largely unoccupied in Champlain's day and served as a buffer zone between Algonquian-speaking tribes such as the Montagnais to the north and the Ho-dé-no-sau-nee, or Five Nations League of the Iroquois, which lived to the south in the Finger Lakes district of present-day upstate New York. This powerful confederation of five tribes—the Mohawk, Oneida, Onondaga, Cayuga, and Seneca—had probably already been in the process of coalescing during the course of Cartier's voyages and initially constituted the Mohawk, Oneida, and Onondaga in the fifteenth and early sixteenth centuries. The addition of the Cayuga and Seneca sometime between about 1590 and 1605 meant the League was far more powerful and potent when Champlain arrived in 1603. The Ho-dé-no-sau-nee fought against neighboring tribes including other Iroquoian groups such as the Hurons, who were also a confederation of four or possibly five closely related, Iroquoian-speaking tribes that formed an association between 1440 and 1630, at least in part, as an alliance against the Five Nations League. Because the Indians of northeastern North America did not necessarily ally with one another on the basis of linguistic or cultural affinity, the Hurons and other Iroquoian speakers, such as the Petuns, considered the League their enemy and formed alliances with Algonquian-speaking tribes, such as the Montagnais and the Algonquins. During Champlain's time, the French became embroiled in these battles and allied with the Hurons and Algonquian speakers against the Ho-dé-no-sau-nee, particularly the Mohawks: the easternmost members of the League with the greatest access to the St. Lawrence Valley via the Richelieu River.[29]

To the west at Green Bay, another alliance had come into existence. The senior partners were the Chiwere-Siouan-speaking Puans who dominated the nearby Algonquian-speaking Menominees. We know far less about these two groups than we do the Iroquois, the Hurons, and the tribes of the St. Lawrence Valley. The reason is that the latter eastern tribes had more intensive and ongoing contacts in the early seventeenth century with Europeans, who produced a rich documentary record. The Puans, Menominees, and other Native groups in the western Great Lakes did not have such relationships with the French until Jesuit missionaries established permanent posts among them in the late 1660s, and those contacts occurred after destructive intertribal wars had significantly altered the ethnic geography of the region from that which existed at the time of Nicolet's voyage. The descriptions of Nicolet's 1634 journey stand as some of the first written sources concerning these Native groups, but they are frustratingly meager.

Thus, we must supplement these scanty records with other sources that elucidate the histories of these communities. Oral traditions are particularly important, but until recently, historians have often rejected them. One early Nicolet scholar, Publius V. Lawson, dismissed oral traditions out of hand. Citing Henry Rowe Schoolcraft, the great chronicler of American Indian history, Lawson argued, "Where reference can only be had to oral traditions, always vague and contradictory, much difficulty arises in deciding on the relative claims of such traditions to authenticity."[30] What many historians have failed to understand is that preliterate societies depend on oral traditions, which include both mythology and what in the Western worldview are considered factual narratives, to accurately preserve a tremendous amount of historical information that is passed down faithfully and with great care from one generation to the next.[31] As with any sources that shed light on the human past, historians must judge how reliable oral traditions are, just as they assess the veracity of written documents. Their assessment includes asking who produced the source, why they produced it, and whether the information provided by one class of sources supports and verifies evidence found in other categories. This methodology is particularly relevant for locating the Puans and Menominees at Green Bay when Nicolet made his journey. Indeed, a strong correlation exists between the Indians' oral traditions, French documents, and archaeological data.

The Ho-Chunks in particular, both in their oral history and mythology, claim their Puans ancestors resided on Green Bay's eastern shore on the Door Peninsula in the early seventeenth century. Charles C. Trowbridge, who served as an American Indian agent at Green Bay in 1823, produced one of the earliest written records of the Ho-Chunks' oral history concerning the Puans. According to his informants:

> They [Puans] first inhabited the Winneebaágoa banks [Red Banks] . . . on the south east side of Green Bay, 12 miles from the mouth of the Fox river. . . . While the nation resided on the borders of the bay, they had but one village, which extended from the Banks to the river rouge [Red River], a distance of nine miles. . . . The Chief of the Thunder tribe [or clan] exercised an immediate and complete

control over that village and his government was so strict that a single family could not leave the village for a hunting excursion without his permission.[32]

The Ho-Chunk chief Caramanee recounted a similar story in 1826, although in more general terms: "Long ago we all lived in one large town. Then our chiefs had influence and our young men behaved well."[33] More than sixty years later, in 1887, Spoon Decorah, a Wisconsin Ho-Chunk elder, related, "It has been told me, by my father and my uncles, that the Winnebagoes [Puans] first lived below the Red Banks, on the east shore of Green Bay. . . . They lived there a very long time. From there they moved to the Red Banks."[34]

About thirty years earlier, Jonathan E. Fletcher collected information from the Nebraska branch of the tribe that was virtually identical to that of their Wisconsin kin:

> The residence of the Winnebagoes [Puans] at a place they call the Red Banks, on the west shore of Lake Michigan, and north of Green Bay, appears to be the earliest event preserved by their traditions relative to their history. . . . The traditions of this tribe extend no further back than their residence at the Red Banks, some eight or nine generations since. . . . The traditions of this tribe refer to the Red Banks on the western shore of Lake Michigan, as the first and great geographical feature connected with them.[35]

Significantly, the oral history of the Ottawas (also spelled Odawa), with whom the Puans engaged in both trade and war, also assert that in the early seventeenth century, the Puans resided at Green Bay.[36]

These secular stories, or *worak* in the Ho-Chunk language, record the factual history of the tribe. Just as important for determining the homeland of the Puans in the early seventeenth century are the *waikan*, or sacred stories. The myths of the Ho-Chunks, like those of all cultures, often recount real historical events cloaked in the mantel of mythological characters and supernatural forces. Thus, it should be no surprise the creation myths of the various Ho-Chunk clans record a genesis at Green Bay. Anthropologist Paul Radin collected many of these creation stories during the early twentieth century. In fact, the testimonies he collected strongly suggest that it was at Green Bay where the remnants of the Puans, in the wake of their war with the Illinois Confederacy in the 1640s, coalesced and became the historic Ho-Chunk tribe. One informant related to Radin the Bear clan origin myth: "In the beginning a bear came walking on the ocean. When he got to the shore he flew off as a raven and alit on the shore. The first being he saw was a Dog clansman. Then he entered a lodge and sat opposite him. . . . They landed at Green Bay, where a great gathering was held of all the clans."[37] George Gale, a Wisconsin writer who researched the Indians of his native state, recorded an analogous Ho-Chunk creation story in about 1850: "*Taw-nee-nuk-kaw*, one of the oldest chiefs of the tribe . . . has the first man created in Heaven and sent down to the earth and landed on the *Moke-kaw-shoots-raw*, or Red Banks, near the head of Green Bay."[38]

Documents produced by French explorers and missionaries who came to Green Bay after Nicolet tell a similar story. The most significant is the narrative of Nicolas Perrot, who traveled throughout the western Great Lakes between 1665 and 1699, including Green Bay. Perrot (some of whose writings were edited by another Frenchman, Charles le Roy, sieur de Bacqueville de la Potherie) noted:

> In former times, the Puans were the masters of this bay [Green Bay], and of a great extent of adjoining country. This nation was a populous one, very redoubtable, and spared no one; they violated all the laws of nature; they were sodomites, and even had intercourse with beasts. If any stranger came among them, he was cooked in their kettles. The Malhominis [Menominees] were the only tribe who maintained relations with them, and they did not dare even to complain of their tyranny. Those tribes [Puans and Menominees] believed themselves the most powerful in the universe; they declared war on all nations whom they could discover, although they had only stone knives and hatchets.[39]

Some of this description is undoubtedly hyperbole; the Puans certainly did not engage in bestiality, but they were known to practice ritual cannibalism, although only upon the bodies of dead enemies. Perrot's narrative also reveals the nature of the alliance between the Puans and Menominees, with the former being the dominant partner. In 1672, the Jesuit missionary Claude Dablon noted the Puans had a long residence in the Green Bay region when he wrote about "the people named Puans, who have always lived here as in their own country."[40]

Archaeological data provides additional evidence of the Puans' residence on the Door Peninsula as well as the region immediately to the west of Lake Michigan, at least to a degree. Archaeologists are unable to link assemblages of archaeological artifacts to historic tribes in the western Great Lakes with an absolute degree of certainty.[41] Nevertheless, most archaeologists believe the Puans and other related Chiwere-Siouan speakers, such as the Iowas, Missourias, and Otos, were the descendants of the prehistoric inhabitants whose artifact assemblages they have labeled Oneota. Carriers of Oneota culture emerged in Wisconsin after about 900 CE and continued their residence into the period of French contact. They practiced corn horticulture and lived in large, populous settlements.[42] Significantly, several sources indicate the Puans were quite numerous at the time Nicolet conducted his westward journey in 1634. Perrot estimated that in the early seventeenth century, the Puans had four thousand to five thousand men, which would mean the population, if one estimates three women, children, and elderly members per warrior, was between sixteen thousand and twenty thousand persons, a population comparable to other agricultural societies, such as the Hurons. Information provided by Fletcher supports these numbers. His informants among the Nebraska branch of the tribe asserted they "had formerly a much larger population than at the present time . . . their number was put down vaguely at four thousand five hundred . . . in 1837."[43]

One school of archaeological thinking that meshes well with the oral traditions and French sources asserts the carriers of Oneota culture in the early seventeenth century consisted of many autonomous yet closely related groups of people who lived in various settlements in eastern Wisconsin. These villages ranged from Green Bay (and possibly as far north as the Strait of Mackinac) southward into northern Illinois and the Chicago region (and possibly as far south as Starved Rock on the Illinois River). While these communities were likely Chiwere-Siouan speakers, they may also have included some Algonquian speakers. Other

Chiwere-Siouan groups, such as the Iowas, lived farther to the west. Only the residents of the populous, hierarchical polity at Green Bay were the Chiwere-Siouan speakers whom the French called the Puans. In fact, the rather significant estimates of this society's population may have included other closely related Chiwere-Siouan groups in addition to the Puans settlements at Green Bay. In the latter half of the seventeenth century, well after Nicolet's visit and especially after their wars with the tribes of the Illinois Confederacy to the south, these communities suffered catastrophic population losses. As mentioned, many scholars believe these remnant populations joined into a single tribal polity later known as the Ho-Chunks, much like the various related communities that composed the Five Nations League and the Hurons coalesced in the decades that separated the voyages of Cartier and Champlain. Thus, the later Ho-Chunk tribe possibly consisted of the vestiges of the Puans who resided at Green Bay in Nicolet's time, related Chiwere-Siouan-speaking groups from other locations, and possibly members of allied Algonquian speaking communities.[44]

Archaeologists have tentatively linked at least two sites in the Green Bay region, Hanson and Astor, to the Puans. These communities may have been part of the Puans polity to which Perrot referred or perhaps were autonomous Chiwere-Siouan communities with social, cultural, and economic ties to the Puans. Spoon Decorah's statement hints that Sawyer Harbor, farther north on the Door Peninsula, may have been such a community, although more archaeological research needs to be conducted at this site in order to confirm this hypothesis. Nevertheless, the archaeological research conducted on the Door Peninsula supports the notion the Puans resided on the eastern shore of Green Bay at the time of Nicolet's visit. The ground has yielded a considerable number of Oneota artifacts, and in the early twentieth century, archaeologists could still observe ancient garden beds that suggested the practice of corn horticulture in the area.[45]

This raises the question of why such a powerful and populous polity emerged along Green Bay's eastern shore. The answer was almost certainly trade. Green Bay is fed by the Fox River, which in turn leads to the Wisconsin and Mississippi Rivers and the interior of North America. At least two decades before Nicolet made his journey, and in all likelihood even two centuries earlier, the Ottawa Indians controlled the trade routes from Lake Huron westward into Lakes Superior and Michigan. The Ottawas definitely traded with the Puans at Green Bay for items that came from the region west of Lake Michigan, such as bison hides. The Puans at Green Bay dominated this interior trade route, which led Paul Le Jeune to observe in 1639 that they were "one of the most important openings for the Western tribes."[46] Considering he wrote this a year before he described Nicolet's voyage, Le Jeune almost certainly received this information from Nicolet. Recent archeological research supports this conclusion and indicates Oneota groups in present-day eastern Wisconsin traded frequently with each other and with Indian communities as far afield as northern Illinois, western Iowa, and southern Minnesota. By the year 1400, the Fox-Wisconsin Waterway, with its northeastern terminus at Green Bay, became the center of this western trade network.[47] Thus, the Ottawas controlled the trade route from Lake Huron to Green Bay where they traded with the Puans who resided along Green Bay's eastern shore. The Puans in turn monopolized the trade with communities to the south and west, most of which were likely other, closely related Chiwere-Siouan groups.

While the Puans almost certainly lived along the eastern shore of Green Bay at the time of Nicolet's visit, much debate continues among scholars concerning the site known as Red Banks on the Door Peninsula. This location figures heavily into many of the Ho-Chunks' oral traditions. During the early nineteenth century, long after the Puans departed this location, white settlers described the remains of an earthen parapet seven feet high and topped by a wooden palisade. Trowbridge's Ho-Chunk informants noted in 1823 that the remains of the parapet were still visible at that time. Officers of the US Army Corps of Engineers even included them on a map based on their surveys of the region in the 1840s. However, these features were already badly eroded at that time. By the late nineteenth century, they were virtually gone; no traces of this parapet exist today. In fact, much of the archaeological record at Red Banks may have washed into the waters of Green Bay. How much remains is largely unknown, as archaeologists have conducted only preliminary surveys of the site.[48] Knowledge of the fortification at Red Banks remained evident in the Ho-Chunks' oral history for many centuries after the site

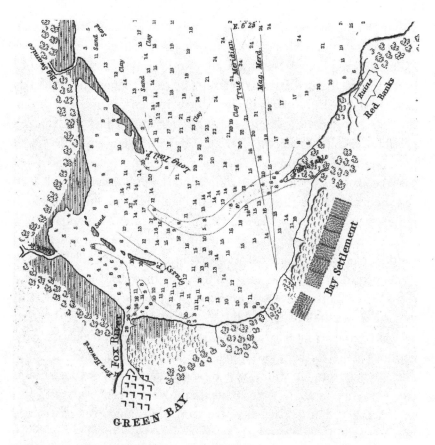

W. G. Williams and J. W. Gunnison's 1844 map, *Chart of Green Bay*, provides evidence of the ruins of the Puans' fortification at Red Banks along the eastern shore of Green Bay. The Puans likely built this fortification during the course of their war with the Illinois Confederacy in the 1640s. If the scale is accurate, the fortification was roughly a half mile in length and a quarter mile in width. COURTESY OF THE CARTOGRAPHIC BRANCH, US NATIONAL ARCHIVES

was abandoned, even among those tribal members who had removed to Nebraska. Fletcher wrote, "Their traditions also say . . . the Winnebagoes [Puans] built a fort—that it was constructed of logs or pickets set in the ground."[49]

Red Banks remains enigmatic because archaeologists have found few artifacts there. Some scholars doubt it was ever a major village site, but the frequent mention of Red Banks in the Ho-Chunks' oral traditions undermines such cavalier dismissals. A tentative conclusion is possible, although only further archaeological research will confirm its plausibility. At the time of Nicolet's visit, the Puans most likely lived in a series of densely populated settlements, all of which relied heavily upon corn horticulture. These settlements stretched from the mouth of the Fox River in the south, northward along the eastern shore of Green Bay on the Door Peninsula (on which Red Banks is located) to the Red River, and possibly as far north as Sawyer Harbor. Along with the Menominees, who lived on the opposite shore of Green Bay, the Puans controlled access to the Fox-Wisconsin Waterway and the hinterlands beyond Green Bay. In the years after 1634, the Puans (and probably related Chiwere-Siouan groups in present-day eastern Wisconsin, and possibly Algonquian allies) became engaged in their war with the Illinois Confederacy, which likely resided in present-day southern Michigan at the time of Nicolet's visit. Under pressure from the Illinois Confederacy, the Puans built a defensive work at Red Banks that they occupied for a relatively short time. This would explain the existence of the parapet as well as the dearth of other archaeological artifacts in the immediate area. The settlement within the confines of this fortification, which may have been a half mile in length and a quarter mile in width, would have been the large village that is frequently associated with Red Banks in the Ho-Chunks' oral traditions. Interestingly, another palisaded structure, built about a century earlier (almost certainly by the closely related Iowas) once stood at the Valley View site near La Crosse, Wisconsin. Archaeological evidence suggests the residents of the Valley View site occupied the site for only a few years at most. This lends credence to the theory Red Banks was a similar site occupied temporarily for defensive purposes.[50]

Their war with the Illinois Confederacy, according to Perrot, reduced the Puans to only about six hundred people from a population that once numbered as many as twenty thousand. If, as some scholars have argued, the remnants of the Puans and the survivors of other Chiwere-Siouan and possibly allied Algonquian communities assembled at this location and coalesced into a new polity that became the historic Ho-Chunk tribe, we can see why Red Banks looms so large in the later oral traditions as the sacred site of the Ho-Chunks' genesis. Moreover, sites near the Mississippi show a marked shift to locations that were more defensible but poorer in natural resources during this period.[51] This suggests these communities (most likely populated by Iowa Indians who possessed alliances and other intimate ties with the Puans) fought against the Illinois Confederacy as well.

An alternative possibility remains tentative pending further archaeological research. Little data currently exists to support the notion that as many as twenty thousand persons lived along the Door Peninsula. However, the stretch of territory north of present-day Lakes Poygan and Butte des Mort known as the Middle Fox Passage shows clear evidence of such a population at the time of Nicolet's visit. In this scenario, the Middle Fox Passage was the center of the Puans polity, and the villages along the Door Peninsula were outlying settlements where the Ottawa fleets conducted their trade with the Puans. If this were the case, the Puans polity would have stretched almost ninety miles in extent, about twice the size of Huronia. Perrot suggested as much when he wrote the Puans were masters of Green Bay "and of a great extent of adjoining country."[52] The archaeological sites along the Middle Fox Passage also show signs of a catastrophic population collapse around 1650, about the time of the tribe's war with the Illinois Confederacy. Early twentieth-century residents in the area uncovered incredible numbers of human bones belonging to men, women, and children.[53] Possibly, the survivors of the conflict consisted primarily of those Puans living in the communities on the Door Peninsula, and thus, when they reconstituted themselves as the Ho-Chunk tribe in the years after the conflict, those villages gained a privileged position in the Ho-Chunks' history, myths, and legends.[54]

The oral traditions of the Menominees indicate they lived on the western shore of Green Bay opposite the Puans in the early seventeenth century. Doing so, according to Perrot, allowed the two groups to create a choke point that controlled access to the Fox-Wisconsin Waterway. At least one scholar has asserted the Menominees' residence at Green Bay occurred after Nicolet's visit, but this argument is based on a single, unreliable French source.[55] Perrot's writings suggest otherwise, as do the tribe's oral traditions. Trowbridge recorded the oral history of the Menominees during his 1823 sojourn to Green Bay, and his Menominee informants maintained they had always resided at Green Bay and once lived in a single village located at the mouth of the Menominee River. The Menominees' origin myths, like their oral history, reflect this historical phenomenon. Trowbridge recorded the creation story of the Menominee Bear clan: "They believe that a *bear*, which inhabited the woods near the Munnoáminnee [Menomonee] river, was at his solicitation transformed, together with his she bear and cubs, by the Great Spirit, into Indians."[56] Significantly, the anthropologist W. J. Hoffman recorded an almost identical version of this myth in about 1890: "When Ki-shä'-manido, the Good Spirit, saw that the bear was still an animal he determined to allow the latter to change his form. The Bear . . . was pleased . . . and he was made an Indian. . . . This took place at mi'-ni-kâ'-ni, Menomoni river, near the spot where its waters empty into Green Bay."[57] The anthropologist Alanson Skinner recorded yet another version of this story in the early twentieth century that is virtually the same as those collected by Trowbridge and Hoffman.[58]

The closely related Noquets lived just north of the Menominees at Big and Little Bay de Noc. They later became part of the Menominee tribe. Augustin Grignon, a man of French and Menominee descent, confirmed this in 1857 when he stated, "The earliest locality of the Menominees, at the first visits of the whites, was at Bay de Noque and Menominee River; and those at Bay de Noque were called by the early French, *Des Noques* or *Des Noquia*."[59] The French Jesuit Pierre-François-Xavier de Charlevoix, after traveling to Green Bay in 1721, asserted the same, although in a much more abbreviated manner, when he noted the Menominees and Noquets spoke "nearly the same languages."[60]

The large settlement on the southern bank of the Menominee River near its confluence with Green Bay known as the Grand Village of the Menominees stood upon the site of present-day Marinette, Wisconsin.[61] As with the Puans' fortification at Red Banks, scholars have confirmed the existence of the Grand Village of the Menominees through ethnohistorical evidence and oral traditions, but firm archaeological data is lacking. Unlike Red Banks, the exact location of the Grand Village is unknown. The extensive development of Marinette during the historic period may well have resulted in the destruction of its archaeological remains. At the time of Nicolet's visit, other Menominee villages almost certainly existed along the western shore of Green Bay. Sites at the mouths of the Peshtigo, Oconto, and Big Suamico Rivers to the south of Marinette indicate the residence of Menominee communities, which may have been satellite settlements of the Grand Village or autonomous communities with ties to it. However, archaeologists caution that only more research will confirm such an assertion with greater certainty.[62] Nevertheless, the French sources, particularly Perrot's narrative, indicate the Menominees were the junior partners in the alliance with the Puans, and the French knew of the ferocity of the latter from information they received from other tribes, particularly the Ottawas, several decades before Nicolet made his journey.

When Samuel de Champlain sailed up the St. Lawrence his first time in 1603, twelve years would pass before he learned of the existence of the Puans. The Five Nations League, given its proximity to Quebec, was a more immediate threat. However, Champlain, in addition to being a soldier, sailor, cartographer, and explorer, was also a superb diplomat. He brought many young men like Jean Nicolet to the New World, and he often employed them as his ambassadors to both friend and foe. To his credit, he managed, at least in the earlier years of his career, to keep the lid on various intertribal rivalries and prevent small-scale raids and acts of violence from exploding into general warfare. Indeed, this accomplishment is an overlooked aspect of Champlain's long career. Undoubtedly, he was a great explorer, and early in his career he searched for the Northwest Passage; he was heir to a long European tradition that sought the riches of Asia and a practical and relatively inexpensive manner by which to obtain them. Yet, he also worked deftly to maintain peace between the warring tribes and secure his tiny French colony on the St. Lawrence. These became his paramount goals, and Jean Nicolet played an important role in realizing them.

2

CHAMPLAIN, EXPLORER OF NEW FRANCE

1603–1616

Samuel de Champlain's early life presents many of the same mysteries as that of Jean Nicolet, although the recent discovery of Champlain's baptismal certificate provides new insights. He was born in 1574, most likely in Brouage, a coastal city in western France, and baptized on August 13 of that year in the city of La Rochelle, within about five days of his birth. His father, Antoine, according to the scant sources that relate to him, was a ship's pilot and a captain in the French navy; two uncles on his mother's side also were naval officers. This had a tremendous influence upon young Samuel, who likely sailed as a young boy with his father. In the 1613 chronicle of his voyages, he wrote that, "Among all the most useful and admirable arts that of navigation has always seemed to me to hold the first place.... This art it is which from my tender youth won my love, has stimulated me to venture nearly all my life upon the turbulent waves of the ocean."[1]

His father's occupation bestowed respectability upon the Champlain family. The addition to the family name of *de*, the particule, was awarded to Samuel as a young soldier in the king's service. The use of the particule was ubiquitous among members of the nobility, and while the evidence is not conclusive, Champlain likely entered its ranks. In France, men who were not born into the hereditary aristocracy could attain such a station through letters of nobility issued by the king, and for many Frenchmen,

No finished portraits of Champlain exist from his lifetime. This steel-plate engraving, one of the most common found in historical works, was actually produced in 1864 by Théophile Hamel and J. A. O'Neil. This engraving in turn was based on a portrait produced in 1654 of the Italian courtier Michel Particelli. Champlain produced only a very small, rough sketch of himself fighting the Iroquois in 1609, but it excludes any details that would allow us to know more about his actual appearance. CHARLEVOIX, *HISTORY AND GENERAL DESCRIPTION OF NEW FRANCE*

the status of bourgeois was a stepping stone to a higher rung on the social ladder. Both Antoine and Samuel adopted the particule and referred to themselves, at various times, as "de Champlain." Although use of the particule by men of bourgeois status was also common, later documents refer to Samuel as a *noble homme* (noble gentleman), a title used by men who were very close to attaining noble status. Other documents indicate that by 1613 he had attained the title of *ecuyer* (esquire), which a *noble homme* usually assumed after becoming ennobled.[2] Thus, the evidence strongly suggests that Samuel de Champlain had acquired nobility.

Champlain's baptismal record also reveals he was born to Protestant parents, although at some point during his adult life he became a Roman Catholic. Brouage at the time of Champlain's birth was in the Huguenot country, and Protestant parents tended to bestow upon their children names from the Old Testament, such as Samuel, while Catholics usually gave their children saints' names. His parents' names, Antoine and Marguerite, strongly suggest that they had been born Catholic and converted to Calvinism. By about age thirty, the historical record indicates, their son had become a Roman Catholic, and a very devout one. In his later years, so deep was his faith, he even had someone read from hagiographies, biographies of the saints, during his meals. Champlain's vision for French North America was that of a populous, well-governed, and economically viable colony that would bring the light of Christ, specifically a Roman Catholic Christ, into the pagan darkness. Indeed, Champlain tightly wove the religious mission of New France into the political and economic goals he formulated.[3]

The extent of his education is another mystery with little documentation. Like Nicolet, Champlain was literate, but his prose, while competent, lacked the flourishes characteristic of men of greater learning, such as his Jesuit contemporaries. His writings demonstrate he had a firm grasp of basic mathematics, although not of geometry or trigonometry. His published maps are evidence he received some training in the craft of cartography, and the sketches that accompany his published works are indicative of some artistic ability. He may have attended an academy in Brouage that taught surveying, mapmaking, and martial skills such as horsemanship and fencing to the sons of the nobility and those from bourgeois families. Many graduates found employment in the army. Champlain possibly learned surveying and cartography from a close associate named Charles Leber, sieur du Carlo, who served as an *ingénieur et géographe ordinaire du roy*: a royal engineer and geographer. Du Carlo was an outstanding surveyor and geographer; of this, there is no doubt. He also had a close relationship with Champlain, although the exact nature of that relationship is unclear; Champlain may have been du Carlo's apprentice. Despite these uncertainties, Champlain's later maps and surveys indicate he had gained these competencies at some point, and he found many opportunities in which to employ those skills throughout his adult life.[4]

Equally important to the arc of Champlain's career was his relationship with the king of France, Henri IV, who ruled from 1589 to 1610. Henri IV bestowed many favors upon the young Samuel even before he began his career as an explorer, including a royal pension that Champlain began to receive as early as 1601 when he was only twenty-seven years old. Usually older men with many years of service to the monarch enjoyed such benefices, including the addition of the title of *sieur*, which, like the particule, did not necessarily indicate nobility. These anomalies have led some historians to conclude Champlain was a bastard child of Henri IV, which is quite possible, given that the great monarch had at least fifty-six mistresses, casual sexual encounters with scores of other women, and at least eleven known illegitimate progeny. The possibility of Champlain being the issue of Henri IV's loins would also explain why he did not enjoy the same close relationship with France's later rulers, Marie de' Medici and Cardinal Richelieu. Nevertheless, while such a conclusion falls within the realm of the possible, it is, like so many other facets of Champlain's life, ultimately unknowable.[5]

Regardless of Champlain's ancestry, his relationship with Henri IV undoubtedly shaped both his career and character. Henri IV came from the ruling family of Béarn in southwestern France, a country that in the future king's youth was riven by disputes between Roman Catholics and Huguenots. His mother raised him as a Protestant. Henri was appalled by the violence that characterized France's religious wars, and during these bloody conflicts, the Valois kings and their supporters forced the young prince, on pain of death, to convert to Catholicism; twice he converted, and twice he returned to the Protestant fold. At the successful conclusion of yet another of France's religious wars in 1589 (commonly known as the War of the Three Henrys), Henri assumed the French throne as Henri IV, the first of the great Bourbon kings who ruled France for the next two hundred years. Four years later, in 1593, and this time of his own volition, Henri IV converted a third time to Catholicism. Many Catholics, who composed the majority of the French population, were rightly skeptical of his sincerity, but it is unlikely that he uttered the notorious phrase attributed to him: "Paris is worth a mass."[6]

Henri IV was not such a shallow and mercenary man. He truly wanted to heal France of the wounds caused by its denominational divisions, and many Protestants, inspired by his example, also returned to the Roman Catholic Church after his conversion. Samuel de Champlain was, possibly, among their number. Like his mentor, Champlain also disliked religious violence and displayed a remarkably progressive, religiously tolerant attitude toward those of different confessions. Like Henri IV, Champlain's Catholic faith continued to blossom as he grew older, but he retained his repugnance for religious intolerance. Nevertheless, as his vision for New France developed during his career, he increasingly believed that establishing a single denomination, the Roman Catholic Church, was vital not only for the moral upkeep of the French who settled in the colony but also for the Indians evangelized by their efforts. This vision was an important cornerstone that shaped his policies toward the Indian people of North America whom he encountered throughout his career. While he certainly desired to convert them to the one true faith, he was nevertheless interested in their aboriginal religious convictions. Unlike many Europeans of his time, he believed that Indians, like all men, possessed souls that longed for the redemptive power of the Christian messiah.[7]

Before he began his career as an explorer, Champlain had already enjoyed many significant experiences and adventures. He participated in the ninth and largest of France's religious wars. It began in 1595 when Spanish, Italian, and Walloon forces invaded the country in support of France's Catholic League, which sought to depose Henri IV and install a more suitable Catholic king. Champlain joined the royal army and served in Brittany. He was an exceptional soldier and even undertook secret missions for the king. He served initially as a *fourrier*, a position equivalent to that of a quartermaster sergeant whose duties included surveying and laying out camps for the army and making maps. He later rose to the rank of ensign. The conclusion of the conflict in 1598 was the closing chapter of France's long series of religious wars, and with his hold over the throne secure, Henri IV issued the famous Edict of Nantes that same year and extended religious toleration to French Protestants.[8]

Champlain accompanied his uncle on a voyage to Spain to return Spanish soldiers who remained on French soil at the war's conclusion. From there, his uncle hired out the vessel to the Spanish government, which employed the ship for an expedition to its colonies in the New World. Champlain accompanied this expedition and, for the next two and half years, he traveled throughout the West Indies and Mexico. He was spell-bound by the sight of Mexico City, the metropolis once known as the Aztec capital of Tenochtitlan. According to Champlain, the thriving capital possessed "splendid temples, palaces and fine houses" as well as "streets extremely well laid out, in which are to be seen the large handsome shops of the merchants full of all sorts of very rich merchandise."[9] He also wit-nessed the darker side of Spain in the New World: the enslavement of Indians to work in the silver mines and the savage punishments inflicted upon those who failed to demonstrate an adequate zeal for the Christian faith. These horrific scenes, like those he observed during the course of France's religious wars, instilled in Champlain a revulsion for religious intolerance and the violence it spawned. Champlain would establish a very different set of relations with the Indians in French North America.[10]

—||—

By 1602, Champlain was in Paris as a member of Henri IV's court at the Louvre, although what role he played is a mystery. He may have worked as a *géographe du roi*, one of the many geographers and cartographers who toiled in the basement of the palace and developed the maps and geo-graphical knowledge of the globe that Henri IV believed were necessary for France to explore new lands and establish lucrative colonies. Cham-plain apparently visited France's Atlantic ports and queried Norman and Breton fishermen about their journeys to North America. He may also have worked in the port city of Dieppe as an *armateur*, a ship's outfitter, who readied vessels for voyages, some of which sailed for the New World. The governor of Dieppe was Aymar de Chaste, an aged naval officer. In 1602, Pierre Chauvin forfeited his monopoly on the fur trade in North America. It now passed to de Chaste, who approached Champlain and offered him a berth on the next voyage to the St. Lawrence, which would set out in 1603. The voyage was to be led by de Chaste's lieutenant, François Gravé, sieur du Pont (who went by the name Pontgravé), a man of great experience who had participated in several previous voyages. Champlain, at the king's request, went along as an observer who "should always make him [Henri IV] a faithful report of all I saw and discovered."[11]

Pontgravé had recently returned from a 1602 expedition to the St. Lawrence with two Montagnais Indians who told Henri IV the

St. Lawrence River extended westward over eight hundred miles and "cut across an infinity of fine lands and lakes, into which a great number of beautiful rivers also flowed."[12] Champlain was probably not present at this meeting, but the Indians' report was likely the basis of Henri IV's instructions to him to learn more about the geography of the St. Lawrence Valley. The king apparently also was acting on information contained in a 1602 treatise written by the Englishman Edward Hayes, who urged his countrymen to settle those parts of North America claimed by France. Hayes also included important geographic information he learned from the works of Cartier as well as Cartier's nephew, Jacques Noël, who was part of his uncle's 1541 expedition and who later returned to the St. Lawrence. According to Hayes, Noël had penetrated the Lachine Rapids at Montreal and traveled to a great interior lake that was freshwater at its eastern confluence with the St. Lawrence River but saltwater at its western extremity, although Noël never made such a claim. Hayes even conjectured the great lake supposedly explored by Noël provided access to the Pacific and "giveth passage unto Cathay [China]."[13] Hayes also believed the St. Lawrence possessed a southern tributary that flowed east toward the Atlantic to a land the English called Norumbega and which today comprises Canada's Maritime Provinces and New England. The English explorer Bartholomew Gosnold had recently visited this region, further raising French suspicions.[14]

Champlain most likely did not read Hayes's treatise. There is no evidence he could read English, and it is clear from his writings at this point in his career he had not even read the writings of Cartier. The great work penned by Champlain of his 1603 voyage, *Des Sauvages* (*Of the Indians*), only mentions Cartier once and mistakenly asserts he never penetrated as far west as the Lachine Rapids, which Cartier accomplished in 1535 and 1541. Nevertheless, members of Henri IV's court evidently knew of Hayes's treatise as well as the 1599 map of another Englishman, Edward Wright, which provided a visual expression of Hayes's text. The Wright map depicted a large lake at the source of the St. Lawrence River that also flowed into a vaguely defined saltwater bay to the north that possibly linked both the Atlantic and Pacific Oceans. It was, in many ways, similar to earlier maps made by Gerard Mercator and other cartographers, except that Wright correctly surmised the great lake drained into the St. Lawrence

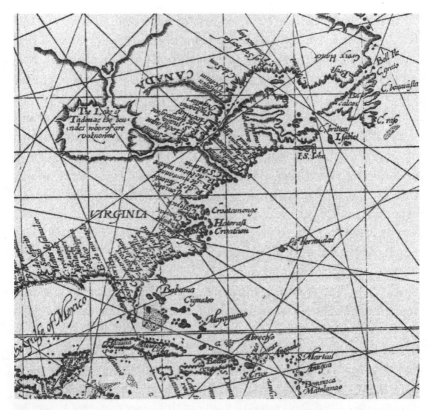

This 1599 map by Edward Wright, like that of Gerard Mercator, illustrates Lake Huron (here labeled *The Lake of Tadouac*). Like Mercator, Wright depicted this lake with a direct link to a hypothetical northern sea that supposedly provided access to the Pacific Ocean. Unlike Mercator, Wright showed the lake having direct links to the Ottawa River and another river that provided access to the Atlantic Ocean. This map, probably more than any other, influenced Champlain's early thinking concerning the geography of North America. NORDENSKIÖLD, *FACSIMILE-ATLAS TO THE HISTORY OF THE EARLY CARTOGRAPHY*

River; he named it Lake Tadouac (as opposed to Mare Dulce or Lac de Conibaz). Like his predecessors, Wright indicated this body of water was accessible via the Ottawa River but also depicted, unlike other mapmakers, a southern tributary of the St. Lawrence called the River Gamas (the present-day Penobscot River), which led directly to the Atlantic Ocean and Norumbega. The Portuguese explorer Estêvão Gomes first explored the river in 1525 and believed it penetrated deep into the interior. However, Wright incorrectly concluded the river was a tributary of the St. Lawrence, which it is not.[15]

Recent research indicates the works of Hayes and Wright as well as the Gosnold expedition shaped the planning for Pontgravé's 1603 voyage, the primary purpose of which was to locate sites for possible settlement; the second priority was trade with the Indians as a means to finance the expedition. Henri IV viewed French settlement of North America as a high priority, given the fact Hayes's treatise and Gosnold's explorations indicated England had its eyes on the North American lands claimed by France. Champlain may not have read Hayes's treatise, but he almost certainly learned about its content; he either saw Wright's map or was informed of what it depicted. Based on what he wrote about the 1603 expedition in *Des Sauvages*, he shared the geographic assumptions of both Wright and Hayes. Interestingly, neither Pontgravé's Montagnais Indians nor the works of Cartier and Jacques Noël mentioned anything about the great inland lake becoming salty at its western extremity. This appears to have been a deliberate falsification on the part of Hayes, who desired to indicate, despite a lack of firm evidence, this lake provided access to the Pacific and thus Asia. Wright followed suit by depicting it as such on his map. In Hayes's and Wright's defense, Mercator and other mapmakers also depicted the lake described by Cartier as emptying into a saltwater body that, it was hoped, provided a water route to the Far East.[16] Champlain perpetuated this error, and almost thirty years passed before he corrected it.

Pontgravé's fleet of three vessels departed Honfleur on March 15, 1603, the flagship being the *Bonne-Renommée*. Three smaller barques and several even smaller shallops were brought along for navigating the shallower waters. The fleet arrived ten weeks later at the harbor of Tadoussac on May 26, 1603. The next day, Pontgravé and Champlain went ashore; it was the first time Champlain's feet touched the soil of what would become Canada. A local Montagnais chief named Anadabijou feted them in grand style at a *tabagie*, or feast. A few weeks later, on June 9, 1603, they attended another grand celebration marking the recent victory over the Iroquois. The assembled Indians included the local Montagnais as well as Algonquins from the Ottawa River and Etchemins, a term that denotes closely related Indians such as the Maliseets, Passamaquoddys, and Penobscots who lived to the south. The allied Indians proudly displayed more than one hundred heads (or possibly just scalps) they had taken in battle and performed several dances as part of the festivities. During one of these dances, the women and girls, much to Champlain's surprise, cast off their garments and "stripped themselves stark naked, showing their privities."[17]

For the next seven weeks, Champlain explored the Saguenay and St. Lawrence Rivers, recording his observations of the land and people he encountered along the way.[18] The contemporary historian would love nothing more than to find a series of letters, a single book, or specific journal entries penned by Champlain that state, unequivocally and in definite language, what exactly he knew about the geography of North America and when he knew it. Unfortunately, one can only pore over his published works and catch glimpses of Champlain's geographic knowledge as well as the assumptions he developed to fill in the gaps when he lacked sound information. Champlain's works about his voyages often reveal, in relatively clear if somewhat abbreviated language, the extent of his knowledge. But just as often, they provide only tantalizing—if not frustrating—hints concerning what he knew. Just as important are the maps he made, for these, even more than his writings, provide visual evidence of his ideas. Yet, even these cartographic treasures occasionally omit details, and while they often illustrate the evolution of his geographic knowledge over the span of his career, they do not always adequately explain why he changed his thinking. Earlier scholars and chroniclers frequently developed muddled conclusions to fill the vacuum left by the historical record. These have served only to obscure the story of Champlain as well as that of his subordinate, Jean Nicolet. Nevertheless, these gaps are not unbridgeable, and the careful investigator can, with patience and persistence, tease the answers from Champlain's documentary legacy.

In mid-June 1603, Champlain explored the lower Saguenay River, which the Montagnais described as leading to Lac St. Jean to the northwest. Beyond Lac St. Jean, according to his Montagnais informants, lay "a sea which is salt." Champlain surmised, "It is some gulf of this our sea [the Atlantic], which overflows in the north into the midst of the continent."[19] The Montagnais described Hudson Bay, although no European had yet entered this vast body of water, much less laid eyes upon it; that would not occur for another seven years. Champlain also learned the

Montagnais had developed lucrative trade relationships with the Indians, particularly the Cree, who lived farther up the Saguenay, and the Montagnais jealously guarded their monopoly with these communities. If these Indians were to receive European goods, they would do so from Montagnais middlemen, not the French. Wisely, Champlain did not press them on the issue and satisfied himself with seeing only the lower Saguenay River.[20]

Edward Hayes argued Englishmen would learn as much by questioning the Native inhabitants as they would from exploration. Champlain took this advice to heart. By June 22, 1603, Champlain and a party led by Pontgravé—which almost certainly included Montagnais guides, possibly the two men Pontgravé took to France the year before—reached the future site of Quebec. His guides also led him up the "river of the Iroquois," today known as the Richelieu River, which fed into the St. Lawrence and which the various Indian nations of the St. Lawrence Valley traveled to fight their enemies among the Five Nations League. Champlain traveled only as far as the Saint-Ours Rapids about fourteen miles upstream, but his guides informed him the river eventually broadened into two large lakes (Lake Champlain and Lake George). After making a portage, this river led to another (the Hudson River), which, according to Champlain, led to the Atlantic and "the coast of Florida."[21] Florida in the minds of Champlain and other Frenchmen consisted not only of the present-day peninsula but also of a substantial part of the Atlantic coast all the way up to present-day New England and even the Canadian Maritime Provinces and just as often overlapped with the English conception of Norumbega.[22] Nevertheless, he was developing a clearer idea of the actual geography that served him well several years later when he explored these areas.

On July 2, 1603, Champlain and his party reached the Lachine Rapids. Finding he could go no farther, he asked the Indians there—Algonquins who most likely lived to the north along the Ottawa River—to draw a map of what lay beyond the rapids. They indicated more rapids were located up the St. Lawrence River, which ultimately led to a lake "which may extend some 80 leagues [168 miles] in length. . . . They told us that at the end of that lake the water is wholesome and the winter mild."[23] The Algonquins were describing Lake Ontario. The length Champlain recorded was quite a bit smaller than the actual size of the lake, which, if one traverses the northern shore from east to west, is about 230 miles. Champlain provided all his inland measurements in leagues, which in his writings average about 2.1 miles. At the western end of this lake, according to the Algonquins, was another rapid, Niagara Falls, "that is somewhat elevated," and this led to another lake "which may extend some sixty leagues [126 miles] in length" and "that the water in it is very wholesome."[24] The Algonquins in this case described Lake Erie; Champlain was a bit more inaccurate in his estimate, since its actual length is about 248 miles. The Algonquins indicated they had been as far as the St. Clair River but "they had not gone any farther and had not seen the end of a lake that is located at some fifteen or sixteen leagues [31 to 34 miles] from where they were" on the St. Clair. They continued, "Neither had those who had told them about it seen anyone who had seen it, forasmuch as it is so big that they will not risk setting out into the open, for fear that some storm or gale might surprise them."[25]

This third lake was Lake Huron, and Champlain pressed them for more information, but his lack of knowledge of his informants' language served only to instill faulty information in his mind that reinforced the already flawed information he had culled from Hayes's treatise and Wright's map. He wrote the water in this third great lake, Lake Huron, was, according to the Algonquins, "very bad, like that of this sea."[26] How the Algonquins' testimony was translated is unknown, but Champlain's less-than-perfect understanding of what they were saying led him to make several specious conclusions. First, he asserted that Lake Huron as his informants described it was "the South Sea [Pacific Ocean], being salty as they say." Just as amazing to the modern reader, he also wrote that Lake Erie had "only such a small discharge" at Niagara Falls.[27]

On July 9, 1603, Champlain and his party stopped at the Île d'Orléans and questioned another group of Algonquins about the geography of the St. Lawrence. Like the first group, they depicted what they knew by drawing a map. They also described the series of rapids that led to Lake Ontario, which, according to these Algonquins, "measures some hundred and fifty leagues in length [315 miles]," an estimate that now made the lake quite a bit longer than it actually is. After portaging around Niagara Falls, the Algonquins asserted they entered into "another very big lake

[Lake Erie], which may be as big as the former."[28] They admitted they had only been to Lake Erie a few times. However, they had heard from others that "at the end of the said lake there is a sea [Lake Huron], whose end they have not seen, nor have they heard that anyone else may have seen it; but they say that there, where they have been [Lake Erie], the water is not bad." Champlain questioned them concerning the flow and outlets of these lakes; this second group of Algonquins stated Lakes Erie and Huron, to their knowledge, only flowed eastward into the St. Lawrence River. He also learned their enemies, the Iroquois, lived only about 100 to 130 miles from Lake Ontario, making the St. Lawrence a dangerous passage beyond the Lachine Rapids.[29]

The next day at Île aux Lièvres, he met another Algonquin; this would be his third meeting with members of the tribe. This young man provided a very different description. Like the first group, he described the Ottawa River as well as the various rapids on the St. Lawrence. According to Champlain, the young Algonquin asserted that "they enter a very large lake, which may measure some three hundred leagues [630 miles] in length." If the young Algonquin meant Lake Ontario, he provided a gross overestimation of its size. He went on to say the water on the eastern end of the lake was "drinkable," but as one pushed westward, "the water is still worse" and the western end was "totally salty." He gave a better account of what presumably was Niagara Falls as being "a league [2.1 miles] in width," over which an "exceedingly great current of water descends." Unlike the first two groups, this Algonquin described the second body of water beyond the first lake in terms that indicated a much greater size; he asserted it was "a sea so great that they have not seen the end of it or heard tell of anyone who may have seen it." In fact, it was much like the first two Algonquin groups' description of Lake Huron rather than the actual second body of water as one travels westward, Lake Erie. Champlain asked him if there were any mines of which he knew, to which the young Algonquin replied the "good Irocois [the Hurons]" told his people there was "in the northern parts, a mine of pure copper." This statement referred to the copper the Hurons received through trade networks with tribes that had access to the copper mines of either Lake Huron or Lake Superior.[30]

Champlain concluded by noting all three accounts were generally the same, "only differing very little from each other . . . and they differ somewhat concerning the path, some making it shorter and others longer." He concluded, based on the reports of the water increasing in salinity as one pushed westward, the third body of water, Lake Huron, "must be nothing other than the South Sea [Pacific Ocean]" which Champlain estimated to be "some 400 leagues [about 840 miles]" from the Lachine Rapids at present-day Montreal.[31]

So, what are we to make of Champlain's conclusions? As indicated by the preceding statement, Champlain believed that the St. Lawrence River, which he knew flowed eastward, and the Great Lakes chain from which it flowed, also had a west-flowing outlet to the Pacific Ocean or some bay or estuary thereof. He presumed Lake Huron was either the Pacific or an adjunct of it. Two of Champlain's recent biographers, Conrad E. Heidenreich and K. Janet Ritch, provide a rather pointed criticism, asking, "Had Champlain lost his critical faculties or was he trying to give credence to the salty western end of Lake Ontario and the sea beyond it that had been postulated by Edward Hayes?"[32] The answer to this question is yes, but a qualified yes. Hayes's treatise and Wright's 1599 map certainly influenced Champlain, but, as has been demonstrated, Wright was hardly the only cartographer who appended to the Great Lakes, imperfectly as they were known, the Pacific Ocean or a saltwater body that was connected to it. Had Champlain lost his "critical faculties" in making what Heidenreich and Ritch label a "silly fabrication" of a body of water, Lake Huron, flowing in two directions? Heidenreich and Ritch rightly state, "It was absurd as claiming that water could flow uphill."[33]

In Champlain's defense, a few lakes do flow in more than one direction and have more than a single outlet, although such lakes are rare and limited to the subarctic regions of North America. Champlain and other Europeans during his age had no knowledge of their existence. One can nevertheless find scattered references that indicate the people of Champlain's time believed such bodies of water existed and, in fact, may have been quite common. In addition to Hayes's treatise and Wright's 1599 map, the writings of two of Champlain's contemporaries, Marc Lescarbot and Gabriel Sagard, also contain references to lakes and even rivers that were believed to flow in opposing directions. Heidenreich and Ritch are correct when they surmise this belief in the existence of a lake that flowed in two directions was largely a product of wishful thinking on the part of Champlain, but other Frenchmen and Europeans also shared this notion in the hope the Northwest Passage might be realized via the St. Lawrence River and Great Lakes.[34]

It is unclear how the Algonquins' verbal testimony was translated at Champlain's three meetings, but the imperfect translations probably led in part to the specious conclusions he drew from these inquiries. In many Algonquian languages, the words for "bad water," "muddy water," and "stinking water" are virtually identical to those used for "saltwater" or "seawater." In the Algonquin language proper, *Winipik* refers to "salt-water" but, just as important, can refer also to "bad-smelling water."[35] Thus, what the various Algonquin parties told Champlain was not that the water became saltier as one pushed westward. Then to what did they refer? Given the imperfect descriptions left by Champlain and the less-than-adequate translations he received, any conclusions are necessarily tentative, but the Indians apparently described the declining quality of the freshwater as one journeyed into the western Great Lakes. In the 1920s, Nellis Crouse provided a tantalizing theory when he proposed the testimony provided by the young Algonquin at Île aux Lièvres described not the route up the St. Lawrence River through the lower Great Lakes and thus to Lake Huron, which the first two groups of Algonquins had communicated, but a route up the Ottawa River to Lake Huron. Thus, the lake the young man reportedly described as "totally salty" at its western extreme was Lake Huron, not Lake Ontario. If this is true, then the rapids he described were the Sault Ste. Marie Rapids rather than Niagara Falls, and the great sea he described beyond Lake Huron was Lake Michigan or possibly Lake Superior.[36]

If correct, Crouse's theory explains quite a few mysteries. For example, assuming the young Algonquin actually meant the water became not "salty" but instead "bad" or "smelly" as one pushed westward into Lake Huron, what exactly did he mean? Crouse conjectured, with a healthy dose of caution, that the young man actually narrated a journey up the Ottawa River to Lake Huron and then along Huron's north shore, past Manitoulin Island and the Sault Ste. Marie Rapids, and then into Lake Michigan and Green Bay (coincidentally, the same route Jean Nicolet traveled in 1634). Crouse noted, "one hundred leagues [210 miles] beyond which the water was said to be bad . . . is in all probability, though we cannot be certain, a vague reference to the upper *Baye des Puans*, or Green Bay in Lake Michigan, inhabited by the Ouinipeg (Winnebago) Indians, whose name was so long associated with salt or ill-smelling water."[37]

Crouse is certainly on firm ground here, for numerous historical accounts attest to the malodorous waters of Green Bay. A few examples illustrate this point. In 1660—a period when the Great Lakes were far better known to the French—a Jesuit, most likely Gabriel Druillettes, described Green Bay as "'the lake of the stinkards,' not because it is salt like the water of the Sea,—which the Savages call Ouinipeg, or 'stinking water,'—but because it is surrounded by sulphurous soil, whence issue several springs which convey into this lake the impurities absorbed by their waters in the places of their origin."[38] Thirteen years later, another Jesuit, Jacques Marquette, wrote something very similar about Green Bay:

> This bay bears a Name which has a meaning not so offensive in the language of the savages; For they call it *la baye sallé* ["salt bay"] rather than Bay des Puans,—although with Them this is almost the same and this is also The name which they give to the Sea. This led us to make very careful researches to ascertain whether there were not some salt Water springs in This quarter . . . but we found none. We conclude, therefore, that This name has been given to it on account of the quantity of mire and Mud which is seen there, whence noisome vapors Constantly arise, Causing the loudest and most Continual Thunder that I have ever heard.[39]

Even two centuries later, an American army surgeon, William Beaumont, wrote in 1827 that the water of the Fox River, which fed into Green Bay, was "unfit for any other use than washing . . . the uncommon lowness of the waters and the consequent exhalations from the decaying animal and vegetable matters spread upon the adjacent swamps and prairies."[40] Observations about the sulfurous odors emanating from Green Bay and Lake Michigan were common several generations later as white settlers entered the region in the nineteenth century.[41]

These accounts illustrate that Indians who spoke Algonquian languages used the same words to describe the saltwater of the sea and malodorous freshwater. Moreover, the foul-smelling water at the head of

Green Bay flowed past the homeland of the Puans. For this reason, their Algonquian-speaking neighbors bestowed upon them the unflattering name *Ounipigou*, or, in English, Winnebago: "People of the Stinking Water." The French, translating this term into their own language, called them *Puans* or *Puants*: the "Stinkards."[42]

Given the nature of the impure, smelly water the Fox River bequeathed to Green Bay and, by extension, the northern portion of Lake Michigan, Champlain's young Algonquin likely described a voyage from Lake Huron to Lake Michigan. Even the first group of Algonquins at the Lachine Rapids asserted the water of Lake Huron, to their knowledge, was "very bad, like that of this sea."[43] They, too, may have referred to the waters that issued from Green Bay and into Lake Michigan, which then flows into Lake Huron. Crouse's theory is not without its problems; the young man's description of the various rapids that one must pass to move upriver bears a stronger resemblance to the St. Lawrence River than the Ottawa River. Nevertheless, scholars cannot reject Crouse's speculations out of hand, particularly since they explain the disparity between the reports of the first two groups of Algonquins when compared to that of the young man at Île aux Lièvres. Crouse's work also answers several questions posed by Heidenreich and Ritch, who candidly note, "It is difficult to believe that an Algonquin who had been as far as Niagara Falls could concoct such a story, unless he was prompted. Did Champlain want to be told of a passage west to saltwater? Did Champlain invent all this? Or did he get this information from European verbal or printed sources, such as Edward Hayes?"[44]

Champlain almost certainly wanted to find a passage to the Pacific Ocean; he was heir to many generations of explorers before him who, seduced by the riches of the Far East, sought a passage through or around the vastness of the North America. The testimony Champlain received in 1603 would be a critical component of his geographical theories concerning the continent, but only a component. He continued to develop his ideas as his store of information increased. Champlain finished his explorations in 1603 by examining the southern shore of the Gulf of St. Lawrence eastward to the Gaspé Peninsula. He attempted to learn more about the river systems, particularly those that might lead inland from the Atlantic coast to the large lake described by his earlier Indian informants. It was yet more proof that Hayes's treatise and the Wright map had deeply influenced his thinking. He wrote, "It would be a great asset if someone could find some passage on the coast of Florida that would come out near the above-said great lake where the water is salty, both for the navigation of the vessels that would not be subjected to so many perils as they are in *Canadas* [the St. Lawrence River valley], and for the shortening of the route by more than three hundred leagues [630 miles]."[45]

—ıı—

In late August 1603, Champlain began the return voyage to France. He made his report and presented Henri IV with a map of his explorations; unfortunately, the map has been lost. According to Champlain, he reported "upon the means of discovering the passage to China without the inconvenience of the northern icebergs, or the heat of the torrid zone."[46] Champlain learned that Aymar de Chaste had died while he was away. Pierre Dugua, sieur de Mons, a Protestant nobleman, became the new leader of France's North American project. While Pontgravé and Champlain explored the St. Lawrence, an English trade expedition under the command of Martin Pring had sailed to New England and traded with the various Indian communities of Cape Cod. Pring sought to examine possible sites for future trade. Much like that of Gosnold, Pring's expedition likely came to the attention of the French court and shaped the next major French effort. The St. Lawrence would wait; de Mons and Henri IV decided it was essential for the French to blunt English designs on the Atlantic coast by establishing French colonies in Acadia, another somewhat vague geographical expression that included present-day Nova Scotia and New Brunswick. By his royal commission, de Mons would build fortifications, establish settlements, explore the Atlantic coast, and develop strong relations with the resident Indian nations. Once again, Champlain asked for and received Henri IV's permission to accompany the expedition and report all he observed.[47]

For the next three years, Champlain was a member of de Mons's expedition. The interval between his return from the St. Lawrence and his departure to Acadia in April 1604 was undoubtedly busy. In addition to acquiring more competence with various navigational and cartographic instruments, he did quite a bit of reading concerning Cartier and other

Europeans who had conducted explorations of North America. When de Mons's fleet reached Acadia in May 1604, he and Champlain, along with the crews of three French ships, spent several weeks exploring the north Atlantic coast and finally decided upon Isle Sainte-Croix (present-day Dochet Island in the St. Croix River in Maine) for their settlement. In the process of searching for the site, Champlain became the first person to survey this coast extensively. He later produced many high-quality maps and charts of the various harbors that added considerably to Europe's knowledge of the area; he also debunked a fable. In the early sixteenth century, Europeans had developed the myth of the City of Norumbega on what is today the Penobscot River. The name of the supposed city also applied to the entire region. Over time, the myth grew, and soon Norumbega was a city with streets wider than those in London and whose citizens wore baubles of gold, silver, and pearls. Upon exploring the river, Champlain quickly surmised the glories of Norumbega were mere legends. He also learned of the various rivers that allowed one to ascend northward and the portages to other river systems that fed into the St. Lawrence. Still, he hoped to find a river like the River Gamas that directly linked the St. Lawrence with the Atlantic. He wrote that he desired nothing more than to explore farther southward down the coast and make "new discoveries towards Florida."[48]

The next spring, Champlain received his wish. The settlement on Isle Sainte-Croix was a hellhole; the winter was more difficult than anyone expected, and thirty-five of the seventy-nine colonists died of scurvy. About twenty others were near death by the early spring of 1605. Clearly, a new site was required. Champlain and de Mons once again explored the coast, and this time they pushed south all the way to Cape Cod. Champlain continued to query the members of the various Indian tribes he met, a task made easier by the inclusion of Indian guides who knew the local languages. When he lacked translators, Champlain communicated with signs and had the Indians make charcoal sketches. De Mons later settled upon a new site across the Bay of Fundy called Port-Royal (present-day Annapolis Royal, Nova Scotia).[49]

The forty-five survivors of Sainte-Croix received another fifty colonists in the summer of 1606. That year, Champlain explored the coast of present-day New England with an expedition under the command of Jean de Biencourt, sieur de Poutrincourt, in 1606. To make life more pleasant at Port-Royal, Champlain founded the Ordre de Bon Temps (Order of Good Cheer), which organized great feasts and entertainments. Good relations also existed with the local Mi'kmaq Indians, but alas, the seeming success of Port-Royal was not to last. In May 1607, a French vessel brought news that de Mons's trading company, which had funded the colonization project, had failed; by August the colonists abandoned the settlement and departed for France. While he was able to fulfill his desire for exploration during his three years in Acadia, Champlain had not discovered any great rivers that might serve as the Northwest Passage, nor had he found any of the great mineral wealth that Acadia was rumored to possess.[50]

The failure of Port-Royal turned out to be a blessing for Champlain, for de Mons was willing to make another attempt at founding a colony, but he wanted to stay in France to protect his interests from enemies in the court. He needed a man in North America to be his lieutenant with the vision required to make his new project work; he chose Champlain. The fur trade would be the economic engine of this new colony, and Champlain convinced de Mons the St. Lawrence Valley offered the best possibilities. The colonists whom Champlain recruited included Étienne Brûlé and possibly Nicolas Marsolet, two of Champlain's "young men" who, like Jean Nicolet later, lived among the Indians and learned their languages and cultures upon their arrival in Canada. Champlain departed France in April 1608 and arrived in June at Tadoussac after a five-year absence. Afterward, he sailed westward looking for the ideal site to plant his settlement. He finally decided upon Quebec, and on July 3, 1608, he and his small number of colonists began to build their post where the St. Lawrence narrowed to a choke point. Champlain judged the site would be easy to defend and provided an excellent spot to control traffic on the river.[51]

Quebec became a base from which Champlain was able to conduct additional explorations of the interior of North America as well as an important center of trade and diplomacy. The Algonquins and Montagnais whom he met throughout 1608 made it clear they wanted French assistance in combating their enemies, the Five Nations League of the Iroquois. Champlain agreed, thus cementing an alliance that was to bring great benefits as well as grave dangers to the budding colony. Champlain was eager to explore the North American interior, but before he could assist France's newest allies or journey deep into the heart of the continent, he first had to lead the small colony of thirty-one settlers through the winter, and a hard winter it was. By the spring of 1609, seven had died of scurvy and another thirteen of dysentery. Unlike the St. Lawrence Iroquois in Cartier's day, the local Montagnais apparently did not know of the curative properties of white cedar, or if they did, they did not share this information with the French. Of those settlers who lived through the winter, only eight enjoyed good health; the others suffered from illness. Nevertheless, the little colony survived, and Champlain was determined to fulfill his promise to his allies.[52]

Thus, in late June 1609, Champlain departed Quebec with a small number of Frenchmen and a large body of Montagnais, Algonquin, and Huron warriors and traveled down the Richelieu River. The expedition, in his mind, was as much a martial exercise to fulfill his promise as it was a journey of exploration. On July 14, 1609, Champlain finally set his eyes upon a large, shimmering lake he named after himself: Lake Champlain. He spent two weeks exploring the lake as his Indian allies waited patiently for the moon to wane and the nights to become darker. On the night of July 29, Champlain and his allies penetrated deep into the Mohawks' country at the southern end of Lake Champlain near a place that would gain renown several generations later: Ticonderoga. There, the French and Indian war party met a group of Mohawks, who, upon being sighted, began to construct a fortification. Throughout the night, both parties exchanged verbal harangues. The next morning, Champlain, his wheel-lock arquebus at the ready, moved behind the body of Indian warriors. The Mohawks, about two hundred strong, must have sensed an easy victory against a party of only about sixty. When the St. Lawrence Indians were about fifty yards from the Mohawks, they called Champlain forward. Champlain later wrote, "I was within some thirty yards of the enemy, who as soon as they caught sight of me halted and gazed at me. . . . I took aim with my arquebus and shot straight at one of the three chiefs, and with this shot two fell to the ground. . . . This frightened them greatly. . . . Seeing their chiefs dead, they lost courage and took to flight."[53]

In addition to providing a visual image of Champlain fighting the Iroquois with his Indian allies, this depiction of a 1609 battle is the only definite likeness of Champlain produced of him during his lifetime. He is shown in the center firing his arquebus.
WHI IMAGE ID 134115

After the battle, Champlain explored the chute that led to nearby Lake George. He even had his Algonquin allies query several Mohawk prisoners they had captured. From them, Champlain confirmed something he had learned five years earlier: it was possible to travel to the south end of Lake George and reach the Atlantic via a portage to the Hudson River. Little did he know that another great explorer, the Englishman Henry Hudson, would, a few months later, sail up the river that bears his name in the hope that it might provide the much-sought-after Northwest Passage. Champlain also witnessed firsthand the tortures the various tribes of Indians in northeastern North America inflicted upon their enemies when his allies took one of the Mohawks and began to burn him with hot brands. They proceeded to pull out his nails, burnt his fingers and penis, flayed the scalp from his head, and pierced his limbs to tear the tendons from his bones. Champlain was amazed at the remarkable composure the prisoner exhibited, relating "he bore it so firmly that sometimes one would have said he felt scarcely any pain."[54]

Champlain offered to dispatch the prisoner with his arquebus, but his Indian allies refused because, they argued, the victim would feel no agony if he were simply shot. They relented only when Champlain continued to demonstrate his displeasure, but even after Champlain shot the man as an act of mercy, the Indians desecrated the corpse. Champlain noted:

> When he was dead, they were not satisfied; they opened his body and threw his bowels into the lake. Afterwards they cut off his head, arms and legs. . . . They did another awful thing, which was to cut his heart into several pieces and to give it to a brother of the dead man to eat and to others of his companions who were prisoners. These took it and put it into their mouths, but would not swallow it.[55]

The Indians' culture of war was far different from that of Europeans, who fought in well-drilled units deemed indispensable to maneuvering large numbers of men. Moreover, the power to make war in European states was firmly lodged in the hands of the sovereign. Indian warfare in northeastern North America, on the other hand, was a means by which individual warriors gained recognition, and while Indian tribal councils occasionally mustered large bodies of men to fight their enemies, small groups of individuals, of their own volition, frequently raided enemy villages. Thus, the decision for war rested not with a distant monarch but with members of the community. Although Indian war parties were well organized and disciplined, Indian men largely fought as individuals once a battle commenced and saw warfare as the means by which they earned individual honor.[56]

The treatment of captives also served important cultural functions. The Iroquois in particular engaged in "mourning wars" whereby prisoners replaced deceased relations. Captives were often adopted and became something of a reincarnation of the departed; women and children frequently fulfilled this role. Scalps taken from the dead even served this purpose and were "adopted" by the community. The scalp of a defeated enemy, and in some cases the entire head, also became trophies of war, and the manhood of a defeated warrior passed to the victor, thus enhancing his social prestige. Male captives were often tortured as a means of avenging earlier losses of community members. In a sense, the captive became an adopted member of the community through ritual torture and was even addressed as a relation by captors who sought redress for relatives lost in a similar manner to their adversaries. Torture also produced a sense of social cohesion, as it clearly defined those enemies who were "the other" and in the process delineated those in the community who were part of the "collective 'we,'" as historian Denys Delâge has argued. Of course, Europeans in Champlain's time also practiced grim spectacles of public torture and execution, but these were directed against wrongdoers within the society who had failed to respect the divinely ordained power of the monarch. According to Delâge, the body of the condemned in European torture became the means by which the sovereign demonstrated to his or her subjects "the existence of a dissymmetry, an irrevocable imbalance of power."[57] Thus, as with war, European monarchs maintained a monopoly over punishment for crimes, not the community, as was the case with the Indians whom Champlain encountered.

Because of the decentralized nature of Indian warfare, Champlain saw it a destabilizing phenomenon that had to be curbed if he was to realize his dream of building a great network of trade in the St. Lawrence Valley and the Great Lakes. He may have gone to war with his Indian allies in 1609, but this was simply part of his larger plan of demonstrating to the Five Nations League the kind of military force the French could bring to the battlefield. He hoped his actions would convince the Iroquois to come to Quebec to discuss peace with the French and their Indian allies, who, like the Iroquois, often clamored for war. Champlain later wrote he wanted his Indian allies to "make peace . . . with the Iroquois, in view of the advantage it would be to them to travel freely up the Great River [the St. Lawrence] . . . instead of being in terror from day to day of being massacred and taken prisoners."[58]

—｜｜—

After the battle, Champlain returned to Quebec and then France, for de Mons had ordered him to return, presumably to assist in finding new investors. Champlain remained for six months before returning to Quebec in April 1610. Almost as soon as he returned, the Montagnais asked his assistance in another campaign against the Iroquois. Champlain agreed but this time demanded something in return: he wanted the Montagnais and Algonquins to assist him in his explorations of the saltwater body to the north (Hudson Bay) and the large sea to the west (Lake Huron). The Indians agreed, and Champlain soon departed with yet another war party. Champlain and his allies only had to travel to the mouth of the Richelieu River where the Mohawks had built a fortification. Champlain brought four French arquebusiers whose heavy volleys took their toll. About one hundred Mohawks were killed and the remaining fifteen survivors taken prisoner. Afterward, he returned to Quebec to continue supervising the construction of the settlement. In June 1610, he learned that an assassin had murdered Henri IV. To add insult to injury, de Mons once again ordered Champlain to return to France to assist in the management of his trading company, which, like all such companies, was the principal means of financing French colonial enterprises during much of the sixteenth and seventeenth centuries. The new king, Louis XIII, was only nine years old, and his mother, Queen Marie de' Medici, acted as his regent. Unlike her deceased husband, she had little interest in North America and even less in developing a strong relationship with Champlain. During his time in France, Champlain married Hélène Boullé. As was common in France in Champlain's time, Hélène was much younger, at twelve years of age, than her new husband, who was thirty-six. Her family had connections that Champlain believed would be important to the success of his North American project. The marriage contract specified that the union would not be consummated for two years, during which Hélène continued to reside with her parents.[59]

Between 1611 and 1615, Champlain frequently shuttled between Old and New France. His presence back home was often needed to maintain support for the colonial venture. On his return to the St. Lawrence in May 1611, he sailed westward with the intent of learning more about the river. He spent much of June and July 1611 near the Island of Montreal and met with the Algonquins and Hurons, who brought along one of Champlain's "youths," most likely Étienne Brûlé, whom he had left with the Hurons and Algonquins many years earlier. The Indians were not prepared to assist him in exploring the Ottawa or St. Maurice Rivers toward Hudson Bay as they had promised earlier. Champlain had little choice except to learn more about the regional geography by once again questioning the Indians. During one meeting with the Hurons and Algonquins, Champlain asked them about the source of the St. Lawrence River. He learned a great deal but, unfortunately for the modern researcher, did not record many details. He wrote:

> They told me many things, both of the rivers, falls, lakes, and lands, and of the tribes living there. . . . Four of them assured me that they had seen a sea, far from their country, but that the way to it was difficult. . . . They told me also that during the preceding winter some Indians had come from the direction of Florida, beyond the country of the Iroquois, who were familiar with our ocean. . . . In short they spoke to me of these things in great detail, showing me by drawings all the places they had visited. . . . And as for myself, I was not weary of listening to them, because some things were cleared up about which I had been in doubt until they enlightened me about them.[60]

Champlain's very general description does not allow us to know if the "sea" to which the Indians referred was one of the Great Lakes or Hudson Bay, and thus, it is impossible to determine what things "were cleared up" in his mind.

Fortunately, Champlain made two maps that record his geographical knowledge at this point. By September 1611, he was back in France and published a new work, *Les Voyages du Sieur de Champlain* (*The Voyages of Sieur de Champlain*), which included a map, *Carte Geographique de la Nouvelle Franse*, that shows, in exquisite detail, those parts of the Atlantic coast and the St. Lawrence Valley he had explored. His depiction of the Great Lakes is less accurate and is based on information he had received from the Indians. The map clearly shows Lake Ontario and lists its length as "15 *Journees des canaux des Sauvages*" (fifteen canoe journeys of the Indians), while the next lake is depicted as 300 leagues (630 miles) in length. While this body of water should be Lake Erie, it almost certainly depicts Lake Huron as it matches the description Champlain received from the young Algonquin at Île aux Lièvres in 1603. Champlain did not depict the western end of this lake, thus subtly hinting it led to the Pacific Ocean. He also produced another map in 1612, *Carte geographique de la Novelle franse en son vray moridia*. Significantly, this second map depicts Hudson Bay, which Henry Hudson had explored only two years earlier in 1610.

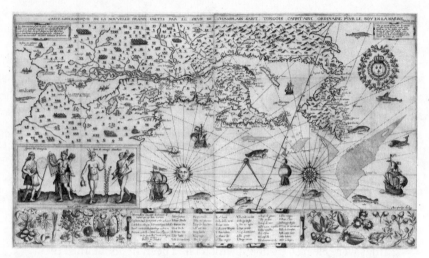

Champlain's depiction of the Great Lakes in *Carte Geographique de la Nouvelle Franse* (1612) is largely inaccurate. It was based on his interviews with various Algonquin and Huron informants in 1603 and 1611 and not on direct oberservation. His depiction of the Atlantic coast is much more accurate, as Champlain extensively charted this region between 1604 and 1607 as part of the expedition led by Pierre Dugua, sieur de Mons.
LAVERDIERE, *OEUVRES DE CHAMPLAIN*

Champlain based his rendering of this great saltwater body on a map made by the Dutch cartographer Hessel Gerritsz, who relied on information acquired from Hudson's voyage.[61]

Also during this time, Champlain gained a new superior. The queen, unlike her late husband, had little toleration for Protestants, and thus de Mons stepped aside in favor of a Catholic and a member of the royal family, Henri de Bourbon, Prince de Condé, a nobleman and cousin of Louis XIII who held the title of viceroy of New France. Prince de Condé would be the first of many such viceroys during Champlain's career who, like all his successors, never set foot in New France. That was left to his lieutenant, Champlain, who, about this time, was approached by one of the young men he had left among the Indians. Nicolas de Vignau accompanied Champlain on his 1611 voyage and spent the winter with a band of Algonquins, led by a chief named Tessoüat, who lived on what is today Morrison Island in the Ottawa River. Champlain had hoped that during his time among the Algonquins, Vignau might be able to explore toward Hudson Bay. Vignau returned to France in 1612 and reported

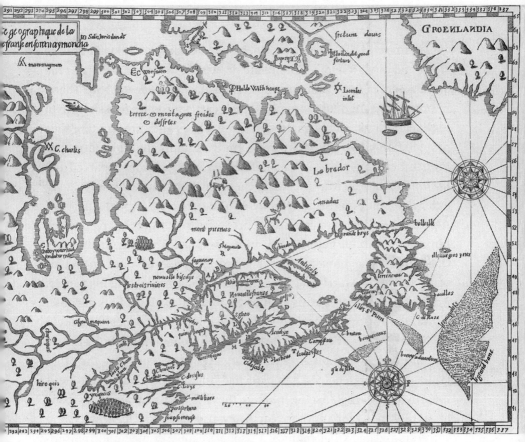

Champlain's 1612 map, *Carte geographique de la Novelle franse en son vray moridia*, like *Carte Geographique de la Nouvelle Franse*, presents a very accurate depiction of the Atlantic coast, which Champlain extensively surveyed from 1604 to 1607. He also included Hudson Bay, which Henry Hudson had explored in 1610 and which the Dutch cartographer Hessel Gerritsz first illustrated cartographically in 1612. This provides evidence that Champlain maintained a keen interest in North American exploration throughout his career. WHI IMAGE ID 134122

to Champlain he had been to the "northern sea" (Hudson Bay) after a seventeen-day journey from the Lachine Rapids and saw the wreckage of an English ship. Champlain noted, "This intelligence greatly delighted me; for I thought I had found close at hand what I was searching for a long way off."[62] Nevertheless, Champlain was skeptical. By this time, he had a better idea of the distances between various points in North America, and he likely believed a journey from the Lachine Rapids to Hudson Bay via the Ottawa River would be longer than seventeen days.[63]

Members of the royal court encouraged Champlain to confirm the story, and in March 1613, Champlain departed France and arrived at the St. Lawrence in April, reaching the Lachine Rapids on May 21, 1613. There, he pressed the Algonquins to fulfill their earlier promise to assist him in his explorations, and he requested three canoes and three guides; they provided only two canoes and one guide. Champlain took along four Frenchmen, including Vignau. The small expedition departed the Lachine Rapids on May 27. Along the way Champlain, as always, took extensive notes on the geography. While traveling, he met a party of Algonquins, who, upon hearing of his desire to explore the river, urged him not to continue because the country was bad. They did not dissuade Champlain, who managed to secure another guide. Champlain and his party arrived at Morrison Island, the home of Tessoüat and his people. After a feast to celebrate his arrival, Champlain explained his purpose. He wanted Tessoüat to provide additional guides and canoes so he could continue upriver to the Nipissings, another Algonquian-speaking people who lived on Lake Nipissing. Tessoüat, after conferring with the other leaders of his band, noted Champlain had failed the previous year to assist them in their war against the Iroquois; they asked Champlain to postpone his explorations for another year. They also said the Nipissings "were sorcerers and had killed many of Tessoüat's people by magic and poisoning, and consequently were not considered friendly."[64]

When Champlain mentioned Vignau had been to the country of the Nipissings (which Champlain likely believed was the gateway to Hudson Bay), Tessoüat became angry and accused Vignau of lying; this only served to confirm what Champlain already thought about the young man. Vignau insisted in private conversations with Champlain he had been to Hudson Bay with a relation of Tessoüat and had seen the wreckage of an English ship and even a young Englishman whom the Indians had taken prisoner. However, Tessoüat asserted with great anger that Vignau was "a brazen liar; you know well that every night you slept alongside of me and my children. . . . You are a miserable wretch whom he [Champlain] ought to put to death more cruelly than we do our enemies."[65] While Champlain doubted Vignau's story, he harbored doubts about Tessoüat as well. Under pressure from both Champlain and Tessoüat, Vignau admitted that he was lying and had concocted the story simply so he could return to Canada. With a heavy heart burdened by disappointment, Champlain departed Tessoüat's village and was back at the Lachine Rapids by June 17, 1613. There, Champlain abandoned Vignau to fend for himself. What became of Vignau afterward is unknown.[66]

But was Vignau lying? Some historians believe he was not. There had, indeed, been an English expedition to Hudson Bay in 1610–1611 under Henry Hudson, and a mutinous crew abandoned Hudson, his seventeen-year-old son, and seven loyal members of his crew in a small boat. Champlain definitely knew of Hudson's expedition and thus understood this part of Vignau's story was true. Moreover, it is possible to ascend the Ottawa River and travel to Hudson Bay via a series of portages. However, the first Frenchmen to accomplish this feat in 1686 required eighty-two days of travel; traveling the same route in seventeen days as Vignau stated would have been a Herculean accomplishment. Similarly, in 1671–1672, the first Frenchmen to reach Hudson Bay by traveling north up the Saguenay River from Tadoussac arrived after a journey of forty-five days. So if Vignau's story were true, even if he stretched the truth about the number of days it took to get to Hudson Bay, why would he have recanted? Certainly, the heavy pressure and threats of death issued by Champlain and Tessoüat might have led him to panic and change his story.[67] But why would Tessoüat have lied?

The sad saga of Nicolas de Vignau exposes the weaknesses of the alliance that Champlain had concluded with the St. Lawrence Indians. Champlain saw the pact as the means by which he could use their knowledge to further his goals of exploration. The Indians, on the other hand, saw it as the means by which they could exploit the French and their weapons in their wars against the Iroquois. However, they were reluctant to assist Champlain in his explorations for several reasons. First, the Montagnais and Algonquins acted as middlemen between the French and Indian communities northward toward Hudson Bay. Taking Champlain to these tribes would have given the French direct access and undermined what the Indians saw as a lucrative trade position. Taking a man such as Vignau was one matter; he was young and lacked experience. Champlain was older, more experienced, and in a far better position than any of his young men to develop relationships with more distant tribes. Throughout Champlain's writings, it is clear the Indians, when pressed to assist him in exploration, made excuses as to why they could not. They would press Champlain for military assistance first; they would urge him to wait another year or more to explore; they would be unable to furnish canoes or guides. Thus, there is a very good chance Tessoüat rather than Vignau was lying. In fact, Tessoüat insisted the Nipissings were the enemies of the Algonquins when in fact they were not.[68]

Champlain returned to France and remained for two years, once again taking care of the various financial arrangements required to maintain his vision for New France. He formed a new group of investors that remained under the leadership of Prince de Condé. Champlain never actually held the title of governor; that was reserved for the viceroys appointed by the king, although many people often referred to Champlain as the governor of New France. He was technically the commander who served as a subordinate of the various viceroys. Champlain served in this capacity from 1612 until his death in 1635. He wrote another book of his travels and began preparations for his return to the St. Lawrence in 1615; in many ways, this journey would be the culmination of his career as an explorer. He departed Honfleur along with his old friend Pontgravé and four Récollet priests, members of a Franciscan order who would be the first Catholic clergy in New France. On June 2, 1615, Champlain reached Quebec and later met the Algonquins and Hurons at Rivière-des-Prairies by the Island of Montreal. Once again, they urged him to assist them in fighting the Iroquois; once again, he agreed and asked for their assistance in his explorations. He noted going on the warpath was, in itself, a quite valuable way "to go and examine their territory, and to help them in their wars, in order to induce them to let me see what they had so often promised me," namely, the "western sea," or Lake Huron.[69]

In July 1615, he and his party, along with ten Hurons, departed Rivière-des-Prairies and began to ascend the Ottawa River toward the Huron country, land occupied by the Hurons in the area of the Penetanguishene Peninsula in present-day southeastern Ontario. Fortunately, Champlain and his allies would set off from here on their military expedition. He would finally see the great western sea! One of the Récollets and twelve Frenchmen had departed earlier. By July 26, 1615, Champlain was at Lake Nipissing and among the Nipissing Indians. Contrary to Tessoüat's statements two years earlier, Champlain found them friendly and accommodating during his two-day visit. Several days later, Champlain entered the broad expanse of Georgian Bay of Lake Huron. There he met the Cheveux releves, the High Hairs, or as they are better known, the Ottawas. A confederation of four closely related Algonquian groups, the Ottawas stretched in an arc from Georgian Bay, along the southern shore of Manitoulin Island and the opposite shore at Saginaw Bay, and west toward the Strait of Mackinac. They were traders who, more so than any other tribe in the Lake Huron basin, traveled westward to trade with distant Indian communities. Champlain met with one of their chiefs and asked him about the geography of the region, particularly to the west. It would be one of his most enlightening discussions concerning North American geography. Champlain wrote, "I asked him about his country, which he drew for me with charcoal on a piece of tree-bark."[70] He did not describe the drawing, but he reproduced it in cartographic form a year later.

By August 1615, he was in the Huron country, where he remained for two weeks before going on the warpath. What was Champlain's reaction upon seeing Lake Huron, the vast, freshwater body that he once believed was the Pacific Ocean? Surprisingly, he wrote virtually nothing, only mentioning he now called it Mer Douce, the Freshwater Sea. Why was his reaction so subdued? He probably already knew this fact before he arrived. During his earlier trips to the St. Lawrence, he often met with the young men he had left there, several of whom had been to the Huron country. He probably learned Lake Huron was a freshwater body in 1611 when he met with one of his young men, most likely Étienne Brûlé, who had spent 1610–1611 among the Hurons. Champlain expressed more astonishment toward the Hurons themselves, as they had a significantly larger population than their hunting-and-gathering allies. Champlain estimated the Hurons' population to be thirty thousand, although it may have been closer to twenty-one thousand. The Hurons produced so much corn the tribe was a net exporter of food, which they traded for peltries with their Algonquian-speaking neighbors, such as the Nipissings, Ottawas, and Algonquins. He visited several of the Hurons' palisaded villages, particularly Cahiague, where the warriors gathered for the campaign against the Iroquois. Champlain also learned more about the liberal sexual practices of the Hurons, noting that "a shameless girl came boldly up to me, offering to keep me company, which I declined with thanks, sending her away with gentle remonstrances."[71]

The war party departed on September 1, 1615, with five hundred warriors and between ten and thirteen French arquebusiers. They traveled by water across the eastern end of Lake Ontario, the second of the Great Lakes Champlain saw. The campaign, however, experienced several problems. When Champlain's Algonquin and Huron allies captured a small party of Onondagas, they immediately began to torture one of the women. When Champlain expressed his disgust and insisted they stop, an Algonquin, incensed at Champlain's interference, grabbed an Iroquois infant and bashed its head against a tree. As Champlain learned, the Indians of northeastern North America did not always distinguish between combatants and noncombatants, and women and children were sometimes fair game in Native warfare. The war party came to an Onondaga town, most likely at the southern end of Lake Onondaga where Syracuse, New York, now stands. Champlain was impressed with what he saw, for the town had strong defenses: four palisades of interwoven timbers in excess of thirty feet in height. Such defensive structures were common to the villages of the Five Nations League, and in some cases, the poles were as thick as twenty-four inches. The Hurons palisaded their villages as well. Archaeological evidence indicates the Iroquois had built such defensive structures as early as 900 CE, another indication of how long warfare had plagued the region. Toward the top of the palisades were galleries where warriors could shoot arrows and other projectiles upon their enemies.[72]

Champlain developed a plan by which his Indian allies would lure the Onondaga men outside of their walls, and then the French arquebusiers would unleash their volleys against them. But alas, the plan crumbled when small parties of allied warriors engaged the Onondagas early. The Onondagas scattered when the arquebusiers fired and retreated safely within the confines of their palisades. Because the French weapons could not penetrate the thick timbers, Champlain came up with a solution: he would have the Indians and French construct an elevated platform known as a *cavallier* that would allow the arquebusiers to fire over the top of the Onondagas' palisades. This ingenious siege engine worked, but it was

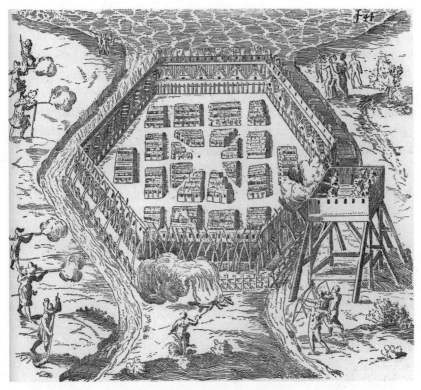

This engraving of Champlain's 1615 battle against the Onondagas clearly depicts the great palisades that surrounded the village of the Onondagas where Syracuse, New York, now stands. In addition to the French arquebusiers who participated in the battle, the engraving also illustrates the elevated *cavallier*, or platform built by the French to fire over the top of the palisades. WHI IMAGE ID 134125

not enough to land a decisive blow. Two Onondaga arrows found their mark—one in Champlain's leg and another in his knee—which caused excruciating pain. While prolonged sieges were common in European warfare, the Indians avoided them. After almost a week of inconclusive fighting, Champlain's allies, sensing they could accomplish little more, withdrew from the battle.[73]

Champlain spent the winter of 1615–1616 recuperating in Huronia and learned more about the regional geography, particularly from the Nipissings, who promised Champlain they would take him northward toward Hudson Bay. However, an Algonquin chief dissuaded them, citing the need to have the Nipissings present at a council to moderate a dispute between the Algonquins and Hurons. Upon learning his Indian allies had cancelled yet another expedition, Champlain plaintively noted, "If any one was sorry it was I; for I had quite expected to see that year what in many other preceding years I had sought for with great solicitude." He continued, "I had such positive information . . . from these people trading with others whose habitation is in those northern parts and who form a considerable division of those tribes in a country of abundant hunting and where there are many large animals."[74] Most likely, he referred to the Cree Indians who lived in the subarctic regions to the north. There was one consolation; the Nipissings told him about a tribe that lived about forty days' journey to the west with whom they traded. Champlain noted, "I saw several skins . . . and by their drawings of their shape I judged them to be buffaloes [bison]."[75] The Nipissings almost certainly referred to the Puans.

Champlain later gleaned more information from the Hurons about this mysterious tribe as well as another, more enigmatic society. What he heard must have come as a surprise, perhaps even a shock. Champlain wrote:

> The savages to whom we have access are at war with other tribes to the west of the said great lake [Lake Huron], which is the reason why we could not have fuller knowledge of it [the region west of Lake Huron], except that several times they told us that some prisoners from a hundred leagues [210 miles] off related to them that there were people there white like us and similar to us in other respects, and through their intermediary they had seen the scalp of these people which is very fair, and which they value highly because of their saying they were like us. Regarding this I can only think that those whom they say resemble us, are people more civilised than themselves.[76]

Clearly, Champlain heard about two different groups of people. The first— the tribe with whom the Indians were at war—was very likely the Puans, for we know from other French sources the Puans were the dominant power at Green Bay along with their allies, the Menominees. Despite their ferocious nature, other sources indicate the Puans also traded with the

Indian nations of Lake Huron when it suited their interests. This would explain how the Nipissings acquired bison hide shields from them.[77]

But what of the fair-skinned people described by the Indians with whom Champlain conversed? The Native communities on the eastern shore of Lake Huron were describing a more distant tribe with which they had no contact: the Mandans on the upper Missouri River. During the nineteenth century, the myth arose in Great Britain and the United States that the Mandan Indians, often called the "white Indians," were the descendants of the Welsh Prince Madoc, who arrived in North America in 1170; however, the origins of this legend went back much further. In the 1730s, Assiniboines, Crees, and French fur traders described the Mandans in the same fashion as the Indians with whom Champlain spoke. Scholars continue to argue about how this myth concerning the Mandans grew, not only among Europeans but also among North American Indian societies. Certainly, the large subterranean lodges of the Mandans were unique; as far as physical characteristics, the Mandans may have possessed genetic characteristics that led to significant variations in skin tone as well as premature graying of the hair. Nevertheless, the Mandans were simply another American Indian society.[78]

Several historians have proffered that Champlain believed the Indians with whom he spoke might have been describing the Chinese rather than the Mandans, and that this was one of his motivations for ordering Nicolet on his famous journey many years later.[79] However, Champlain's writings do not support such a conclusion. Champlain never expressed a belief in the existence of a supposed Chinese colony west of the Great Lakes region anywhere in his writings; he only wrote that one would need to see the people described by his Indian informants "in order to know the truth of it. . . . Only time and the courage of some persons of means, who can or will undertake to assist this project, can decide in order that one day a full and complete exploration of these parts may be made in order to obtain certain knowledge of them."[80] While his mention of "some persons" seems to allude to Nicolet's future voyage (a claim made by earlier historians), the context indicates Champlain was talking only in general terms. Moreover, Champlain, when he sent Nicolet westward in 1634, definitely wanted him to make contact with the Puans as well as gather information on the Indian nations that lived farther to the west.

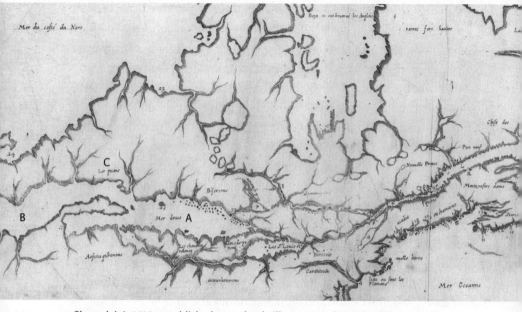

Champlain's 1616 unpublished map clearly illustrates Lake Huron (A), or Mer Douce (the Freshwater Sea), as Champlain labeled it. To the west stretches Lake Michigan (B), although Champlain gave it an east-west orientation rather than the lake's well-known north-south orientation. It was the first map to depict Lake Michigan as well as the first written document to record the existence of the Puans (C). COURTESY OF THE JOHN CARTER BROWN LIBRARY AT BROWN UNIVERSITY

However, he did not believe by that late date, and in fact never believed at all, that a colony of Chinese settlers lay only a few hundred miles farther west of Lake Huron.

The most important source for understanding Champlain's knowledge of North American geography at this time after his 1615–1616 journey is a map he made after he returned to France in September 1616 and which only came to the attention of scholars in 1953. Champlain never completed the map, nor was it published during his lifetime. Nevertheless, it illustrates what geographical information he received from the Indians on the eastern shores of Lake Huron, particularly from the Ottawa chief who sketched a map of the country to the west with charcoal. The two lakes that Champlain saw are both on the map: Mer Douce (Lake Huron) and Lac St. Louis (Lake Ontario). It also shows a diminutive and unnamed Lake Erie. While the proportions and shapes are not exact, Champlain connected the lakes in their proper sequence and accurately showed them flowing eastward into the St. Lawrence River.[81]

He also added a new lake to the west of Lake Huron. Several scholars have asserted this lake, due to its east-west orientation, is Lake Superior, and the strip of land between them is the Keweenaw Peninsula. However, as Conrad E. Heidenreich has demonstrated, this is actually Lake Michigan, and the strip of land separating it from Lake Huron is the Lower Peninsula of Michigan. Either the Ottawa chief did not mention the eventual southward turn one took as they traveled along the northern shore of Lake Huron into Lake Michigan, or Champlain failed to note it. Thus, Champlain's sketch of Lake Michigan exhibits the same east-west orientation as Lake Superior. Champlain also did not learn of the Door Peninsula that juts out into the northwestern corner of Lake Michigan, thus creating Green Bay. One of the key pieces of evidence that demonstrates this body of water is Lake Michigan is that Champlain wrote *Les Puans* on the seeming northern shore of the lake. Champlain's 1616 map stands as the earliest document that records the existence of the Puans. If we turn the 1616 map ninety degrees counterclockwise, we see the rough outline of Lake Michigan emerge, and the Puans are located where they lived at the time: on the northwestern portion of Lake Michigan at Green Bay. We even see two small indentations on the top of Lake Michigan that are Big and Little Bay de Noc.[82]

The map also demonstrates Champlain still held out hope the Great Lakes provided for the Northwest Passage, for the new lake on the 1616 map stretches westward toward the Pacific Ocean. In fact, it appears to be some great bay or estuary of the Pacific. Champlain's 1616 map, in many ways, was simply an updated version of Edward Wright's 1599 map and Edward Hayes's 1602 treatise. As mentioned, these works, in part, led Champlain to conclude after his 1603 expedition that Lake Huron was the Pacific Ocean or an extension thereof. After standing on the shores of this great freshwater sea in 1615, this idea was no longer tenable, but he was able to extend this possibility to the new lake of which he learned from the Ottawas. Thus, he clung tenaciously to his dual-drainage theory of the Great Lakes chain, and his dream of finding the Northwest Passage remained alive. Moreover, it is clear Champlain continued to stay abreast of the voyages of other explorers of his day, as his 1616 map depicts Chesapeake Bay on the Atlantic coast, a body of water Champlain may have learned about from John Smith's 1612 map of this region.[83]

Champlain remained in France for most of 1617 and part of 1618. By this time, not everyone involved in the project of New France saw the need to establish a settled colony. Most of the investors simply wanted to make money from the fur trade, which continued to be profitable. While in France, Champlain wrote a petition to the chamber of commerce as well as a letter to King Louis XIII outlining the advantages of colonizing New France and the tremendous resources to be found there, including rich fisheries, vast forests, and plentiful supplies of furs. In his petition, he wrote, "In addition to all these things one may hope to find a short route to China by way of the river St. Lawrence; and that being the case, it is certain that we shall succeed by the grace of God in finding it without much difficulty."[84] In his letter to the king, Champlain wrote, "One cannot doubt but that this would be the means of reaching easily to the Kingdom of China and the East Indies, whence great riches could be drawn."[85] He went on to say there existed "the South Sea [Pacific Ocean] passage to China and to the East Indies by way of the river St. Lawrence . . . and which river issues from a lake about three hundred leagues [630 miles] in length, from which lake flows a river that empties into the said South Sea."[86]

Champlain believed additional exploration was required to find the Northwest Passage, but after 1616, others would conduct such voyages. His journey to Huronia and Iroquoia in 1615 and 1616 was the last such expedition he undertook; afterward, his duties were that of a colonial administrator. After 1616, he continued to shuttle between France and Quebec, although his visits to New France increased in duration. His duties as the commander of the colony became all consuming, and his priorities shifted as well. After 1616, he focused primarily on securing the future of New France from the dual threats of the Iroquois and other European powers. Rather than accompanying his Indian allies on war parties as he had done earlier in his career, he went on a diplomatic offensive after 1616 to ensure they stayed at peace with the Iroquois.[87] Just as we must understand the evolution of Champlain's geographic knowledge during the span of his career, we must also understand the development of his plans for the colony of New France if we are fully to understand the mission of Jean Nicolet.

3

CHAMPLAIN, COMMANDER
OF NEW FRANCE

1616–1634

From 1616 to 1620, Champlain was primarily in France engaged in the endless court dramas concerning the administration of New France. He made only two short visits to the St. Lawrence in the summers of 1617 and 1618. His 1618 visit had been particularly valuable because he traveled to Trois-Rivières, where he met many Indians with whom he had become well acquainted over the last decade. He also had the opportunity to meet with members of Indian communities that resided farther north on the St. Maurice River and with whom the French had previously not had contact. Champlain gave them presents to draw them into the French trade network. As always, the Indians sought Champlain's promise the French would assist them in their wars against the Iroquois. In return, Champlain sought the Indians' assurances of continued trade with the French.[1]

While at Trois-Rivières, Champlain encountered Étienne Brûlé, whom he had not seen since 1615, just prior to the military campaign Champlain conducted against the Onondagas. Champlain had ordered Brûlé to travel to the Susquehannock Indians and recruit five hundred warriors for the battle. Now, in 1618, Champlain demanded to know why Brûlé had failed to appear. Brûlé explained when he arrived at the Susquehannock village of Carantoüan (most likely located at what is present-day

Athens, Pennsylvania), he was able to raise five hundred warriors, but the Indians' delay in making preparations resulted in Brûlé and the Susquehannocks arriving two days after Champlain and his allies had departed. Brûlé went back to the country of the Susquehannocks and spent the fall and winter exploring their country. He had traveled on a river that "discharges on the coast of Florida" and led to the ocean; there, Brûlé paddled "past islands and the coasts near them."[2] Thus, Brûlé had become the first Frenchman to journey southward on the Susquehanna River into the broad waters of Chesapeake Bay. In the spring of 1616, he traveled back to Huronia but became separated from his guides and fell into the hands of the Senecas. Upon determining Brûlé was French, the Senecas treated him as an enemy, torturing him by pulling out his fingernails and burning him with hot brands. He was saved only when his tormentors spied an Agnus Dei medallion on his neck. Brûlé told them this symbol of the Lamb of God was a powerful talisman that would invoke the wrath of his deity. When a sudden thunderstorm propitiously appeared, the Senecas opted for discretion and ended their tortures. They treated Brûlé as a guest thereafter, and he later resumed his journey to Huronia.[3]

Given the circumstances, Champlain was ready to forgive Brûlé for his failure. Several years earlier, Champlain had ordered Brûlé to conduct additional explorations. However, during the course of the conversation, he learned Brûlé "would have proceeded farther to explore the lie of these regions as I had given him instructions," but continued rumors of war among the tribes on the eastern shore of Lake Huron prevented him from doing so.[4] Presumably, Champlain's directive to Brûlé meant an expedition either north toward Hudson Bay or farther westward into the Great Lakes. Brûlé promised he would undertake such a journey as soon as it was feasible. Champlain noted with no small amount of satisfaction this "pleased me from the hope of succeeding better by this means in continuing and forwarding" such journeys of discovery.[5] Brûlé would not fail to disappoint Champlain—at least not with his explorations.

During his return to France in the summer of 1618, Champlain began work on another book, *Voyages et descouvertures faites en la Nouvelle France, depuis l'année 1615* (*Voyages and Discoveries Made in New France since the Year 1615*). The book was primarily a propaganda piece designed to curry favor with King Louis XIII and win his support for France's North

American project. Champlain largely succeeded and felt confident enough to return to New France for an extended stay in 1620. Thus began, in earnest, his long tenure as a colonial administrator. He spent the majority of his remaining years, until his death in 1635, in the colony of New France as its commander. In this role, he focused on the day-to-day management of the colony. With the assistance of the Récollet priests and later the Jesuits, he maintained religious observance among the colony's settlers. He acted as the chief justice, enforced the laws and decrees of the king, and punished those who did not abide by them. The colonists' welfare was a constant concern, particularly since the population depended almost completely on supplies brought from France, and disease—especially scurvy during the winter months—hovered like a specter over the colony.[6]

In fact, Quebec's population in 1620 consisted of a mere forty-six souls, and the diminutive settlement never held more than one hundred persons before 1629. The various merchants who invested in the companies that profited from the fur trade consistently resisted Champlain's efforts to send more settlers, as they believed large-scale settlement would be detrimental to the trade. The small number of buildings and dwellings at Quebec required constant repair. Quebec in 1620 was not so much a settlement as it was a trading post dominated by a cluster of buildings known as the Habitation. This consisted of a storehouse, a pigeon loft, and three interconnected wooden structures that served as a residence for the permanent inhabitants. Upon his return, Champlain had a fortification erected upon the bluff overlooking Quebec, and in 1624 he replaced the first Habitation with a more substantial structure built of stone.[7]

Champlain's other major duty was diplomatic and required maintaining strong relations with New France's Indian allies as well as finding additional Native communities with which to trade. He had largely accomplished this goal by 1620 with the Montagnais, Algonquins, Nipissings, Ottawas, and Hurons. Expanding the French trade network to new tribes required exploration. Champlain by this time was in his mid-forties and no longer able to withstand the physical rigors such journeys required, but more significantly, his duties at Quebec did not allow him time to pursue such adventures. Certainly, the commissions he received from the various viceroys from 1612 onward required him to conduct

The original Habitation at Quebec was made of wood and consisted of a storehouse, a pigeon loft, and three buildings that served as residences for the permanent inhabitants. In 1624, Champlain had the original Habitation replaced with a more substantial structure made of stone. WHI IMAGE ID 134126

explorations with the goal of finding the Northwest Passage. The commission he received in 1612, for example, ordered him "to carry on discoveries and explorations . . . in order to try to find, through the said country, the easy route to the country of China and the East Indies."[8] By contrast, the commission Champlain received in 1625 required him only "to have explorations made . . . in order to endeavor to find the easiest way to go through the said country to the Kingdom of China and the East Indies."[9] He did not have to make such journeys himself; he only had to ensure they were "made," and that implied employing younger men more fit for the task.[10]

Hence, the young men Champlain sent out to learn the various languages and customs of the tribes became the principal explorers who conducted new journeys of exploration from 1616 onward. This was not their only responsibility, nor even their most important. Their foremost duty was to maintain the relationships Champlain had developed with the Indians so they continued to trade with the French. Jean Nicolet became one of these young men after his arrival in New France in 1619. Like his colleagues, Nicolet accompanied fleets of Native canoes each year from the distant lands of the far-flung French trade network and brought them to the St. Lawrence River to barter with the various traders of the companies that had secured monopolies on the fur trade. Champlain's young men, called *truchements* or interpreters, often received significant compensation for their services. Brûlé received one hundred gold pistoles each year for ensuring the Hurons came to trade. This was equivalent to one thousand livres, the principal unit of French currency. Converting the livre or any other currency from this period into contemporary monetary values is difficult, but, as a comparison, a common laborer at Quebec during the same period received a mere seventy-five livres (in addition to free food and lodging) for two years of work. Thus, Brûlé secured a rather sizeable purse from the French traders.[11]

In addition to substantial salaries, the *truchements* had other benefits. They could trade for themselves and on their own accounts, as Nicolet did during the eight or nine years he spent among the Nipissings. According to Jesuit sources, he also maintained his own cabin. Other rewards were less tangible, but, for young Frenchmen who often bristled at the strict morality of Christian Europe, they were no less significant. More specifically, the *truchements* were at liberty to indulge in sexual relations with Indian women. The various Native societies to which the French were allied had much less restrictive sexual mores, and their members engaged freely in premarital intercourse. Once married, divorce was easily realized even if a union produced children. In such cases, the children stayed with the mother, thus freeing the father of any responsibilities. Brûlé was particularly libertine in his conduct. Champlain wrote Brûlé was "very vicious in character, and much addicted to women."[12] Even Nicolet, who in his later years married a French woman and earned the respect of the Jesuits for his Christian piety, had a daughter with a Nipissing woman while he lived among the tribe.[13]

The *truchements* were not the only Frenchmen to brave the interior of North America; Roman Catholic missionaries did so as well. The

Franciscan Récollets believed the sedentary Hurons offered the best possibilities for conversion. However, not more than nine Récollets ever lived in New France at any given time. The small religious order lacked the resources required to have any deep impact upon the Indians of New France. Thus, in 1625, the viceroy, Henri de Lévis, duc de Ventadour, turned to a larger and better-funded religious order: the Society of Jesus, or the Jesuits. The two religious orders had definite differences in their approach to evangelization. The Récollets believed the Indians had to abandon their cultures and languages and embrace those of the French before they could properly accept Christianity. The Jesuits, who had experience with mission work in China and India, believed such seismic cultural disruptions could be counterproductive. However, both religious orders agreed on one thing: the *truchements* were grave obstacles to their efforts. Indeed, men such as Brûlé who lived in the manner of the Indians, dressed like them, and—worst of all—indulged in their decidedly unchristian sexual practices, sowed confusion in the minds of potential converts. Like the Récollets, the Jesuits also believed the Hurons were the best candidates for missionary activity.[14]

The Récollets and Jesuits, like the *truchements*, often made significant contributions to the geographic knowledge of North America during Champlain's career. The Récollet priest Joseph de la Roche Daillon, for example, wintered among the Neutral Indians from 1626 to 1627 in an attempt to bring them directly into the French orbit. However, not only did he fail, his mission enraged the Hurons, who sought to maintain their status as middlemen between the Neutrals and French. Daillon's feckless journey illustrates the ambiguities one encounters when researching many of the explorations conducted by the French during in the early seventeenth century. Daillon was not the first Frenchman to travel among the Neutrals. Brûlé preceded him, likely in either 1624 or early 1625. In fact, Daillon asserted Brûlé's description of the Neutrals' country had been one of the primary motivations for his going. What was significant, however, was Champlain made no mention of Daillon's expedition nor Brûlé's earlier journey in his writings. The reason is uncertain, but it is important to understand several journeys of exploration that occurred between Champlain's return to Quebec in 1620 and his death in 1635 are recorded in other sources (the *Relations* of Jesuits in particular) but are absent in Champlain's writings. This includes the 1634 journey of Jean Nicolet. In fact, after 1620, Champlain recorded only a single mission carried out by an unnamed Frenchman in 1628 to the Kennebec River and the Abenaki Indians.[15]

Had Champlain lost interest in finding the Northwest Passage? At least one of his biographers seems to think so; Marcel Trudel writes the discovery of the Northwest Passage "seems to have interested Champlain less and less, or else he no longer had the leisure to concern himself with it."[16] Certainly, his duties after 1620 distracted him from many of the projects he passionately pursued as a younger man. Moreover, Champlain was not as obsessed with finding a route to China during his career as many scholars and biographers have proffered.[17] He had always been interested in expanding the French trade network as well. Champlain's writings indicate he saw exploration, at least early in his career, as the principal means of finding the Northwest Passage, but they also illustrate he believed it was just as important for the discovery of new Indian communities with which the French could engage in commerce. The 1628 expedition to the Abenakis certainly had such a purpose in mind, as Champlain later wrote, "This journey and discovery gave me great satisfaction through the hope I entertained of the benefit we might derive from it in our time of need, in which these people might be very useful to us."[18]

Another biographer, Conrad E. Heidenreich, believes that in the later years of his career, Champlain was interested in recording only new geographic information he had acquired. He had already learned about the Neutrals and their country during his 1615 military expedition with the Hurons, so nothing that Brûlé or Daillon would have uncovered in the 1620s concerning them or their country was novel. On the other hand, the Frenchman who made contact with the Abenakis in present-day Maine surely met this criterion, for the anonymous explorer left from Quebec and made a series of portages to reach the Kennebec River, which ultimately flows to the Atlantic Ocean. Thus, the charting of this river and bringing a new Indian tribe into the French sphere of influence would have piqued Champlain's interest.[19]

The one possible exception to this theory is that Brûlé acquired additional intelligence that Champlain learned secondhand from the Récollet brother Gabriel Sagard. In fact, this information dramatically changed Champlain's conception of the Great Lakes and his idea of the Northwest Passage. Brûlé's exploits are only vaguely known, for, like Nicolet, we know about him only through the writings of others. Nevertheless, these are enough to conclude Brûlé explored more of North America than did any other Frenchman of his era, certainly more than Nicolet, and even more than Champlain. Brûlé became the first Frenchman and the first European to travel up the Ottawa River and see the vast waters of Lake Huron in 1610; the same is true of seeing Lake Ontario and traversing its waters in 1615. While the Spanish and English preceded the French in reaching Chesapeake Bay, Brûlé was the first to enter it from the north after descending the Susquehanna River, which he did in 1615 or 1616. He was, at least according to the scant sources available, possibly the first European to set his eyes on the Sault Ste. Marie Rapids and Lake Superior in 1623 or 1624. Debate has raged among historians whether Brûlé actually penetrated into the Lake Superior basin and explored any or all of the lake. Everything we know about this voyage comes from the writings of Sagard, who spent a single year among the Hurons from 1623 to 1624. As with several other of Brûlé's journeys, it is impossible to pin down the exact date, but it probably occurred while Sagard was among the tribe. Some scholars doubt Brûlé made the journey at all and speculate he may simply have received information about Lake Superior and the Sault Ste. Marie Rapids from the Ottawas or another tribe during his long residence in Huronia.[20]

In his *Histoire du Canada* (*History of Canada*) published in 1636, Sagard wrote Brûlé and a group of Indians assured him another large freshwater lake lay to the west that emptied into Lake Huron by a waterfall Brûlé named Gaston Falls. The combined length of Lake Huron and this previously unknown freshwater lake was about 840 miles. Gaston Falls, based on Brûlé's description, is today known as the Sault Ste. Marie Rapids, and the freshwater lake beyond the rapids is Lake Superior.[21] Did Brûlé actually enter Lake Superior or travel by canoe along its vast shoreline? Sagard did not state explicitly that Brûlé made such a journey, although he mentioned that Brûlé and another Frenchman named Grenolle secured an ingot of copper from a mine about 160 to 210 miles from Huronia. Some historians have asserted this ingot could only have come from the rich mines of the Lake Superior basin (especially Isle Royale), but the distances provided are securely within the boundaries of Lake Huron, which also has copper deposits. Sagard's statements, at best, allow us to conclude only tentatively that Brûlé stood at the Sault Ste. Marie Rapids and the entrance into Lake Superior, and even that is not certain. The only reason the extent of Brûlé's journey matters is because if he did travel the entire circumference of Lake Superior, it would make him the first European to have stepped foot on the soil that today constitutes the state of Wisconsin, at least if he traveled as far as Chequamegon Bay on the southern shore.[22] Of course, we normally reserve this honor for Jean Nicolet.

Sagard also referred to the Puans. When discussing the Ottawa Indians in the vicinity of Huronia, Sagard wrote that "they travel in groups to several regions and lands, farther away than five hundred leagues [1050 miles] . . . and then from there transport themselves to the tribes all the way to those of the Puants . . . where they trade their merchandise, in exchange for fur pelts, paintings, pottery, and other trivial items they are very interested in acquiring."[23] Sagard also mentioned the Puans in an earlier work he published in 1632, *Le Grand Voyage du Pays des Hurons* (*Long Journey to the Country of the Hurons*). In a list of tribes that would be candidates for evangelization, Sagard included "the Tobacco tribe, the Neutral nation, the province of Fire [Mascoutens], that of the Stinkards [Puans], the Forest nation, that of the Coppermines, the Iroquois, the province of the High-Hairs [Ottawas], and several others."[24] Champlain first mentioned the Puans in his 1616 map; Sagard's works indicate the French had a keen interest in the Puans despite the fact they had not made contact with these Indians in the 1620s.

How Champlain acquired Brûlé's information concerning Lake Superior can be determined with relative certainty: he received it from Sagard upon his arrival at Quebec on July 16, 1624. There he met with Champlain, who later wrote, "Brother Gabriel arrived with seven canoes, to our great joy. He told us all that had happened during the winter he had spent with the savages, and the bad life which most of the Frenchmen had led in the country of the Hurons; amongst others the interpreter Brûlé."[25] Could Champlain have received information concerning Lake Superior from Brûlé? Several factors indicate this was unlikely, not the least of which was the low opinion that Champlain held of his ne'er-do-well *truchement*. After Champlain's meeting with Brûlé in 1618, the next recorded encounter between the two men was the less-than-cordial reunion they had in 1629, the year the English conquered Quebec. Brûlé by this time had turned against the French and assisted the English in their conquest of the French colony. Along with Brûlé, three other Frenchmen, including Nicolas Marsolet, cast their lots with the English and became turncoats. Champlain seethed with rage when he saw them and told Brûlé, "To think of you, brought up from early boyhood in these parts, turning round now and selling those who put bread into your mouths . . . you will be pointed at with scorn on all sides."[26] Thus, it is hard to imagine Champlain and Brûlé had a friendly chat concerning the geography of the western Great Lakes in the summer of 1629.

One may ask why Champlain did not mention in his narrative the information Sagard received from Brûlé. The answer is that Champlain recorded it in another source. After the loss of Quebec in 1629, Champlain spent the next four years across the Atlantic working tirelessly to have the colony restored to France. During that time, he wrote his final great work, *Les Voyages de la Nouvelle France* (*The Voyages in New France*), which he published in 1632. *Les Voyages* reprinted parts of his earlier books and included new material on his later explorations. *Les Voyages* also had a new map titled *Carte de la nouvelle france* (1632). It stands as the final expression of Champlain's geographic conception of the Great Lakes. He did not describe this map in the main narrative of *Les Voyages*, just as he had not described any of the details he learned about Lake Superior from Sagard. However, in the appendix of *Les Voyages*, he included descriptions of various points on his map, *Carte de la nouvelle france*. For point number 34, he wrote:

> Gaston Rapids [Sault Ste. Marie Rapids], nearly two leagues [four miles] in length, emptying into the Freshwater Sea [Lake Huron] and flowing from another extremely large lake [Lake Superior], which together with the Freshwater Sea [Lake Huron] makes a 30 days' canoe journey, according to report of the Indians.[27]

This description is almost identical to what Sagard wrote in *Histoire du Canada*:

Champlain's 1632 map, *Carte de la nouvelle france*, illustrates his final ideas concerning North American geography. In addition to showing Mer Douce (A), or Lake Huron, it also depicts Grand lac (B), based on an amalgam of facts Champlain learned about Lakes Michigan and Superior. Champlain also included rough renderings of Green Bay (C) and the Door Peninsula to the north of Grand lac and, as in his 1616 map, located the residence of the Puans at Green Bay. WHI IMAGE ID 27032

The Interpreter Bruslé [*sic*] and a number of Indians have assured us that beyond the *mer douce* [Lake Huron] there is another very large lake, which empties into the former by a waterfall, nearly two leagues [four miles] across, which has been called the Gaston Falls [Sault Ste. Marie Rapids]; this lake [Lake Superior], with the freshwater sea [Lake Huron], represents about a 30-day trip by canoe according to the Indians' statement, and according to the interpreter [Brûlé] is 400 leagues [840 miles] long.[28]

The similarities are too striking to ignore. Interestingly, Champlain listed the combined length of Lakes Huron and Superior as a thirty-day canoe journey. Sagard did so as well and recorded the distance to be 400 leagues (840 miles). Throughout his writings, Champlain stated the length of Lake Huron was 300 leagues (630 miles), an estimate much longer than it actually is. He first received this measurement in 1603 from the young Algonquin at Île aux Lièvres. Champlain's estimate of 630 miles is quite close to the distance from the mouth of the French River where one enters Lake Huron via the Ottawa River route, along the north-ern shore of Lake Huron, and all the way to the southern tip of Lake Michigan if one travels along the western side of the lake. This is prob-ably the distance to which the young Algonquin referred. The only time Champlain used the longer measurement of 400 leagues (840 miles) is when he referenced another lake to the west of Lake Huron; this was Lake Superior. Moreover, the stated distance of 840 miles is very close to the combined length of these two bodies of water if one travels along the northern shores of both.[29]

An analysis of Champlain's 1632 map also reveals several important factors that bear upon the mission of Jean Nicolet. Champlain described point number 33 on the map as the *Riviere des Puans* (River of the Puans), "issuing from a lake where occurs a mine of pure copper."[30] The map also indicated that at the head of this lake lived *La Nation des Puans*. These two points demonstrate Champlain also included information about Lake Michigan on this map. Then why is there only one lake beyond Lake Huron rather than two? Conrad E. Heidenreich has proposed the most definitive explanation regarding how Champlain expressed his geo-graphical knowledge on his 1632 map, which was an updated version of his 1616 map. Champlain almost certainly learned of Lake Michigan from the Ottawas in 1615, and he acquired knowledge of Lake Superior and the Sault Ste. Marie Rapids from Sagard in 1624. Later he learned about Green Bay, although how and when are unknown; he may have received this information from Sagard, who in turn obtained it from the Indians or Brûlé. Champlain depicted it not as a bay but as a river and small lake on his 1632 map. The "mine of pure copper" on the map likely referred to the copper-rich Isle Royale in Lake Superior; he probably procured this in-telligence from Sagard as well. Champlain simply assumed the two sets of information about two separate lakes (Lakes Michigan and Superior) referred to a single body of water he called Grand lac. Heidenreich writes:

> Knowing of only two large lakes, Champlain placed the sault between
> Lakes Huron and Michigan. Since the first story of the route to the
> *Puan* did not mention a sault and the second mentioned a river and a
> smaller lake, Champlain chose to show that river emptying into *Mer*
> *douce* just east of the *sault*. In this way one did not have to cross a sault

to get to the *Puan*. The route to the *Puan* was now rationalized. One traveled along the northern shore of *Mer douce* and continued along a wide river to a smaller lake where the *Puan* lived. This smaller lake lay north of the large lake (Grand lac), which emptied into *Mer douce* by a *sault*. In actual fact this is a fair description of how to get to the *Puan*. One traveled along the northern shores of Lake Huron and Lake Michigan, through the long and narrow Green Bay.[31]

Thus, Grand lac on the 1632 map was an amalgam of information Champlain knew about both Lakes Superior and Michigan, which he conflated into a single body of freshwater. Just as important, the 1632 map does not even hint Grand lac provided any kind of passage to the Pacific Ocean. This differed from Champlain's unpublished 1616 map, on which the body of water beyond Lake Huron was depicted as possibly a bay or estuary of the Pacific Ocean. He makes no such argument for Grand lac, for a *lac* in French denotes a freshwater body; the word *mer* is used to describe the saltwater seas (Champlain's Mer Douce excepted). Unlike its unnamed counterpart on the 1616 map, Grand lac does not appear to drift westward to the Pacific; its shape hints Champlain believed it to be a closed, inland lake. The inclusion of Gaston Falls (the Sault Ste. Marie Rapids) indicates Grand lac flowed only in one direction, not two.[32] Thus, Champlain depicted Lake Michigan as the destination of Jean Nicolet on his 1632 map with the placement of the Puans at Green Bay, and he indicated he no longer believed this body of water provided direct access to the Pacific.

Did he reject the idea of the Northwest Passage altogether by 1632? Several pieces of evidence suggest Champlain retained this idea, but he did not believe the Great Lakes provided a direct route as his 1612 and 1616 maps suggested. In 1630, as he waited impatiently for the English to restore New France to Old France, he wrote a petition to King Louis XIII:

And moreover, if the way to China which so desired could be found, either through the rivers and lakes, some of which are three hundred leagues [630 miles] long, and if the reports of the people of the country are to be believed, some of these lakes empty into the southern and northern seas, there would be through this a great and admirable outcome, with a shortening of the way of more than three thousand leagues [6,300 miles].[33]

The 1630 petition illustrates Champlain still believed the Northwest Passage might exist, but he did not intimate such a route was possible via the two lakes he knew: Mer Douce (Lake Huron) and Grand lac (his expression of Lakes Superior and Michigan). Champlain's reference to lakes being three hundred leagues (630 miles) in length suggests he was talking about Lake Huron, although he did not depict it as being that long on his 1632 map. He was probably referring to the combined lengths of Mer Douce and Grand lac. Why he did not use the previous distance he had employed, 400 leagues (840 miles), is unclear. What is crucial in the 1630 petition is the language Champlain employed; he did not explicitly assert *these* two lakes provided access to the Pacific, only that *some* lakes might provide for a passage between the Atlantic and Pacific Oceans. This suggests other lakes and rivers were waiting to be discovered.[34]

Champlain presented a similar case in his 1632 book *Les Voyages*, which was much like the 1630 petition: a propaganda piece designed to convince the king and members of the court recovering the colony of New France from the English was a worthy endeavor. In this book, Champlain only once mentioned the Northwest Passage. As in his 1630 petition, he first discussed the many explorers who had undertaken voyages of discovery that had failed to find a route through North America. He concluded by writing "what could not be achieved in one place may in time be found in another."[35] As with the 1630 petition, he did not mention Mer Douce and Grand lac as possible candidates for the Northwest Passage. Probably the most telling example of the shift in his geographic thinking is that, at the conclusion of his 1603 voyage, Champlain confidently told King Henri IV the St. Lawrence River and the Great Lakes chain almost certainly provided a passage through the continent to the Pacific Ocean. When recounting this same voyage in his 1632 work *Les Voyages*, he omitted this passage entirely.[36]

Thus, while Champlain's writings and 1632 map are frustratingly vague, they strongly suggest he believed other yet-to-be-discovered waterways—and not the Great Lakes as he understood them—provided access to the Pacific Ocean. In other words, he no longer embraced his earlier dual-drainage theory of the Great Lakes by the time of Nicolet's 1634 voyage. While this conclusion is secure, it is unknown how extensively Champlain disseminated this information. The Jesuit Paul Le Jeune, writing in 1640 and recounting Nicolet's voyage, noted Lake Superior, of which he had only the sketchiest knowledge, might provide "an outlet towards Japan and China." Nevertheless, he also knew that it was a "fresh-water sea," and the tone of his narrative suggests any outlet it provided toward the Pacific would be via portages with other watersheds separated from that of the Great Lakes.[37] Another Jesuit, Paul Ragueneau, firmly understood by 1648 that two lakes existed west of Lake Huron (Lakes Superior and Michigan), and all three bodies were freshwater, but it is speculative as to whether he knew the Great Lakes comprised a system that only flowed eastward via the St. Lawrence River.[38] The first unequivocal statement to this effect is found in the Jesuit *Relation* of 1659–1660, most likely penned by Gabriel Druillettes.[39] We must give Champlain credit for understanding this as early as 1624 based on the incomplete information he received from Sagard. Nothing in his later works suggests he believed otherwise from 1624 onward, and nothing even remotely implies he believed China or some colony thereof lay at western end of the Great Lakes chain. These same sources illustrate Champlain knew as early as 1615 of the Puans, their warlike proclivities, and the kinds of goods they produced. Champlain also knew the tribe lived within the basin of what we today call Green Bay of Lake Michigan.[40]

—ı⊢—

While it is difficult to coax from Champlain's maps and books a clear idea of his geographical knowledge at any given time, we have no such sources for Nicolet. That is why understanding what Champlain knew and when he knew it is crucial to understanding the nature of Nicolet's journey. It is logical to assume when Champlain ordered him westward, he imparted to Nicolet some idea of where he was going. However, is it possible Nicolet knew even more about the lands to the west of Lake Huron than did Champlain?

Comparing Nicolet's experiences with those of his contemporaries provides an answer. Nicolet spent eight or nine years—likely from 1621 to 1629 or 1630, although one cannot be certain of the dates—among the

Nipissings, who lived in close proximity to the Ottawas. All three tribes spoke related Algonquian dialects with which Nicolet was fluent. He was also fluent in the Iroquoian language of the Hurons. Gabriel Sagard, during his short time in Huronia, noted the Ottawas undertook trade expeditions westward to the Puans, and there is no reason to doubt Nicolet knew this as well, particularly since he lived along the eastern shore of Lake Huron for much longer than did Sagard. During his years among the Nipissings, Nicolet must have learned quite a bit from the Ottawas about this mysterious tribe to the west. He would have known they spoke a language that was neither Algonquian nor Iroquoian. Like Champlain and Sagard, Nicolet would have seen the kinds of products the Ottawas procured from the Puans, and they would not have looked like Chinese wares. Sagard had mentioned seeing furs, earthen pottery, and painted items. While Nicolet was not familiar with the Chiwere-Siouan language of the Puans, he must have perceived their material culture, at least from a European perspective, was not very different from that of the Indians with which he was familiar. Moreover, Champlain learned, after a relatively short interview with an Ottawa chief, that the Puans lived along the shores of another great lake to the west. During his long stay at Lake Huron, Nicolet must have learned quite a bit more about the Puans as well as Lake Michigan. Finally, if Brûlé was able to learn about Lake Superior and the Sault Ste. Marie Rapids during his residence in Huronia, Nicolet could have learned about these bodies of water as well.[41] In fact, Nicolet probably had a better idea of where he was going and the kinds of Indians he would meet than did Champlain.

While it is crucial to understand what both Champlain and Nicolet knew about the Puans and the country in which they lived, it is equally important to understand why Champlain ordered Nicolet to undertake his mission. It was certainly not to locate the Northwest Passage. What, then, was its purpose? To answer this question, we must examine the political, military, and diplomatic situation in the St. Lawrence Valley and the Great Lakes region during the 1620s and the early 1630s. The situation for the colony of New France was quite tenuous during these years, and in 1634, Champlain, as the commander of the colony, faced several grave crises. He simply did not have the luxury of sending Nicolet westward on a journey solely for the purpose of exploration.

Upon his return in 1620, Champlain sought to end the intertribal warfare that disrupted the smooth operation of the French trade network. In Champlain's three military campaigns with the Indians between 1609 and 1615, the Franco-Indian alliance had the upper hand because it possessed firearms wielded by the French. This superiority waned slightly after the Dutch founded Fort Nassau at Albany in 1614 and later Fort Orange in 1624. The Iroquois did not receive firearms from the Dutch until 1639, but they secured metal for arrowheads that rendered useless the wooden armor used by the Indians of northeastern North America. Not everyone in New France wanted peace, particularly French traders, who feared such a move might drive the Hurons and other French-allied tribes into the arms of the Dutch; the Mohawks feared a move toward peace as well, since it might lead to an alliance between their enemies, such as the Montagnais, and the Dutch. Nevertheless, in 1622, the Montagnais and Mohawks extended peace proposals and attended a council at Quebec. A Montagnais delegation later visited the Iroquois. On July 26, 1624, both sides concluded a peace at Quebec. It ended a war Champlain asserted had lasted fifty years. Nicolet conducted a party of four hundred Algonquins to make peace with the Iroquois, although the Jesuit chronicler who recorded this expedition provided no date. It most likely occurred in 1624 as part of Champlain's peace efforts, for Champlain wrote in that year that thirty canoes arrived at the mouth of the Richelieu River, an area under Iroquois suzerainty. Champlain recorded that the Indians who arrived were Hurons rather than Algonquins, but as he was not present at this council, it is possible he simply received less-than-accurate information.[42]

While the 1624 treaty neutralized the Iroquois threat, Champlain also had to placate his Native allies, for by the early 1620s, ruptures appeared in the Franco-Indian alliance. The Montagnais began to bristle at French policies, particularly Champlain's insistence they not trade with the Dutch or English. Although he was able to conciliate them with better prices for French goods, he often handled other situations somewhat arrogantly and treated the Montagnais more like subjects than allies. In 1622, Champlain used his influence to elevate a warrior named Miristou to the principal position of leadership among the Montagnais in the vicinity of Quebec. Champlain believed Miristou would be more compliant

Wooden armor was common among the various Indian tribes of northeastern North America before the arrival of Europeans. Metal arrow tips and firearms that the Indians later secured from Europeans rendered such armor ineffective. WHI IMAGE ID 134138 AND 134141

and sympathetic to French interests. Champlain also tried to get the Montagnais to lead a more settled, agricultural existence at Quebec with the noble intention of increasing their food supply, but the Montagnais resisted and clung to their hunting-and-gathering economy. Furthermore, the allies themselves occasionally had differences that required mediation, such as in July 1623 when the Hurons accused the Algonquins of levying tolls on goods when the Hurons traversed their territory. Champlain arbitrated the dispute to both sides' satisfaction, and the alliance held. In 1624, Champlain, who had made tremendous progress by building up Quebec, making peace with the Iroquois, and maintaining the Franco-Indian alliance, decided to return to France. His young wife, Hélène, likely missed the comfortable life she knew in her home country and had grown weary of her four-year sojourn in North America. Champlain and his wife were back in France in October 1624.[43]

—||—

Champlain remained in France for the next two years. During this time, King Louis XIII appointed Cardinal Armand Jean du Plessis de Richelieu to first minister, a position he held until his death in 1642. Richelieu's vision was to build France into a powerful and prosperous state, and he believed overseas trade was the key. Richelieu, more so than his predecessors, saw trading companies as the means by which France would become a great power. He wanted such companies to engage in commerce in not only Canada but throughout the Americas, the Mediterranean, Asia, and Africa. The new viceroy, Ventadour, reappointed Champlain to the position of commander of New France on February 15, 1625, and asked Champlain to remain in France another year so he could take advantage of Champlain's experience concerning how best to execute his duties. However, affairs in New France went into a steep decline after Champlain's departure. He learned the population of inhabitants dropped from about sixty to forty-three. The buildings and fortifications had fallen into disrepair. Thus, Ventadour instructed Champlain to depart from France in the spring of 1626, and he arrived at Quebec in July of that year.[44]

Champlain, as usual, became a whirl of activity in his efforts to strengthen the colony. One of his goals was to make Quebec self-sufficient in food production. It still relied heavily on supplies brought from France, and the lack of fresh food resulted in scurvy during the winters. Moreover, the local Montagnais, who themselves often ran short of food in the winter, were unable to provide more. Toward that end, Champlain began an agricultural settlement thirty miles upstream on the St. Lawrence at Cap Tourmente to raise crops and cattle. He also had to address a crisis that had arisen with the Montagnais, for a party of Montagnais warriors had killed two French cattle drovers who were hunting in the vicinity of Cap Tourmente in October 1627. The tribal chiefs surrendered three young Montagnais girls to Champlain as hostages as a sign of good faith. They asked only that the children remain alive and well cared for as long as no further acts of violence occurred. The plan was successful, and the killings stopped, but the episode was further evidence the Franco-Indian alliance required constant maintenance and diplomacy.[45]

Champlain also had to repair relations with the Five Nations League. During the winter of 1626–1627, a war party of French-allied Indians broke the 1624 peace and attacked the Iroquois. Much to Champlain's displeasure, he also learned some of his Indian allies had taken their furs to the Dutch, whom he believed encouraged them to attack the Mohawks. It is questionable whether the Dutch actually offered such encouragement; the inspiration may well have come from the Mahicans, who, like the Indians of the St. Lawrence, were enemies of the Mohawks. Nevertheless, the fact New France's allies had traded with the Dutch at Fort Orange in the Hudson Valley was an unforeseen consequence of the 1624 peace, as it provided the French-allied tribes of the St. Lawrence Valley the freedom to traverse the country of the Iroquois. Champlain found it necessary to convene another council with the French-allied tribes at Trois-Rivières in May 1627 to reaffirm the peace with the Iroquois, but affairs in Quebec prevented him from attending. Instead, he sent his brother-in-law, Eustache Boullé, who conducted several diplomatic missions for Champlain during his career, and Émery de Caën, a merchant from Rouen. Both men did their best to convince the Indians to remain at peace, and while the leaders of the various tribes agreed, a group of young men, determined to go to war, eschewed the decision. According to Champlain, the combined entreaties of Boullé, de Caën, and the tribal leaders were not enough "to dissuade nine or ten young hot-heads from undertaking to go on the warpath, which they did in spite of all attempts to prevent them, so slight is the obedience they show to their chiefs."[46]

The incident created another diplomatic crisis when this renegade war party captured two Mohawks along the Richelieu River and began to inflict the usual tortures upon them until a chief, not pleased with the young men's actions, intervened. When Champlain received word of the incident, he immediately departed for Trois-Rivières. At Champlain's urging, the assembled chiefs decided to return one of the prisoners with a delegation from the French-allied tribes and retain the other as a hostage whom they would release upon the safe return of the delegates. A Montagnais chief named Cherououny led the delegation, which, in addition to the prisoner, brought gifts as a sign of goodwill to the Mohawks. Additionally, Champlain sent along one of his young men, Pierre Magnan, who departed Trois-Rivières in July 1627 along with Cherououny, two other Indians, and the prisoner. Champlain's purpose in sending Magnan was to "give more weight to their embassy."[47]

Despite Champlain's best intentions, the mission ended in disaster. An Algonquin with a personal grudge against Cherououny arrived earlier and told the Iroquois the men in the delegation were spies who intended them harm. The Mohawks initially treated Cherououny and Magnan as guests. They then seized the envoys and cut flesh from Cherououny's arms, boiled it in water, and forced the hapless Montagnais chief to eat it. They continued to hack pieces of flesh off Cherououny until he died. Magnan fared no better; the Iroquois applied hot brands and torches of burning bark to his body and tormented him with fire until he burned to death. Despite this failure, Magnan's mission bears a striking resemblance to the journey of Jean Nicolet seven years later. Champlain sent Magnan to make peace between a powerful Indian federation and the Indians allied to the French. He later sent Nicolet on a mission to the Puans that was virtually identical in composition and purpose to that of Magnan. In both cases, Champlain sent Indian delegations as well as Frenchmen who were his personal representatives and ambassadors for the commander of the colony of New France. In fact, Boullé and de Caën also acted as Champlain's diplomats when he sent them to Trois-Rivières to reaffirm the peace made between France's Indian allies and Iroquois.[48] Thus, when we examine how Champlain employed Frenchmen as his personal ambassadors and diplomats in the 1620s, Nicolet's 1634 mission becomes clearer.

Despite these incidents, the frayed peace with the Iroquois held. Another bright spot also appeared on the horizon in 1627: Richelieu formed the Company of One Hundred Associates, or, more simply, the Hundred Associates. It replaced the previous concern under Ventadour and was one in a long line of companies that profited from the grant of a royal monopoly on the fur trade. It was the eleventh such company since the first had formed in 1588; Champlain held commissions from six of them. The Hundred Associates was better funded than the earlier companies, and Richelieu was its chief investor and the viceroy of New France. Champlain was also an investor and now had a financial stake in the success of the colony. Richelieu planned to send four thousand settlers to New France. When one compares the population of New France with those of other nations' North American colonies, it is easy to see why Richelieu was eager to increase the number of colonists. In 1628, the Dutch colony of New Netherland had a population of 270 persons, and the English colonies of Plymouth and Virginia possessed 300 and 1,275 persons respectively. Quebec, Cap Tourmente, and Tadoussac had a woefully diminutive population of 65 souls. Another 21 Frenchmen—missionaries and *truchements*—labored among Indians. The first contingent of 400 colonists embarked for New France in April 1628, and it seemed Richelieu's policies would provide New France with the people and resources needed to compete with the other colonial powers.[49]

But alas, Richelieu's plan foundered on the shoals of a war that almost spelled the end of the colony. England and France became embroiled in yet another conflict in 1626, and the English commissioned sea captains to serve as privateers and plunder French ships. The Kirke family readily accepted the offer. The patriarch was Jarvis Kirke, a merchant of English descent who had operations in England as well as Dieppe, France. His son David along with four brothers assembled a fleet of three vessels in March 1628 that was to intercept French ships headed to North America. They succeeded admirably when they arrived in the St. Lawrence and captured several French fishing vessels and a Basque trading ship. They also seized a supply ship of the Hundred Associates headed for Quebec, a particularly grave development, as Quebec was desperately short of food. As they captured French vessels, the Kirkes integrated them into an even larger fleet of six ships anchored at Tadoussac. From there, David Kirke sent fifty armed men to Cap Tourmente and laid waste to the settlement. Champlain learned of the English presence at Tadoussac and the savage attack against Cap Tourmente on July 9, 1628. The next day, David Kirke sent messengers to Quebec to announce he would remain in the St. Lawrence until the close of navigation and prevent any supply ships from reaching the settlement. He also demanded that Champlain surrender the post. Champlain staunchly refused and promised a "fight to the death."[50]

Kirke had largely procured what he sought that year, namely, French ships and French goods. The fort Champlain had constructed above the heights of Quebec seemed formidable, although Kirke did not know how precarious Champlain's situation was, for Quebec possessed a mere fifty pounds of gunpowder and very little ammunition. Still, believing discretion was the better part of valor, Kirke departed with plans to return the next year and finish what he had started. His fleet then met with an unexpected surprise: four large merchant ships of the Hundred Associates bound for Quebec with much-needed supplies and four hundred French colonists. The French captain put up a valiant fight but eventually succumbed to Kirke's more powerful fleet. Kirke took possession of the supplies and put the passengers on a ship headed back to France.[51]

Over the next year, Quebec's greatest enemy would be not the English or Iroquois but hunger. Adding insult to injury was the fact one small barque slipped through the Kirkes' cordon and brought eleven additional Frenchmen to Quebec: eleven more mouths to feed. Along with the inhabitants who had been at Quebec before the arrival of the Kirkes' fleet, survivors streamed in from Cap Tourmente. Almost one hundred hungry French colonists resided at Quebec. Rations dropped to seven ounces of peas per day, per person. The local Montagnais provided eels and some moose meat, but it was not enough. The French were forced to hunt and gather roots. Miraculously, no one succumbed to scurvy during the winter. By the summer of 1629, the situation became increasingly desperate. At that time, the Kirke brothers returned in force with four well-armed ships. After a parlay, conducted in the formal etiquette characteristic of European siege warfare of the day, Champlain, knowing all was lost, decided capitulation on favorable terms was unavoidable. On July 19, 1629, he surrendered Quebec to the Kirke brothers. In the weeks thereafter, as the French inhabitants boarded ships bound for France, Champlain had his last encounter with Étienne Brûlé when the vessels stopped at Tadoussac. His parting words to Brûlé were, "You run a great risk of being seized and punished."[52] Champlain's words would be prophetic.

Even before the fleet departed Tadoussac, Champlain heard rumors that France and England had ended the war prior to the Kirkes' conquest, a fact he confirmed upon arriving at Plymouth, England, in October 1629. He learned the two countries had signed a peace treaty on April 24 of that year, three months before the Kirkes made their appearance at Quebec. It was music to Champlain's ears, and he traveled to London to see the French ambassador and urge him to petition the English government to have the colony restored to its rightful owners. He gave the ambassador a map of New France that illustrated its boundaries. Unfortunately, it is another of Champlain's maps that has been lost. If Champlain expected a speedy resolution, he was mistaken, for England and France had other outstanding disputes. After five weeks in England, Champlain departed for France, where he remained for almost four years waiting to return to his beloved colony. These years were not without accomplishment; he wrote and published *Les Voyages de la Nouvelle France* and produced his 1632 map. He also wrote his 1630 petition illustrating the bountiful resources in New France, met with King Louis XIII and Richelieu, and pleaded for a rapid return of the colony. In 1632, France and England ironed out the last of their differences and signed the Treaty of Saint-Germain-en-Laye. Richelieu reorganized the Hundred Associates as a stronger, more agile company, but he was reluctant to reappoint Champlain as the commander of New France. He had other men in mind and did not get along particularly well with Champlain. However, when his first choice turned down the position, he issued Champlain a commission. Richelieu was perceptive enough to realize Champlain had a great deal of experience.[53]

The fleet of three ships that departed France in March 1633 included not only Champlain but also 197 French settlers, many of whom were women and 150 of whom were *hivernants* who promised to remain in the colony through the winter. Richelieu finally made good on his promise to produce a stronger, more populous New France. Champlain thus made his twenty-seventh (and final) Atlantic crossing. He arrived in Quebec on May 22, 1633. Little is known of the events in New France during the English occupation, but many French settlers, missionaries, and *truchements* remained in the colony during the four years of the Kirkes' reign. Jean Nicolet was among them. One of his biographers, Henri Jouan, wrote in 1886 that Nicolet "with some other Frenchmen . . . left not a stone unturned to harm the invaders in the minds of the savages."[54]

While such a notion has a romantic tone, such a conclusion has no basis in fact. Because we know Nicolet, like many *truchements*, traded on his own account, he likely conducted transactions with English merchants during the occupation, although like most French residents, he probably stayed in the colony with the expectation it would be restored to France. He most likely resided among the Nipissings and possibly the nearby Hurons during the years of the Kirke brothers' regime.

Nevertheless, the years of the English occupation present at least a three-year span during which we know almost nothing of his activities. Étienne Brûlé was not nearly as lucky. He lived in Huronia during the occupation, but the Hurons had grown weary of him, particularly after he turned against them just as he had against his own countrymen and tried to undermine the Hurons' trade monopoly with the Neutrals. He may also have tried to develop a relationship with the Senecas, members of the Five Nations League and the enemies of the Hurons. Thus, the Hurons tortured and killed Brûlé, although it is unlikely they ate his flesh as the more sensational French accounts later asserted. While both the Hurons and the tribes of the Five Nations League were known to practice ritual cannibalism in much the same manner as the Puans, the Hurons, according to the most reliable sources, simply buried Brûlé's body after killing him. Historians have provided various years for when this act occurred, but in 1633, the Hurons mentioned Brûlé had been killed, so his execution transpired at some point before that time.[55]

—||—

We know more about Champlain's activities upon his return to New France. Quebec had fallen into a shambles during the Kirke brothers' occupancy, and the defensive fort was in particularly appalling condition. Champlain immediately set to repairing it. He wanted to avoid a replay of the events of 1629, and the continued presence of English traders on the St. Lawrence River gave him cause for concern. The Franco-Indian alliance also required repair, for an Algonquin had killed a Frenchman shortly after Champlain's return; he managed to defuse the situation through diplomacy. He also met with the Montagnais and later held a council with the Hurons, whom he urged to renew their ties to the French. However, the Iroquois once again became a threat when they renewed their violence against New France's Indian allies as well as the French themselves. On June 2, 1633, a party of thirty or forty Mohawks attacked Frenchmen who were at Trois-Rivières and killed at least two of them. The largest action occurred in spring 1634 when fifteen hundred Senecas invaded Huronia, killed two hundred Hurons, and captured another one hundred. The situation was apt to spiral out of control, and, unlike in 1624 and 1627, Champlain concluded further peace overtures to the Five

Nations League were futile. The Franco-Indian alliance remained strong, but a renewed war with the Iroquois had the possibility of disrupting the trade that was the lifeblood of the colony. Champlain's Indian allies had expressed concern about the renewed Iroquois assaults. Moreover, the colony was still in a precarious state, and Champlain believed an all-out war against the Iroquois led by the French was the only option. However, except for a small number of pikemen and musketeers to garrison the fort at Quebec, he had, for all practical purposes, no French troops at his disposal.[56]

Virtually all that we know about New France after the restoration comes from sources other than Champlain, particularly the *Relations* of the Jesuits. Champlain wrote only two letters to Richelieu before his death in 1635; in neither does he mention anything about journeys of exploration or finding the Northwest Passage. Both letters focus almost completely on the grave security issues facing New France. In his first correspondence, dated August 15, 1633, Champlain related to Richelieu that the English and Flemish traders who prowled the St. Lawrence still posed a threat to the colony. However, the Iroquois constituted the greatest menace. He told Richelieu that conquering the Iroquois "will only require one hundred twenty men armored lightly in order to avoid arrows, with this there will be two or three thousand savage warriors allied with us, in a year this will allow us to be the absolute master of all these people in bringing to them the order required."[57] Champlain's next letter, and the last he wrote concerning events in New France, was dated August 18, 1634. In it, he listed all the work he had done to rebuild the colony and bolster its defenses. He also reiterated the risks the Iroquois posed toward the colony: "And as every year the French colony grows, it also augments the habitations that terrorize the enemies of the savages, those who try us a great deal by coming to spy from afar on our people . . . and kill them in treachery. In order to vanquish and subjugate them into obedience of his majesty six twenty [120] well-equipped men from France with our savage allies would suffice to exterminate or bring them to reason."[58]

Another source that discusses events in New France in 1633 is a text written anonymously in that year and published in Paris three years later in the periodical *Mercure François*. Several historians have asserted that Champlain authored this document, an assessment that in all likelihood is correct.[59] The text certainly mirrors the contents of Champlain's two letters to Richelieu, especially the particulars concerning the men and arms required to subdue the Iroquois. The author of the 1633 text asserted such a force should be composed of eighty of the finest soldiers wielding muskets and ten men with swords and pistols. It would also possess four sappers with grenades and other explosives required to blow up the palisades of the Iroquois villages, ten halberdiers, ten pikemen, four carpenters, four locksmiths armed with battle-axes and pistols, and two surgeons. Three to four thousand Indian allies armed with axes, steel arrowheads, and even swords supplied by the French would accompany this elite fighting force.[60] Regardless of the authorship of the 1633 text, it provides additional evidence that in the minds of Champlain and other Frenchmen in New France, the Iroquois remained the principal threat to the colony upon its restoration to France. However, despite Champlain's entreaties, Richelieu did not grant his request. The first professional French soldiers in Canada would not arrive until 1665 in the guise of the twelve-hundred-man Carignan-Salières Regiment, which was sent to accomplish the same goal Champlain outlined in his 1633 and 1634 letters: to shatter the military power of the Five Nations League.[61]

While the Iroquois threat to New France and its Indian allies is well documented, far less is known about the Puans and their allies the Menominees. Nevertheless, the meager documentary sources are enough to demonstrate the tribes along Lake Huron's eastern shore were engaged in war with the Puans at least as early as 1615, although the fighting appears to have been sporadic, as the Ottawas also traded with them during the 1620s. We also know the Puans controlled access to Green Bay as well as the entire region to the west that they accessed via the Fox and Wisconsin Rivers. The extant sources describe the Puans as a powerful, populous tribe that ate the flesh of their defeated enemies. This was not merely a tall tale employed by the Puans to instill fear in their enemies, although it certainly accomplished this goal. Various sources confirm the practice of ritualized cannibalism, including later Ho-Chunk oral traditions as well as those of the Iowa Indians with whom they shared a common ancestry. The Puans' massacre of an Ottawa party mentioned by Nicolas Perrot most likely occurred in the early 1630s, possibly 1633. The alliance the Ottawas and other tribes in the Lake Huron region had with the French may have prompted the Puans to commit this massacre. Perrot wrote, "The Outaouaks [Ottawas] . . . sent to them envoys, whom they [Puans] had the cruelty to eat. This crime incensed all the nations [Indian tribes], who formed a union with the Outaouaks, on account of the protection accorded to them by the latter under the auspices of the French, from whom they received weapons and all sorts of merchandise."[62] According to an earlier Jesuit writer, this union of French-allied tribes that formed against the Puans included the Hurons.[63]

Champlain did not reveal anything about this dangerous new threat in his writings, but it was almost certainly the reason he sent Nicolet on the diplomatic mission to the Puans in 1634. As Champlain's letters to Richelieu clearly illustrated, he was intensely concerned with the threat of the Five Nations League of the Iroquois to the south of Quebec. He also had another, powerful tribe to the west that presented a peril to the still-delicate security of New France and its Indian allies along the shores of Lake Huron. This new threat demanded immediate diplomatic action; therefore, Jean Nicolet would serve as Champlain's diplomat. Champlain composed his final letter in August 1634 while Nicolet was still conducting his westward journey to the Puans. Why did he make no mention of Nicolet's journey in this letter? Any conclusions are ultimately speculative, but it was likely because Champlain did not yet know what the outcome of this diplomatic mission would be.[64] Moreover, as will be seen, Champlain, even if he learned the details of this mission later, died before he was able to provide a detailed report to Richelieu.

4

NICOLET JOURNEYS WESTWARD

1634

The Jesuit Paul Le Jeune related the voyage of Jean Nicolet in a little less than two pages in his 1640 *Relation*, while his colleague, Barthélemy Vimont, required about the same amount of space in his 1642–1643 *Relation*. Le Jeune's narrative was not so much a description of Nicolet's journey but instead was based on a report Nicolet wrote concerning this expedition and consisted almost exclusively of the names of the tribes that lived in the western Great Lakes. To the modern researcher, it is exasperatingly ambiguous in its brief descriptions of the various points Nicolet passed as he traveled to his destination. Yet, it is the only source that details his route. In this, Le Jeune must be forgiven, for Nicolet was the first Frenchman to pass through these regions, and no place names had been assigned to these locations (at least not by the French). Vimont's narrative describes what occurred when Nicolet arrived at his destination, but it, too, is frustratingly vague.[1]

Why so paltry a documentary record? One must bear in mind the purposes for which the *Relations* were written, for they were not simply day-to-day chronicles of events. Rather, they were propaganda pieces that illustrated, often in broad, sweeping terms, the Jesuits' activities in New France so as to influence supporters and attract potential benefactors in Old France. Their authors frequently took center stage in the narratives, eager to establish their authority as witnesses of the heroic and holy works done for the greater glory of God deep in the forests of North

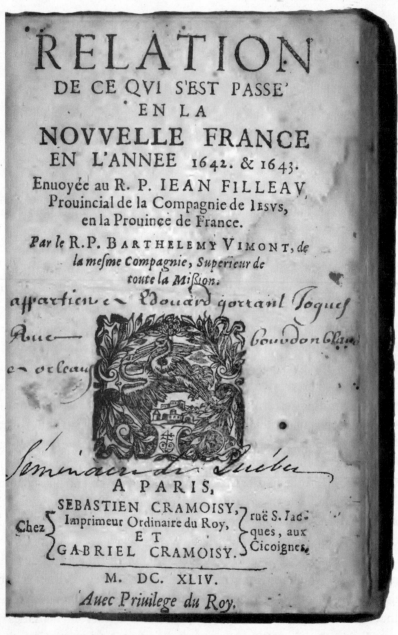

·RELATION·
DE CE QVI S'EST PASSE'
EN LA
NOVVELLE FRANCE
EN L'ANNEE 1642. & 1643.
Enuoyée au R· P. IEAN FILLEAV,
Prouincial de la Compagnie de IESVS,
en la Prouince de France.

Par le R.P. BARTHELEMY VIMONT, de
la mesme Compagnie, Superieur de
toute la Mission.

A PARIS,
SEBASTIEN CRAMOISY, ⎱ ruë S. Iac-
Chez ⎰ Imprimeur Ordinaire du Roy, ⎰ ques, aux
        ⎱ E T   ⎰ Cicoignes.
        ⎰ GABRIEL CRAMOISY. ⎰

M. DC. XLIV.
Auec Priuilege du Roy.

Title page of Barthélemy Vimont, *Relation de ce qvi s'est passé en la Novvelle France, en l'année 1642 & 1643*. The *Relations* of the Jesuits were annual publications that recorded the religious order's activities in North America as well as other events. Vimont's 1642–1643 *Relation* provides the most detailed description of Jean Nicolet's 1634 mission to the Puans. COURTESY OF THE JOHN CARTER BROWN LIBRARY AT BROWN UNIVERSITY

America as they labored among pagan tribes that could be seemingly both noble and cruel. In doing so, the Jesuits who penned these works aspired to develop deep, intimate connections with their readers, who, as coreligionists, sought validation for their faith in an age of confessional rivalries in the wake of the Protestant Reformation. Not surprisingly, the Jesuits' *Relations* often read more like devotional tracts than official reports.[2]

Le Jeune's and Vimont's narratives provide more gaps in information than they do unassailable facts, and historians have little choice but to employ interpolation, extrapolation, and sometimes well-informed speculation. What has hindered researchers from fully understanding the nature of Nicolet's mission is many of these speculations are not only wrong but have been presented as facts, and successive generations of historians have accepted these assertions as rock-solid conclusions and have repeated them to the point they stand as unquestioned dogmas. Thus, to understand the story of Nicolet, we must look critically at the evidence as well as scholars' interpretations of this evidence so we can determine their legitimacy. We must judge which are the strongest arguments and which are little more than pet theories. Even these conclusions will not stand as immutable truths, but, at best, they will be generally accepted interpretations of the evidence. As with so many narratives historians weave to penetrate the mists of the past, the saga of Jean Nicolet cannot be known any other way. Ideally, historians would love nothing more than to articulate a seamless account about Nicolet's voyage in the same manner as the life of Samuel de Champlain. However, even Champlain's life story, which is far better documented, suffers many gaps. Attempting to produce a flowing narrative of Nicolet's journey as though it were based on incontrovertible facts would be intellectually dishonest. Therefore, to proceed, it is best to frame Nicolet's expedition as a series of questions that beg to be answered.

The first two questions we must address are these: Who ordered Nicolet on his westward mission, and when did he depart? Both questions are intimately related, but, unfortunately, Vimont did not provide answers to either query. He wrote only that Nicolet "was delegated to make a journey to the nation called People of the sea [Puans], and arrange peace between them and the Hurons."[3] The passive construction of this sentence does not indicate who issued the order or when. It hardly seems possible to consider anyone but Champlain; however, scholars have argued for other candidates. The answer depends on when Nicolet departed. Emery de Caën, who served as the commander of the colony during Champlain's absence from 1624 to 1626, arrived in New France on June 29, 1632, and received Quebec back from the Kirkes on July 13, 1632. He then commanded the colony for almost a year until Champlain's return on May 22, 1633. If Nicolet undertook his journey before Champlain's arrival, either one of the Kirke brothers or Emery de Caën might have sent him.[4]

The Kirkes are easily eliminated as candidates, however, because the entire family was motivated purely by the lure of profit. Jarvis Kirke and his sons did not become privateers in 1628 because of any great patriotic desire to fight for England; they only sought to plunder French ships and monopolize the fur trade once they took Quebec. Only scant documentation relates to the Kirkes' administration of Quebec, but it is known they cared little for the Indians or the French who remained in the colony. Unlike Champlain, they did not have any grand vision for New France; they saw it only as a source of revenue and squeezed every bit of wealth they could from it. Before Champlain departed from the colony in 1629, he warned David Kirke that his conquest might be illegal, as rumors were already afloat that the war had ended before the Kirke brothers appeared on the St. Lawrence River. For this reason, the Kirkes almost certainly realized their occupation might be short; their fears were confirmed in 1632 when Emery de Caën arrived. Thus, they probably did not invest many resources in the colony between 1629 and 1632, and definitely not after they lost power in 1632. Between their conquest in 1629 and de Caën's assumption of command in 1632, it is difficult to imagine the Kirkes were concerned with events on the far western fringes of the colony or a war the French-allied Indians had with some distant tribe.[5]

What about Emery de Caën during his time as commander of the colony? Marcel Trudel insists Nicolet conducted his journey sometime between 1629 and 1633, possibly under orders issued by de Caën between 1632 and 1633 or, more likely, by the Kirke brothers between 1629 and 1632. Trudel maintains that no evidence shows de Caën issued such an order (which is true) but suggests the Kirke brothers are better candidates despite the lack of concrete evidence in their case as well. Trudel says one of the people who remained at Quebec during the Kirkes' occupation was a Frenchman named Gros Jean de Dieppe (Big John of Dieppe). Trudel believes this may have been Nicolet. While such a man was at Quebec in 1629, there is no indication he was Nicolet, particularly since Nicolet hailed from Cherbourg, not Dieppe. Trudel also states that during the English occupation, the Kirke brothers sponsored a journey of four hundred leagues (840 miles) into the interior of North America, and this may have been the mission led by Nicolet. However, the English document that describes this expedition mentions nothing about where it went, who led it, or its purpose. Moreover, Vimont's chronology is clear: Nicolet was first appointed as an agent and interpreter of the Hundred Associates and then ordered to journey westward to the Puans. Only Champlain had the power to make this appointment, not the Kirke brothers or de Caën. Trudel also writes Nicolet might have embarked on his mission at the urging of the Hurons. However, Vimont's statement that Nicolet "was delegated to make a journey" suggests someone in a position of authority issued the orders, and Nicolet was never under the authority of any Indian society.[6]

Trudel offers another possibility to make his case that Nicolet conducted his journey in 1633 rather than 1634. The Hurons went to Quebec in the summer of 1633 to trade. Since Nicolet served as their interpreter, Trudel argues, he also would have come and then could have received his appointment as an interpreter for the Hundred Associates as well as Champlain's order to conduct his mission.[7] While the Hurons definitely traveled to Quebec and arrived on July 28, 1633, and while it is possible Nicolet was with them, no pieces of evidence—no documents of any kind—prove beyond any doubt he accompanied them.[8] The anonymously authored narrative of events in New France in 1633 mentioned in the previous chapter provides an alternative and stronger version of this argument, but even this source is ambiguous. It states that on June 20, 1633, a *truchement* arrived at Sainte-Croix, a trading post erected about thirty-five miles upstream from Quebec, along with a group of Nipissings. The *truchement* sent word he wanted to meet with Champlain, who left Quebec after receiving the message and hastened to Sainte-Croix. Lucien Campeau asserts the *truchement* was Nicolet and that the meeting resulted in

Champlain ordering him on this mission, a theory championed by Champlain's most recent biographer, David Hackett Fischer.[9]

However, the *truchement* in the text is unnamed. It is certainly possible it was Nicolet, but the 1633 text does not state or even suggest Champlain sent the unnamed *truchement* on any sort of mission, and it does not mention the Puans. The Nipissings and Hurons had problems with the Iroquois on the Ottawa River as well as conflicts with other tribes in the Lake Huron region; these facts are evident in this text. However, to say, on the basis of this document, that Nicolet received his appointment and orders to conduct his mission in the summer of 1633 is to read far too much into the evidence it presents. We know from Vimont's *Relation* only that Nicolet was recalled and appointed as an agent and interpreter for the Hundred Associates prior to his journey.[10] This could just as easily have happened in 1634 as in 1633. Nevertheless, Campeau and Fischer make a compelling case that Champlain ordered Nicolet westward in 1633, and no sources preclude such a conclusion. Thus, scholars must seriously consider the possibility Nicolet conducted his journey in that year.

Nevertheless, the evidence provides a stronger case that Nicolet conducted his voyage in 1634. The only documentation that accounts for Nicolet's whereabouts indicates he lived among the Nipissings until 1629 or 1630; the next we hear of him is at Trois-Rivières on July 7, 1634. From there, he departed for the Huron country with the Jesuit Jean de Brébeuf, a group of Hurons, and Algonquins from Allumette Island. Two other parties of Jesuits and Frenchmen, most of whom were *truchements*, left Trois-Rivières on July 15 and July 23. Nicolet may have traveled with one of these parties, although Brébeuf's *Relation* suggests he traveled with the first on July 7, 1634. Brébeuf arrived in Huronia on August 5, 1634, after a journey of thirty days. For reasons Brébeuf did not fully explain, Nicolet was delayed at Allumette Island and arrived in Huronia with one of the other parties sometime between August 15 and August 19, 1634. Over the course of two weeks, members of all three parties assembled at the Huron village of Ihonatiria on the northeastern portion of the Penetanguishene Peninsula. From there, Vimont picks up the story and says Nicolet departed from Huronia on his journey to the Puans.[11] Champlain was at Trois-Rivières in the late summer of 1634, supervising the building of a fort and trading post there. The exact dates Champlain supervised the work at Trois-Rivières are unclear, but he arrived back at Quebec on August 3, 1634. Thus, both he and Nicolet were at Trois-Rivières at roughly the same time.[12]

Another piece of evidence Trudel presents to argue Nicolet made his journey sometime between 1629 and 1633 is a passage in a *Relation* written by Paul Le Jeune. According to Le Jeune, an interpreter who departed earlier with one of the parties from Trois-Rivières between July 7 and July 23, 1634, turned back after reaching Allumette Island. Later, the hapless *truchement* met Champlain at Quebec and related the difficulties of the journey. Trudel insists this was Nicolet, in which case he would never have made it to Huronia in 1634 or conducted his mission to the Puans that year. However, Le Jeune never mentioned the name of the interpreter, and Brébeuf recorded that Nicolet had arrived in Huronia in August 1634. Brébeuf's somewhat equivocal language is the cause of the confusion. It is useful to quote his *Relation* and examine what he wrote about his first two weeks in Huronia:

> I was occupied some two weeks in visiting the villages, and bringing together . . . all our party. . . . Among all the French I do not find any who had more trouble than Father Davost and Baron; the Father from the wicked treatment of his Savages, Baron from the length of the journey. He occupied forty days on the road. . . . Jean Nicolet, in the voyage that he made with us as far as the Island [Allumette Island], suffered also all the hardships of one of the most robust Savages. Being at last all gathered together, we decided to dwell here at Ihonatiria, and to build here our cabin.[13]

Trudel takes Nicolet's difficulties to mean that, upon reaching Allumette Island, he turned back to Trois-Riviéres. However, the context of Brébeuf's narrative indicates Nicolet, like other members of the three parties, may have had a difficult time at Allumette Island, but he did not turn back. The language implies Nicolet, along with the Jesuit Ambroise Davost and a man named Baron, made it to Huronia despite their struggles, although it took them ten to fourteen days longer than Brébeuf. The fact Brébeuf knew the details of Nicolet's troubles suggests he learned of them from Nicolet upon his arrival. As for the *truchement* who turned back at Allumette Island, his identity remains a mystery. Brébeuf never provided the exact number of men who made up the three parties. His *Relation* indicated the first two parties totaled nine people; he accounted for the members of the third party simply by saying "the rest" departed. He named only six of the persons who departed in all three parties and never stated how many of them made it to Huronia.[14] Thus, it is a tremendous leap of logic to say Nicolet returned to Trois-Rivières in 1634 when the number of men who departed (and most of these men were not named) and the number who arrived are unknown.

To summarize, here is what we can glean from the available evidence. In July 1634, we know Nicolet was at Trois-Rivières, about the same time Champlain was there. Presumably, at that time, Champlain appointed him to serve as an interpreter and agent for the Hundred Associates. It is also presumed Nicolet informed him about the conflict between the French-allied tribes (particularly the Ottawas) and the Puans, and Champlain ordered him westward to make peace. Champlain may have imparted to Nicolet the geographic information needed to make the voyage, although this would have been unnecessary, as Nicolet's Indian guides almost certainly had made the journey before, and Nicolet probably knew more about the Puans and their country than did Champlain. From Trois-Rivières, Nicolet followed the Ottawa River route to Allumette Island, where he was delayed. He arrived in Huronia ten to fourteen days after Brébeuf, who had arrived on August 5. From there, he conducted his journey to the Puans, and the very earliest he could have departed was August 15, 1634. The weakest of these conclusions is the presumption Nicolet met Champlain at Trois-Rivières, but documentation exists that confirms both men were there about the same time. Absolutely no evidence exists that he met with either Emery de Caën or any of the Kirke brothers between 1629 and 1633 or that he met Champlain in 1633. While Champlain definitely met a *truchement* at Sainte-Croix in June 1633, we cannot conclude with any certitude it was Nicolet.

What was Champlain's reason for sending Nicolet to the Puans? In 1634, Champlain may still have believed the Northwest Passage existed somewhere in the interior of North America. However, as demonstrated in the previous chapter, his later writings suggest he did not believe the Great Lakes as he understood them provided such a passage. Moreover, his final commission, issued by Richelieu in 1629, made no mention of finding the Northwest Passage, thus indicating it was not a priority. It did state he was to "govern the said tribes as you may judge proper . . . to the advantage of the said Company [the Hundred Associates]."[15] His letters to Richelieu in 1633 and 1634 reveal the security of New France was Champlain's greatest concern, and the Iroquois posed a grave threat to the colony. He had asked Richelieu to send 120 soldiers, but Richelieu sent none. Thus, Champlain had virtually no military resources at his disposal to address this or any other threat. He could not afford a war between New France's Indian allies and the Puans. As he had learned through experience, maintaining the Franco-Indian alliance required constant diplomacy. While he frequently assisted his allies in their wars as a means of keeping the alliance strong, he also sought to have them make peace. New France's Indian allies along the shores of Lake Huron were engulfed in a new war, and if he did not do something to assist them, the alliance with them might be threatened. Negotiating peace between them and the Puans was the only realistic option. His young *truchements* had served as his ambassadors in the past. Nicolet had done so with the Iroquois in the early 1620s, and Pierre Magnan attempted a similar mission in 1627.[16] Nicolet was the perfect candidate to send as a diplomat to arrange a peace with the Puans.

Vimont stated that Nicolet "embarked in the Huron country, with seven Savages."[17] Who were these seven "Savages"? While it would be common sense to conclude they were Hurons, almost certainly some Ottawas accompanied Nicolet, and possibly the entire party was composed of Ottawas. As Gabriel Sagard had noted a decade earlier, they were the only tribe known to have a trade relationship with the Puans. Thus, the Ottawas knew the route to the Puans' country and possessed the experience required to make the journey. The Hurons were agriculturalists, and while they traded extensively with Iroquoian tribes to their south and Algonquian communities to their north, they were not known to trade with tribes as far away as the Puans. Evidence suggests Huron men often traveled with Ottawa parties on their westward journeys; one Jesuit chronicler suggested they did so, and Huron men often traveled in pursuit of adventure as well as trade. Some Hurons may have traveled with Nicolet. We know from Nicolas Perrot the Puans had attacked an Ottawa party at some point in the past, but Vimont asserted the Puans were at war with the Hurons. The Hurons' inclusion in the alliance that formed to make war against the Puans may well have occurred because the Ottawa party the Puans attacked had included Hurons as well. Another consideration is Vimont's use of the word *Huron*. This may not have described a specific group of Indians but referred instead to all the tribes serviced by the Jesuits' Huron mission, including the Ottawas.[18]

What route did Nicolet travel to the Puans' country? The answers to this question separate those scholars who believe he traveled to Lake Superior from those who assert he journeyed to Green Bay of Lake Michigan. Le Jeune made a list of the tribes Nicolet encountered and began by describing the Indians on the eastern shore of Lake Huron who were already well known to the French, such as the Hurons, Nipissings, and Ottawas. Moving westward along the northern shore of Lake Huron, Le Jeune described several of the tribes Nicolet met, such as the Amikouai (Amikwas, known as the Nation of the Beaver) on the northern shore of Lake Huron opposite Manitoulin Island and the Oumisagai (Mississaugas), who lived on the Mississagi River on Lake Huron's northwestern shore. Both were Algonquian speakers. Le Jeune next mentioned the Baouichtigouian, another Algonquian group whose name meant "People of the Rapids" and upon whom the French would later bestow a name with a similar meaning in their language: the Saulteurs. Le Jeune described them as "the nation of the people of the Sault, for, in fact, there is a Rapid [the Sault Ste. Marie Rapids], which rushes at this point into the fresh-water sea [Lake Huron]."[19]

Up to this point, Le Jeune's description clearly illustrates the intrepid Frenchman traveled along the northern shore of Lake Huron. However, Le Jeune wrote two other passages that were more ambiguous. After describing the Baouichtigouians, he went on to say, "Beyond this rapid we find the little lake, upon the shores of which, to the North, are the Roquai [Noquets]." After this sentence, Le Jeune wrote, "Passing this smaller lake, we enter the second fresh-water sea, upon the shores of which are the Maroumine [Menominees]; and still farther, upon the same banks, dwell the Ouinipigou [Puans]."[20]

These two statements have caused tremendous controversy. Some scholars argue "Beyond this rapid" in the first passage means Nicolet negotiated the Sault Ste. Marie Rapids and entered Lake Superior. Even more so than Champlain's 1632 map, this short bit of text has led adherents of what is known as the Lake Superior thesis to conclude Lake Superior was Nicolet's final destination.[21] The debate hinges largely upon a single French phrase used by Le Jeune, *au delá*, which in the English edition of Le Jeune's *Relation* is translated as "beyond." Scholars have long criticized many of the English translations found in the edition of the *Jesuit Relations* edited by Reuben Gold Thwaites between 1896 and 1901. The translation of *au delá* would appear to be yet another term the team of translators working under Thwaites's direction improperly interpreted, as this phrase can have two connotations in French. It can mean "beyond" as in "move through," or it can mean "past" as in "travel past" or "move past."[22] If used in the former context, Nicolet would have gone through the Sault Ste. Marie Rapids and into Lake Superior. Supporters of this theory assert the "little lake" mentioned by Le Jeune refers to Whitefish Bay of Lake Superior and "the second fresh-water sea" refers to Lake Superior itself.[23] However, Le Jeune almost certainly used the term *au delá* in the latter context to infer Nicolet went past the rapids but did not go through them. This means as Nicolet and his guides paddled toward Lake Michigan, the Sault Ste. Marie Rapids would have been to their right; they did not go through them but went past them.

This fact is confirmed by a third and far less ambiguous passage Le Jeune wrote later in his *Relation*: "Sieur Nicolet, who has advanced farthest into these so distant countries, has assured me that, if he had sailed three days' journey farther upon a great river which issues from this lake, he would have found the sea."[24] To what river and sea did he refer? This passage has also perplexed scholars who have studied Nicolet, even those who believe he went to Green Bay. John Gilmary Shea was the first scholar to "rediscover" Nicolet through the Jesuits' *Relations* and in 1852 wrote a short description of his journey. Shea first advanced the idea that Nicolet ascended the Fox River in present-day Wisconsin and that the "sea" to which Le Jeune referred was the Mississippi River. In fact, Shea postulated Nicolet actually traveled all the way to the Mississippi. Consul W. Butterfield built upon this conclusion in 1881, although he did not have Nicolet traveling as far. Butterfield argued Nicolet traveled all the way to the portage of the Fox and Wisconsin Rivers. Had Nicolet made a three-day journey down the Wisconsin River, Butterfield argued, he would have reached the Mississippi.[25]

Shea's and Butterfield's interpretation of Le Jeune's passage was, like other aspects of Nicolet's saga, repeated to the point it became orthodoxy in some quarters. In the 1920s, Louise Phelps Kellogg modified this argument by stating the three-day journey instead referred to a sojourn down the western shore of Lake Michigan, then into the Chicago River, which at times of high water connects to the Des Plaines River. Nicolet then would have proceeded to the Illinois River, the length of which was a three-day journey to the Mississippi. Kellogg, like Butterfield, asserted the Mississippi was the "sea" of which Le Jeune wrote. Kellogg's argument has even attracted contemporary supporters. More recently, Ronald J. Mason also has argued the Mississippi was the "sea," and either the St. Croix or Bois Brule Rivers would have been the "great river."[26] However, these conclusions strain credulity. Nicolet had seen the St. Lawrence River; it is hard to believe he would have described the Chicago, Des Plaines, Fox, Illinois, Wisconsin, St. Croix, or Bois Brule Rivers as "great" by comparison. Even Mason admits the St. Croix and Bois Brule Rivers are not "deserving of the adjective 'great.'"[27] Could it have been a mistranslation and Nicolet confused the Indian words for "river" and "sea"? This is doubtful, given his fluency in Native languages.

Instead, what Nicolet described were the St. Mary's River and Lake Superior. Le Jeune stated the "great river" flowed out of a large lake, and it was a three-day voyage on this river to this "sea."[28] The St. Mary's is truly a great river about sixty miles long and over a mile wide in places. It carries the waters of Lake Superior to Lake Huron via the Sault Ste. Marie Rapids, which, in Nicolet's time, dropped twenty-two feet over the course of nine hundred yards, thus creating a tremendous torrent. Claude Dablon, one of Le Jeune's Jesuit successors, described the St. Mary's River and the Sault Ste. Marie Rapids in 1670 and left no doubt that seventeenth-century Frenchmen found both the river and rapids to be impressive works of nature:

What is commonly called the Sault [Sault Ste. Marie Rapids] is . . .
a very violent current of waters from Lake Superior . . . these waters
descending and plunging headlong together, as if by a flight of stairs,

over the rocks which bar the whole river. . . . This entire extent making a beautiful river, cut up by many Islands, which divide it and increase its width in some places so that the eye cannot reach across. It flows very gently through almost its entire course, being difficult of passage only at the Sault.[29]

Thus, after paddling to the entrance to the St. Mary's River, Nicolet and his guides continued southeast toward Lake Michigan. Certainly, his guides were intimately familiar with the western Great Lakes and no doubt would have informed Nicolet that if one proceeded farther up the river, one would see the Sault Ste. Marie Rapids and Lake Superior. Most likely, Nicolet traveled past the southeast end of St. Joseph Island, which separates the St. Mary's River into northern and southern channels. The distance to the Sault Ste. Marie Rapids and Lake Superior is about the same for both channels (roughly sixty miles) and a three-day journey traveling by canoe. This fact is confirmed by another voyage conducted 186 years later by the American Indian agent Henry Rowe Schoolcraft and Lewis Cass, the governor of Michigan Territory. In 1820, they departed Mackinac Island with a party of four canoes and arrived at the Straits of St. Mary between the Upper Peninsula of Michigan and Drummond Island where the south channel begins. From there, they departed on June 14, 1820, and arrived at the Sault Ste. Marie Rapids the same day. They had a council with the local Indians that required them to spend two days at Sault Ste. Marie. Schoolcraft and Cass resumed their journey on the morning of June 17. To negotiate the rapids, their canoes carried only half loads over the churning waters while the soldiers who accompanied the party carried the remaining baggage by land over the half-mile portage. This task consumed an entire day. The next day, they traveled the remaining length of the river into Lake Superior. Thus, Schoolcraft and Cass required three days of travel on the St. Mary's River to arrive at Lake Superior.[30]

As Le Jeune's third passage makes clear, Nicolet did not ascend the St. Mary's River and did not enter Lake Superior. However, what about the "little lake" and the "second fresh-water sea" mentioned in Le Jeune's first and second passages? Mason, the most recent adherent of the Lake Superior thesis, insists this chronology and the hydrography upon which

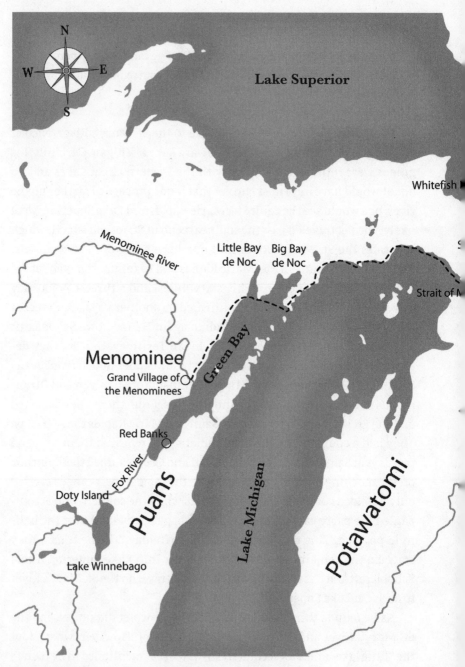

Route of Jean Nicolet to the Puans. MAP BY JAMES CRAWFORD

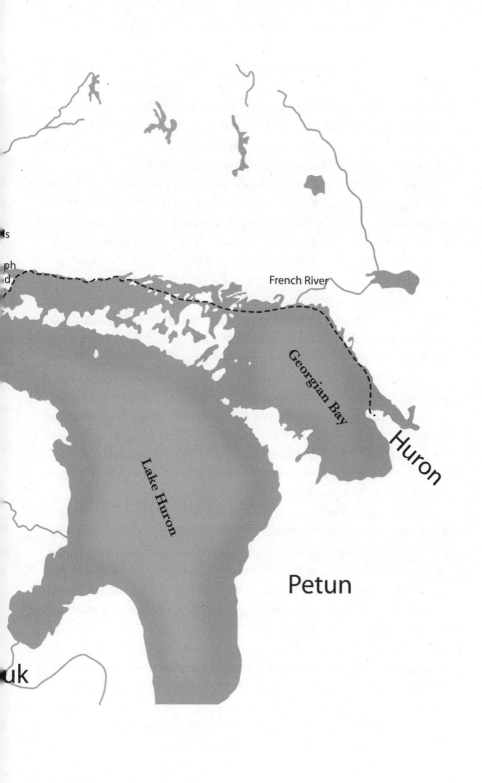

it is based can only be applied to Whitefish Bay (the "little lake") and Lake Superior (the "second fresh-water sea"), which lies beyond it. Had Nicolet traveled to Big or Little Bay de Noc, Mason argues, he would have had to enter Lake Michigan before he entered the "little lake," which is the opposite of how Le Jeune described Nicolet's route. In fact, every advocate of the Lake Superior thesis has made this argument.[31]

Le Jeune's text, a source even Mason admits is beset with "omissions, errors, and ambiguities," is so vague, any number of reasonable explanations can account for this seeming lack of coherence.[32] An alternative explanation is the "little lake" described by Le Jeune was Big or Little Bay de Noc, and Green Bay itself was the "second fresh-water sea" beyond Lake Huron. No previous scholar has presented this theory, and it is based on how Nicolet would have viewed Lakes Huron and Michigan as he traveled through them. Modern people have the advantage of having seen maps that accurately depict the geography of these inland seas, particularly the Strait of Mackinac that separates Lakes Huron and Michigan. Nicolet had no such resource at his disposal; it is doubtful he even saw Champlain's very tentative maps. Thus, Nicolet likely did not sense he was entering another body of water as he passed through the Strait of Mackinac. As one travels by water along the northern shore of Lake Huron, the southern shore of the lake comes into view long before one passes through the strait, which is quite wide at five miles and looks to be little more than a narrows within Lake Huron.[33]

It is telling that neither Nicolet nor Le Jeune mentioned the Strait of Mackinac. Nicolet likely assumed what we today regard as the northern portion of Lake Michigan was simply a western extension of Lake Huron. In fact, this is what the Ottawas believed, if Champlain's 1616 map is an accurate rendering of the charcoal sketch he received earlier from an Ottawa chief. Even into the 1660s, when the Great Lakes were much better known, some Frenchmen still described Lake Michigan as a western extension of Lake Huron. Many contemporary geographers also consider them a single body of water.[34] If this was also the case with Nicolet, the first features that presented a definite change of geography to his eyes were the enclosed spaces of either Big or Little Bay de Noc: the first "little" lake. From there, he traveled south into Green Bay, the "second fresh-water sea," which is a large and discernable body of water, since both the eastern and western shores are visible as one traverses its length.

Conrad E. Heidenreich presents another possibility. Heidenreich argues Le Jeune confused the incomplete information he possessed concerning Lakes Michigan and Superior when he wrote this chronology, and thus, he conflated the hydrographies of the two bodies of water. That Champlain made the same mistake on his 1632 map makes this a plausible explanation.[35] A final possibility, which assumes Nicolet understood Lake Michigan was a separate body of water from Lake Huron, is either he or Le Jeune simply confused the original sequence. Le Jeune's earlier writings reveal he did not receive detailed information about Nicolet's journey until about two years after Nicolet had completed it. Le Jeune wrote in April 1636, "I have some memoirs from his [Nicolet's] hand, which may someday appear, concerning the Nipisiriniens [Nipissing Indians]."[36] These memoirs, which have not survived, almost certainly were the basis for Le Jeune's 1640 description of Nicolet's travels. Given the time that elapsed between Nicolet recording the events two years after they had occurred and Le Jeune's transcription of Nicolet's journey four years after that, it is entirely possible either one or both men improperly recorded the sequence of the journey.

In the end, Le Jeune's text is only one source that answers the question of where Nicolet made his landfall. To use this as the sole or even principal piece of evidence for arguing he traveled to Lake Superior forces one to ignore the third passage in Le Jeune's account that accurately describes the hydrography of the St. Mary's River and the Sault Ste. Marie Rapids. The same passage also emphatically states Nicolet did not ascend this river or enter Lake Superior. Arguing Nicolet went to Lake Superior rather than Green Bay of Lake Michigan also requires one to disregard a wealth of historical, ethnographic, and archaeological data that unequivocally places the Puans and Menominees at Green Bay during the early 1600s.

Scholars have used other sources in addition to Le Jeune's narrative to support the Lake Superior thesis. Many historians believe the body of water depicted to the west of Lake Huron on Champlain's 1616 and 1632 maps is Lake Superior rather than Lake Michigan, and since Champlain marked the homeland of the Puans on the northern shore of this lake, Nicolet must have journeyed to Lake Superior. As discussed in chapters 2 and 3, the lake directly to the west of Lake Huron is Lake Michigan on Champlain's 1616 map, and Grand lac on the 1632 map is a composite of facts that Champlain possessed concerning both Lakes Michigan and Superior, although the features of Lake Michigan predominate. This oversight has resulted in rather tortured and implausible arguments. Marcel Trudel has asserted the River of the Puans on the 1632 map is actually the Nipigon River and the small lake is Lake Nipigon; Larry Dever has presented a similar argument for Wenebegon Lake. Ronald Mason, on the other hand, argues the Attiovandarons listed on another map produced in about 1641, *Novvelle France*, are the Puans, and this map and Champlain's 1632 map place them along the shores of Lake Superior. However, all three of these arguments are based on a flawed understanding of Champlain's 1632 map. Moreover, Conrad E. Heidenreich and the Iroquoian linguist John Steckley conclude the Attiovandarons on the 1641 map were part of the Iroquoian Neutral tribe farther to the east, not the Puans.[37]

All of these arguments also ignore the fact there is no evidence the Puans ever lived in the Lake Superior basin and a great deal of evidence, as presented in chapter 1, they did not. What is amazing is the circular logic some scholars have employed to prove their interpretation of the maps is correct: they insist, despite other evidence to the contrary, the Puans must have lived in the Lake Superior basin in the early seventeenth century. Why? Because Champlain's maps say they were there! Other scholars have been more careful but have proffered the equally erroneous conclusion the term *Puans* in the early French sources referred not to the Chiwere-Siouan speakers whose progeny later were known as the Ho-Chunks but to an Algonquian-speaking group in the region of Lake Superior. However, the same sources to which these scholars refer assert the Puans were not Algonquian speakers.[38]

Why did Nicolet not conduct an exploration of Lake Superior on either his outward or return journeys? Kellogg in particular puzzled over this question and rationalized a seemingly satisfactory answer. She asserted Nicolet "would not have hesitated to take the three days' journey" if this mysterious sea had been as close as Le Jeune noted; she blamed Le Jeune for misunderstanding the report of Nicolet, who must have stated "he would have found *the way* to the sea" rather than the actual body of water.[39] Both Kellogg and Butterfield saw Nicolet as a great explorer, and the florid language they employed illustrates this view. Butterfield wrote, "The bold Frenchman fearlessly threaded his way along its [Lake Huron's] northern shore . . . the courageous Norman was not satisfied with a visit to the Winnebagoes [Puans] only. He must see the neighboring tribes."[40] Kellogg cited Butterfield frequently in her examination of Nicolet and adopted Butterfield's interpretation that, first and foremost, Nicolet was an explorer: "Nicolet's Norman blood must have leapt within him, as like his Viking ancestors he breasted the waves through unknown seas, apparently as broad and untamed as the billows of old ocean."[41] Kellogg's sweeping prose conjured up images of Leif Eriksson as the surf sprayed over the side of his dragon-headed longboat when he spied the distant forests of Labrador. Butterfield's Nicolet was a heroic, larger-than-life figure who lusted to see the lands beyond the horizon.

As romantic as these visions are, they are, alas, inaccurate. Nicolet's Jesuit biographers, Vimont and Le Jeune, despite the brevity of their narratives, paint a far more accurate picture of the man. He was, first and foremost, Champlain's agent, and that was the image Nicolet had of himself. He did not explore Lake Superior or any of the other places Butterfield imagined because that was not the purpose of his voyage. He served as a diplomat to a distant, unknown Indian society that threatened the western frontier of New France. His career before this mission is also illustrative of the portrait we have drawn of Nicolet. Until his journey to Green Bay, he had never been any place another Frenchman had not been before. Étienne Brûlé had been the first Frenchman to see all the places and people Nicolet saw: the Ottawa River, Lake Huron, the Nipissings, the Ottawas, and Huronia. Even Champlain had walked in Brûlé's footsteps before Nicolet. We know from Vimont, on the other hand, that Nicolet played a key diplomatic role in the 1620s as part of Champlain's peace efforts with the Iroquois.[42] Thus, Nicolet was an agent and diplomat, and his actions upon reaching the Puans' country reinforce this image. Champlain sent him to make peace with the Puans; acquiring new geographic information was tangential to this task. He learned of Lake Superior during the course of his travels but did not explore this vast body of freshwater because that was not part of his mission.

—|I|—

Before we examine where Nicolet made his final landfall, we should first ask another question: How long did it take Nicolet to travel to his destination? Benjamin Sulte estimated the trip took ten weeks each way, or seventy days per leg for a total of 140 days. Sulte also speculated Nicolet spent the winter at Green Bay and did not return to Quebec until July 1635. However, there is no evidence he spent the winter in the neighborhood of Green Bay and strong evidence he did not. Vimont makes no such claim and states that after the Nicolet concluded the peace, he returned immediately to Huronia. Moreover, Sulte's estimate of ten weeks travel for both the outward and return legs of the journey is far too long. Based on the available evidence, Nicolet's westward journey by canoe started in Huronia and terminated at either Big or Little Bay de Noc on the north side of Green Bay. This trip is about 450 miles if, from Huronia, Nicolet traveled along the northern shores of Georgian Bay and Lake Huron and the northwestern shore of Lake Michigan as Le Jeune's text indicates.[43]

How long would this journey have taken? We can use Jean de Brébeuf's 1634 voyage for comparison. Brébeuf went from Trois-Rivières to Huronia, a distance of about six hundred miles (a considerably longer voyage than that of Nicolet), in thirty days. The route included numerous portages that slowed his party significantly. His descriptions of the difficulty of the journey and the ability of the Indians to make such arduous voyages are instructive. Brébeuf related the canoe voyage entailed a total of thirty-five portages that sometimes required his party to carry their goods and canoes as many as six miles, and some portages required as many as four trips back and forth to complete. He compared one of the rapids his party portaged to "the Cataracts of the Nile, as they are described by our Historians."[44] He noted the Indians made this journey subsisting on little more than a gruel made of corn and fish they occasionally caught. The Indians paddled continuously, and the French, not inured to such demanding physical labor, often struggled to maintain the same pace. Brébeuf developed a great deal of respect for the Indians' strength and stamina. Yet, despite these difficulties, it took Brébeuf and the Indians with whom he traveled only thirty days to reach their destination. Thus, they averaged about twenty miles per day, a speed that was comparable to other known rates of travel achieved by American Indians who plied the waterways of northeastern North America.[45]

Using this information, we can conservatively assume Nicolet's journey, which was shorter and required no portages, also took thirty days per leg. If we assume after Nicolet arrived in Huronia on August 19, 1634 (the latest date possible according to Brébeuf's *Relation*), it might have taken him at least a week to make preparations. Therefore, he would have departed Huronia on August 26 and arrived at Green Bay on September 24. Again, if we are conservative and assume he spent two weeks among the Puans and Menominees to complete his diplomatic mission, he would have departed Green Bay on October 8 and returned to Huronia on November 7. His arrival date would have been just in time to avoid the more difficult possibility of traveling in winter. Sources from this period indicate that, in most years, the earliest frosts occurred in the first two weeks of October, and the snows began in the middle to the end of November. In some cases, the snow began to fall in late October, but this was atypical. So, if Nicolet arrived back in Huronia on November 7, 1634, he would have just avoided the winter weather. Even more important, his Indian guides would have wanted to return to their homes before the onset of winter, since this was their principal season for hunting.[46] The importance of the winter hunts for Indians is another significant piece of evidence that supports the conclusion Nicolet did not spend the winter of 1634–1635 at Green Bay. Not only was it possible to travel to Green Bay and back to Huronia before the onset of winter; his Indian guides would have insisted on returning in time to prepare for their hunts.

The date of November 7 is a conservative appraisal of Nicolet's return. We obtain a more liberal estimate if we again use Brébeuf's journey as a metric and assume Nicolet, like Brébeuf, averaged about twenty miles per day. If so, it would have taken Nicolet about twenty-three days each for the outward and return journeys. Thus, if he departed Huronia on August 22 (assuming he arrived there on the earlier date of August 15 and took a week to prepare), Nicolet would have made landfall at Green Bay on September 14. If he stayed for one week rather than two and then departed on September 25, he would have arrived back at Huronia on October 14. Considering he did not have to make all the portages that plagued Brébeuf, he might well have achieved a greater distance each day.[47]

Champlain mentioned that after he completed his 1609 military action with his Indian allies, he and his companions traveled home by canoe and "every day we made twenty-five or thirty leagues [about 52.5 to 63 miles] in their canoes, which was their usual rate."[48] If Nicolet achieved a similar rate (57.75 miles per day on average) on both the outward and return journeys, he would have had considerably shorter voyages of about eight and a half days each. That means if he left Huronia on August 26 (the later date), he would have arrived at Green Bay on September 4, and if he stayed two weeks, he would have been back in Huronia on September 27. If he stayed only one week at Green Bay, he would have been back by September 20 and would have been able to return to Trois-Rivières, assuming it would have taken him thirty days to travel there from Huronia, before the onset of winter. However, this scenario was unlikely, since the Huron fleets that departed to the St. Lawrence to trade with the French left in the summer. Thus, upon his arrival back at Huronia, regardless of when it occurred, Nicolet almost certainly spent the winter there. Vimont hinted at this when he wrote Nicolet did not return to Trois-Rivières until "some time later."[49] Thus, Sulte's estimate of seventy days each way is unrealistic. It is unlikely Nicolet spent the winter at Green Bay. He likely remained in Huronia during the winter of 1634–1635 and departed to Trois-Rivières in the summer of 1635. This assertion is supported by the fact the next time Nicolet appears in the historical record, he was serving as an interpreter at Trois-Rivières on December 9, 1635.[50]

Why did Nicolet go to Big or Little Bay de Noc or somewhere along the northern shores of Green Bay and not directly to the location of the Puans? Security was almost certainly the reason. He was visiting a tribe with whom his Indian guides were at war. To land directly in the heart of the Puans' country could have been suicidal. The sheltered coves of either Big or Little Bay de Noc would have been perfect places to hide their canoes, which were the only means by which to return to Huronia. We get a firm idea of this tactic when we examine the actions of Champlain's Indian allies in 1615 when he accompanied them on their military expedition against the Iroquois. Champlain wrote, "We went by short stages as far as the shores of the lake of the Onondagas [Lake Ontario]. . . . We paddled some fourteen leagues [about thirty miles] in order to cross to the south side of the lake, towards the enemy's country. The savages hid all their canoes in the woods near the shore. We went by land some four leagues [about eight miles] along a sandy beach."[51] Champlain related that after the battle, the war party returned to the location where they hid the canoes: "We succeeded in reaching the shore of the aforesaid lake of the Onondagas and the place where our canoes were hidden, which we found all intact; for we had been afraid lest the enemy might have broken them up."[52]

What did Nicolet and his guides do after their arrival at the north end of Green Bay? According to Vimont, "They fastened two sticks in the earth, and hung gifts thereon, so as to relieve these tribes from the notion of mistaking them for enemies to be massacred."[53] What Vimont described was a calumet ceremony, an important act of diplomacy among tribes in the Great Lakes that signaled Nicolet's peaceful intent. The gifts would have included tobacco and a ceremonial pipe or calumet, the smoking of which indicated the parties involved sealed a treaty of peace between them. Vimont went on to say, "When he was two days' journey from that nation, he sent one of those Savages to bear tidings of the peace, which word was especially well received when they [most likely the nearby Menominees] heard that it was a European who carried the message."[54] From this, we can easily discern Nicolet kept the bulk of his party at the north end of Green Bay and sent one man to take his message to the Puans' allies, the Menominees. Why? Very simply, he was taking no chances. If his messenger had been killed, the remainder of his party would have had to make a hasty retreat back to Huronia. Vimont also made it very clear that after the messenger came back, Nicolet and his Indian guides left their canoes at the north end of Green Bay and proceeded on foot: "They [the Menominees] despatched several young men. . . . They meet him; they escort him, and carry all his baggage."[55] Thus, Nicolet traveled by land with the young men sent by his hosts. Nicolet and his party left their canoes at the original point of arrival as a security measure, and Nicolet may have left a few of the Indians who accompanied him there as well.

To where did Nicolet and his Indian guides walk? This is another hotly debated issue. Some purported sites where Nicolet met the Puans are easily dismissed. The theory Nicolet landed at Keweenaw Bay of Lake Superior, for example, is negated by the fact the Puans resided at Green Bay. Moreover, the principal champion of this theory, Ronald Stiebe, an adherent of the Lake Superior thesis, bases his argument largely upon a misreading of Champlain's maps and his refusal to agree with the accepted interpretation of the archaeological data that concludes it was Algonquians and not Puans or other Chiwere-Siouan speakers who resided at Keweenaw Bay during this period.[56]

Robert L. Hall, on the other hand, has argued Nicolet landed at a site in the Calumet River drainage near Chicago. Hall presents archaeological data that suggests the Puans lived in this location in the 1630s and dismisses Green Bay as a possibility because, he argues, the site of Red Banks was too small to have supported a population of twenty thousand. However, Hall bases his argument, in part, on the description of a much smaller mound complex about five hundred yards in diameter (the Speerschneider site on the Door Peninsula) that he mistakes as the remains of the parapet that once surrounded the fortification at Red Banks. Archaeologist Charles E. Brown in 1909 confirmed the Speerschneider mounds were not part of the Red Banks complex. Moreover, while Chiwere-Siouan speakers likely lived in the Calumet River drainage at the time of Nicolet's journey, these were not the Puans, as Hall argues. Various sources indicate that when the French and Ottawas referred to the Puans, they referred only to an Indian society that lived around Green Bay. Hall ignores these sources as well as later Ho-Chunk oral traditions and French sources that place the Puans at Green Bay at the time of Nicolet's visit. The Ho-Chunks' oral traditions undermine Hall's argument that the copious amounts of wild rice in the Calumet River drainage would have supported a large Puans population. Unlike Algonquian populations that relied on wild rice as a staple, it was never a major source of food for the Puans or their later progeny, the Ho-Chunks. Charles C. Trowbridge wrote in 1823 that the Ho-Chunk people "gather the wild rice in common with other indians [sic] . . . but it cannot be considered as a very considerable part of their subsistence."[57]

Historians who argue Nicolet entered Green Bay of Lake Michigan have not reached a consensus either. John Gilmary Shea first advanced the idea Nicolet landed at Green Bay, although he did not specify where; several other historians and anthropologists largely repeated his argument.[58] In 1905, Arthur C. Neville argued Red Banks was the location of Nicolet's landfall, since the Puans lived there at the time of his visit. His theory won quite a bit of acceptance in historical circles.[59] Neville became

The historical marker at Red Banks was placed at the site in 1909 due largely to the efforts of Arthur C. Neville, a prominent citizen of Green Bay who served as mayor of the city from 1888 to 1889. Neville also did a great deal of research into the early history of the Green Bay area, and he believed Jean Nicolet's landfall occurred at the Red Banks site. PATRICK J. JUNG

entangled in a dispute with another Nicolet scholar, Publius V. Lawson, who advanced the theory Nicolet did not land at Red Banks but at another Puans village on Doty Island in Lake Winnebago. Even today, two historical markers celebrate Nicolet's landing in Wisconsin: one at Red Banks and another at Doty Island.[60]

However, several factors illustrate Lawson was mistaken. He believed Nicolet conducted his two-day journey by canoe down the Fox River to Doty Island rather than on foot. Vimont's description allows for such a loose interpretation, but what undermines Lawson's theory is that all the evidence he presents for Nicolet's destination refers to an eighteenth-century Ho-Chunk village on the site that post-dated Nicolet's voyage by almost a century. Archaeological work done on Doty Island has confirmed a historic Ho-Chunk village stood at this location from the 1720s to the 1830s, but this was long after the journey of Jean Nicolet. While the site may have been occupied at the time of Nicolet's journey, this is by no means certain. The archaeological data is ambiguous and offers no hints as to whether the possible prehistoric or protohistoric occupants were Puans, other Chiwere-Siouans, or Algonquian speakers who had a

NEAR THIS SPOT LANDED
1634
FIRST WHITE MAN IN WISCONSIN
JEAN NICOLET
MET THE WINNEBAGO TRIBE
HELD EARLIEST WHITE COUNCIL

—

ERECTED BY
WOMAN'S CLUBS OF MENASHA
1906

Publius V. Lawson was a prominent citizen of Menasha, Wisconsin, who served six terms as mayor from 1886 and 1896. As a prolific researcher into the history of the Fox River valley, he led the effort to place this momument on Doty Island in Menasha in 1906 that immortalized Nicolet's supposed visit to the Puans village that Lawson argued was on the site at the time. PATRICK J. JUNG

relationship with the Puans.[61] Thus, the archaeological evidence erodes much of Lawson's argument.

Nevertheless, the historical marker at Red Banks is, in all likelihood, wrong as well. As discussed in chapter 1, the Puans probably did not occupy Red Banks at the time of Nicolet's journey. Other evidence suggests Nicolet did not visit this location or any Puans villages in the Green Bay region. So where did Nicolet go after arriving at Green Bay? The answer lies in a single passage in Vimont's *Relation*; when Nicolet arrived at the Indians' village, they called him, "Manitouiriniou,—that is to say, 'the wonderful man.'"[62] The word *manitouiriniou* is Algonquian and not derived from the Chiwere-Siouan language of the Puans. Several authors have presented this as further evidence to argue Nicolet visited Algonquian Indians along the shores of Lake Superior and not the Chiwere-Siouan-speaking Puans.[63] However, the term recorded by Vimont is not just Algonquian but more specifically is Menominee. The root word, *manito*, in Algonquian languages means "ghost" or "spirit," but it can also denote people or things that possess extraordinary attributes or power. The Menominees almost certainly had heard stories about the French before Nicolet's arrival, so they did not believe he was a spirit or a god. Nevertheless, they knew very little about the French, and Nicolet would have aroused great curiosity. Thus, it is not surprising the word they used to describe him reflected this interest. The Menominee word *manitouiriniou*, which is a conjugated form of *manito*, can mean "he does wonders" or "he has supernatural powers."[64] This key piece of evidence indicates Nicolet proceeded to a village populated by Menominees, and the Grand Village of the Menominees (present-day Marinette, Wisconsin) would have been the most likely candidate based on Vimont's description.

Why did Nicolet visit the Grand Village of the Menominees and not the Puans' settlements around Green Bay? This question requires a bit more speculation, but at least it is informed speculation. Nicolas Perrot, in recounting the early history of both the Puans and Menominees, described them as allies. The positions of their village sites on opposite sides of Green Bay allowed them to control access to the bay. Perrot gave additional credence to this assertion when he noted the two tribes were "masters of this bay."[65] A few Nicolet scholars, such as Butterfield, have inferred Nicolet made a stop in this Menominee village, but none has argued it was Nicolet's final destination. Vimont noted Nicolet's Indian hosts carried his baggage, which implies they were on foot, and Nicolet "was two days' journey from that nation."[66] The distance from Big and Little Bay de Noc to the Grand Village of the Menominees was about fifty miles, which means Nicolet, his Indian companions, and his hosts walked about twenty-five miles per day to reach their final destination. This may seem like a considerable distance, but considering Indian men had tremendous stamina, as Brébeuf learned, it was not impossible. The Indian warriors with whom Champlain fought regularly marched fifteen or sixteen miles per day, and in armies throughout history, well-conditioned soldiers have marched twenty miles a day on average and thirty miles or more per day when necessary. Furthermore, Nicolet might have made his landfall quite a bit south of Big and Little Bay de Noc, which would have made the distance to the Grand Village of the Menominees shorter.[67] Why did Nicolet and his guides travel to the Grand Village of the Menominees? In all likelihood, it was because the Grand Village was a neutral location. The Menominees were allies of the Puans, but Perrot made it clear the Puans and not the Menominees had been the aggressors against the French-allied tribes. Thus, both Nicolet and the Puans would have been more amenable to conducting peace talks there. This would have required the Puans to cross Green Bay to attend the council, although some Puans may already have been at the Grand Village when Nicolet arrived. We know more than just Menominees were at the council, for Vimont stated that "news of his coming quickly spread to the places round about, and there assembled four or five thousand men."[68] Surely, this council included the Puans from across the bay.

—||—

What did Nicolet wear when he arrived at the Menominee village? We now examine what has been the most serious historical error committed in the story of Jean Nicolet; a fiction that has been repeated so many times it truly has become historical dogma; a fabrication that has done the most to undermine and sabotage the efforts of scholars to develop a clear understanding of Nicolet's mission and Champlain's purpose in sending him. According to Vimont, Nicolet "wore a grand robe of China damask, all strewn with flowers and birds of many colors."[69]

Before we examine the fiction, it is best to first present the truth. China damask did not denote a style of robe; instead, it was a kind of silk known as *damas de la Chine* in French. It was originally made in China and introduced to Europe by way of Damascus. Due to the great demand for this fabric, Europeans, by the 1100s, began producing large quantities of silk, including *damas de la Chine*, and the French city of Lyon became a major manufacturing center by the mid-1400s. One source describes *damas de la Chine* as "a rich silk fabric with woven floral designs made in China and introduced into Europe through Damascus."[70] Silk weavers in France ornately embroidered their fabrics. One historian writes, "The tool of the highly skilled workman traced the most varied designs, such as flowers, small crosses, foliage, and nosegays" on satin and silk.[71] Both

Peasants Making Silk, Carrying and Spreading Cocoons, a painting by Giuseppe Maria Crespi (Bologna 1665–1747), depicts seventeenth-century Europeans producing silk. Jean Nicolet's cape undoutedly was made from silk produced in Europe during this time.
COURTESY OF THE GROHMANN MUSEUM AT THE MILWAUKEE SCHOOL OF ENGINEERING

descriptions sound much like Nicolet's garment, which was "strewn with flowers and birds of many colors."[72] Nicolet's robe was undoubtedly crafted from *damas de la Chine* produced in Europe, most likely in France or possibly Italy. Some raw silk from China was imported into Europe during Nicolet's time, but Europeans produced the vast majority of this material in Europe for Europeans. Small numbers of finished garments such as robes and liturgical vestments arrived in Europe from China during the seventeenth century, but these were confined exclusively to Portugal, which possessed the important trading post of Macau in China. There is no evidence any of these garments found their way to France during the early seventeenth century.[73]

What did Europeans and Frenchmen make with silk, specifically *damas de la Chine*, in Nicolet's time? The English translation of Vimont's narrative describes Nicolet's garment as a "robe," but a better word would be "cape." In the early seventeenth century, European men of the nobility

Men of noble and bourgeois rank during the age of Nicolet frequently wore capes such as those presented here for formal state functions. Nicolet's diplomatic mission to the Puans in 1634 would have been the kind of event that would have been appropriate for such outerwear. PLUVINEL, *L'INSTRUCTION DU ROY ENL'EXERCICE DE MONTER À CHEVAL*

and bourgeoisie who wanted to dress in high fashion regularly wore capes as outerwear for what one historian calls "full dress Court occasions."[74] This perfectly correlates with the atmosphere and purpose of Nicolet's mission to the Puans as well as his position; he served the commander of New France as an envoy to a powerful Indian nation. He was also a bourgeois gentleman who would have wanted his dress to properly reflect his social status. Vimont described Nicolet's garment as a "*grande robbe*," but it was improperly translated into English as "grand robe." Rather than "grandiose" or "splendid," Vimont used the French word *grande* in its usual meaning of "large."[75] Thus, the term "large cape" is a more accurate translation that describes the item of clothing men wore for formal affairs in Nicolet's day.

Of course, by the middle of the nineteenth century, when historians rediscovered the Jesuits' *Relations* and the story of Jean Nicolet, such garments had long since gone out of fashion. They read Vimont's *Relation* and imagined Nicolet wearing a Chinese-style robe. Thus began the greatest fiction in the Nicolet saga. The first historian to intimate Nicolet wore a Chinese robe was Benjamin Sulte, who in 1876 wrote Nicolet possessed "the belief that these people were not far from the Chinese, or they must have known them, [and Nicolet] had put on a great robe of Chinese damask."[76] From this point on, the myth of the Chinese robe swelled in scope. Consul W. Butterfield in 1881 expanded upon Sulte's interpretation and was the first to assert the purpose of Nicolet's visit was to find the Northwest Passage. He also wrote, "But, why thus attired? Possibly, he had reached the far east. . . . Possibly, a party of mandarins would soon greet him and welcome him to Cathay [China]."[77]

Butterfield's book was the first full-length biography of Nicolet's life and career, and it did much to spread the myth of the Chinese robe. By the time Henri Jouan wrote his essay on Nicolet in 1886 (which was translated into English two years later), the idea had passed into orthodoxy. Jouan asserted, "The Chinese costume that Nicolet wore in his first interview with the 'People of the Sea' [the Puans] indicates that he expected to see some mandarin come to meet him."[78] Some scholars questioned the idea but could not find an alternative explanation as to why Nicolet wore a Chinese robe, so they simply repeated the story and added further legitimacy to the fiction. Louise Phelps Kellogg in 1925 wrote, "It seems hardly possible that Champlain with his knowledge of geography expected his envoy would reach China on this expedition. He apparently was in doubt concerning these 'people of the sea,' and thought they might be a colony from the Orient."[79]

Even more than the words of scholars, the paintings produced by artists who enshrined Nicolet's voyage in visual images solidified this idea in the minds of future historians and members of the public. One of the first artists to depict Nicolet was E. W. Deming, who painted Nicolet meeting the Indians at Green Bay wearing a long robe that was unmistakably Chinese in its design. His painting, completed in 1907, was reproduced many times, including on a 1934 postal stamp commemorating Nicolet's landfall. A succession of artists, such as Franz Rohrbach, Hugo Ballin, and William McCloy, followed suit. Their paintings hang in the Brown County, Wisconsin, courthouse; the Wisconsin governor's conference room in the State Capitol Building; and the Wisconsin Historical Society respectively. In 1951, Sydney Bedore, a sculptor, produced a towering bronze likeness of Nicolet overlooking Red Banks and wearing a suspiciously oriental robe, thus bestowing further legitimacy upon two fictions concerning Nicolet. Over time, these paintings and Bedore's sculpture would be reproduced in scholarly articles, history books—both

E. W. Deming's 1907 painting, *The Landfall of Jean Nicolet*, aptly illustrates that the mistaken notion of Nicolet wearing a Chinese robe during his mission to Green Bay had become well established by the early twentieth century among both historians and the general public. WHI IMAGE ID 1870

serious works of scholarship and popular histories—elementary school texts, and other media.[80] Even the most careful and scrupulous historians (the present author included) have been led astray by the enduring myth of the Chinese robe.[81]

While the myth of the Chinese robe has been the principal source of the notion Nicolet sought the Northwest Passage, the moniker Paul Le Jeune bestowed upon the Puans is another. When translating the Algonquian word *Ouinipegou*, Le Jeune decided to forgo the usual French translation of *Puans* or "stinkards" and opted instead to use the term *Gens de Mer*, or People of the Sea:

> We enter the second fresh-water sea, upon the shores of which are the Maroumine [Menominees]; and still farther, upon the same banks, dwell the Ouinipigou [Puans], a sedentary people, who are very numerous; some of the French call them the "Nation of Stinkards," because the Algonquin word "ouinipeg" signifies "bad-smelling water," and they apply this name to the water of the salt

The US Post Office issued this commemorative stamp as part of the 1934 tercentennial celebration of Jean Nicolet's landfall at Green Bay. COURTESY OF THE MILWAUKEE PUBLIC MUSEUM

sea,—so that these peoples are called Ouinipigou because they come from the shores of a sea about which we have no knowledge; and hence they ought not to be called the nation of Stinkards, but the nation of the sea.[82]

At the beginning of this passage, Le Jeune stated the Puans and their neighbors the Menominees lived along the shores of a "fresh-water sea." His mention of "the water of the salt sea" was only another reference to the fact Algonquian speakers used the same words to describe both salt-water and foul-smelling freshwater. The full context indicates Le Jeune knew the Puans resided along the shores of a sea composed of malodorous freshwater and not saltwater, but later historians working on the puzzle of Nicolet's journey misread this passage and assumed it was more evidence Nicolet was searching for a saltwater outlet to the Pacific Ocean: the fabled Northwest Passage.[83]

This was simply another fiction that further obscured the nature of Nicolet's mission and reinforced the myth of the Chinese robe. What is worse, several contemporary historians have embellished the already illusory narrative by adding additional details that even Sulte, Butterfield, and Jouan had not extrapolated from Vimont's narrative. James A.

Sydney Bedore's 1951 statue of Jean Nicolet originally stood at the Red Banks site. In 2009, it was moved to Wequiock Falls County Park in Door County, Wisconsin. WHI IMAGE ID 39915

Clifton, a renowned scholar noted for his meticulous research, asserts that in addition to his Chinese robe, Nicolet also wore a mandarin's cap during his visit. Ronald Stiebe, on the other hand, writes, "An Asian robe accompanied Champlain's return to New France" in 1633 so Nicolet would be properly attired when he met the representatives of the Ming emperor.[84] Not a shred of evidence exists to support either assertion.

—⫫—

While these fictions have obfuscated what we know about Nicolet, they have also limited our understanding of Champlain. Many scholars, even those who have looked at his cartographic works such as the 1632 map, have asserted or at least suspected Champlain must have continued to harbor a desire to find the Northwest Passage, even toward the end of his career. They have commented on how extensively Champlain wrote about his desire as a younger man to find the Northwest Passage, but they have failed to discern or have chosen to ignore that in his 1632 book

Champlain mentioned the Northwest Passage hardly at all. Instead, Champlain discussed at length his dream of building a prosperous, populous colony. Moreover, his commission from Richelieu in 1629 clearly stated he was to do just that. Even if historians have noticed Champlain's waning interest in the Northwest Passage, they have been reluctant to concede he no longer believed, or at least had serious reservations about, the Great Lakes providing a water route to the Pacific Ocean. Why? Because he supposedly sent one of his *truchements*, Jean Nicolet, westward with a Chinese robe! Even Kellogg, who doubted Champlain could have been so geographically naive, made exactly this argument.[85]

Some Nicolet historians have also taken Champlain's earlier writings out of context. The best example involves the passage he wrote after his sojourn in Huronia during the winter of 1615–1616 when an Indian informant told him people with light skin and hair, later determined to be the Mandans, lived farther to the west. Many scholars have either ignored or overlooked the passage that comes later when Champlain expressed his skepticism: "One would need to see them [the fair-skinned people] to know the truth of it."[86] He never expressed any belief they were Chinese; instead, he expressed skepticism regarding the claim. In fact, throughout his career, Champlain required evidence before he accepted any seemingly fantastic tales. He had looked for the riches of Norumbega and not found them; he had read of Jacques Cartier searching for gold and diamonds and bringing home rocks.[87]

Thus, Champlain was neither naive nor gullible; experience had made him a skeptic. Nevertheless, part of the dynamic that has kept these fictions alive is the innate human desire to believe we are better, more advanced, even smarter than the generations that preceded our own. Dressing Jean Nicolet in a Chinese robe and sending him to Green Bay thinking the people he was to meet would be Chinese gives people in the modern age a sense of superiority. They imagine Frenchmen almost four centuries ago who lacked the profound knowledge of our own time as simple rubes only a century or two removed from the darkness of the Middle Ages. Publius V. Lawson was the most notorious offender, for he asserted Nicolet, and by extension Champlain, expected "the mythical China lay upon the shores of Winnebago Lake, the supposed 'China Sea.'"[88] This statement assumes Champlain believed Asia and North

America were part of single landmass. Such a belief may have existed among some cartographers in the early sixteenth century, but by the time Champlain was born, this idea was already withering, and the explorations of Ferdinand Magellan and Francis Drake had assigned this notion to the ashbin of history by the time Champlain was learning the art of navigation as a youth. Even a casual glance at his writings reveals he never entertained such a preposterous notion.[89]

A final question no previous scholar has ever asked is this: Even if Nicolet believed he was going to meet Chinese mandarins who represented the Ming emperor, what purpose would it have served for a Frenchman to wear a Chinese robe? Such an article of clothing certainly would not have disguised the physical features of his face and the fact he was European. The Chinese had seen Chinese robes before; Nicolet would not have been showing them anything novel. The first European to reach China by sea was the Portuguese ambassador Fernão Pires de Andrade in 1517. He arrived as a European, in a European ship, wearing European clothing.[90] Would Jean Nicolet, another European diplomat in a similar situation, not have done exactly the same thing? To conclude otherwise is to defy both common sense and reason. Once we unmask the myth of the Chinese robe, the other fictions this error has sustained begin to unravel. We no longer can use this illusion to shore up other fictions, such as Nicolet looking for the Northwest Passage or his superior, Champlain, believing that China lay just beyond Lake Huron. All these arguments turn to dust.

At this point, we should again summarize what we know. Nicolet departed Huronia, most likely in August 1634, and arrived at Green Bay, probably in September. He traveled along the northern shore of Lake Huron, paddled past the St. Mary's River along the southeastern shore of St. Joseph Island, and probably made his landfall at or near Big and Little Bay de Noc. After hanging gifts and a calumet on sticks as signs of his peaceful intent, he sent a messenger to announce his arrival. He and his guides hid their canoes near the landing site to ensure they had the means to return to Huronia in case the mission failed. The nearby Menominees sent a delegation to acknowledge their willingness to host a council between Nicolet and the Puans. The Menominees had their young men carry his baggage, probably to the Grand Village of the Menominees where Marinette, Wisconsin, now stands. Upon arriving, Nicolet donned a silk cape, not a Chinese robe. He was dressed for a formal occasion in a manner fitting his position as an envoy of the commander of New France. This was the principal task; any new geographic information he learned was peripheral to his primary mission of making peace between New France's Indian allies and the Puans. Of these conclusions, the assertion he entered Lake Michigan rather than Lake Superior is secure, as there is an overwhelming amount of evidence indicating the Puans and Menominees resided at Green Bay. The assertion Nicolet initially went to Big or Little Bay de Noc is somewhat tenuous, but these bodies of water fit the description of Le Jeune's "little lake." The conclusion he went to the Grand Village of the Menominees is more speculative, but we know a major Menominee village existed there, and the residents greeted Nicolet with the word *Manitouiriniou*, which is of Menominee derivation.

What did Nicolet do after he donned his silk cape? This is another reason why examining the career of Samuel de Champlain is crucial to understanding Nicolet's mission, for Champlain's earlier actions provide a template that explains much of what Nicolet did. Vimont wrote, "No sooner did they perceive him than the women and children fled, at the sight of a man who carried thunder in both hands,—for thus they called the two pistols that he held."[91] When Champlain accompanied his Indian allies to war in 1609, one of his goals was to show their Iroquois enemies the powerful weapons the French possessed. Nicolet undoubtedly had the same purpose in mind when he conducted the demonstration of his pistols, for, like the Iroquois in 1609, the Puans and Menominees were unfamiliar with Europeans and their firearms.[92] Nicolet's demonstration was obviously effective, as many Indians fled upon hearing them fired; wearing his ornate silk cape would have added to the spectacle.

Nevertheless, he was not there only to cow the Puans; he was there to negotiate a treaty. Given the fact Nicolet brought baggage, it is safe to assume he gave the assembled Puans and Menominees trade goods as presents. Again, Champlain's actions provide context. When the Iroquois extended peace proposals to the Montagnais in 1622, Champlain urged his allies to send a delegation to make peace. The Iroquois had brought one hundred beaver skins as gifts and a sign of their earnest intentions. Champlain, in turn, gave the Montagnais thirty-eight beaver skins to present to the Iroquois as a sign of good will. Champlain noted this was "the purpose of making presents to their enemies on their arrival, as is the custom."[93] He also sent gifts along with Pierre Magnan on his ill-fated mission to the Iroquois in 1627. Champlain frequently took presents on journeys of discovery in the event he might bring new Indian communities into the French trade network. He also provided gifts to tribes already allied to the French in order to maintain their allegiance. Giving presents was an important aspect of Indian diplomacy not only between the French and the Indians but also between Indian tribes. Giving gifts served to end existing disputes and ensure friendly relations continued to exist.[94]

After his demonstration of French weaponry, the remainder of Nicolet's diplomatic mission was a success. Vimont devoted only two sentences to the rest of the visit, the first of which described the four to five thousand Indians who assembled from the immediate area to see Nicolet. Vimont also wrote, "Each of the chief men made a feast for him, and at one of these banquets they served at least sixscore [120] Beavers."[95] Champlain experienced similar festivities designed to cement and maintain good relations with New France's Indian allies. Upon his first step onto Canadian soil at Tadoussac in 1603, the assembled Montagnais, Algonquins, and Etchemins hosted a *tabagie*, a feast where they asked Champlain for French assistance in their wars with the Iroquois. Solemn speeches and the smoking of a calumet preceded the feast, which consisted of moose as well as bear, beaver, seal, and wild fowl. Champlain wrote he found "their grand Sagamore [chief] named Anadabijou . . . and some eighty or a hundred of his companions, making a *Tabagie* (that is to say, a feast). He received us very well, after the fashion of the country, and made us sit down beside him, while all the savages ranged themselves one next the other on both sides of his lodge."[96]

About one thousand Indians assembled two weeks later for another great *tabagie* that, according to Champlain, was much like the first. During his time in New France, Champlain attended many such festivities, which, like presents and the smoking of a calumet, served to establish amicable relations between Indian nations and maintain strong bonds between alliance partners. During times of war, such feasts served to celebrate victories over an enemy. Champlain hosted many feasts with those tribes allied with the French in order to maintain their loyalty. His

Indian allies even held feasts when they took prisoners as a prelude to inflicting torture. We should not underestimate the importance of these events, for Champlain noted a feast was "no small favour amongst them." He was reluctant to go to one feast after having already eaten but he attended anyway "in order not to commit a breach of the manners of the country."[97]

Vimont recorded the number of assembled Indians at Nicolet's feast to be between four and five thousand, while another Jesuit with whom Nicolet spoke recorded a total of three thousand. Even if the lower figure is correct, the number was considerable. We know little of the Indians who lived in the western Great Lakes during this period, but such gatherings were not unusual, nor was it unknown for the Indians of the Lake Huron region and Ottawa Valley to venture as far west as the Puans and beyond. Le Jeune wrote in 1640, "We have been told this year that an Algonquin, journeying beyond these peoples [the Puans], encountered nations extremely populous. 'I saw them assembled,' said he, 'as if at a fair, buying and selling, in numbers so great that they could not be counted.'"[98]

We have only tantalizing glimpses of how far Indians traveled within the waterways of northeastern North America, but these are enough to illustrate how Nicolet was able to learn as much as he did about the tribes outside the Green Bay region. In addition to the Puans and Menominees, Nicolet, according to Le Jeune, also learned of the Naduesiu (Santee Sioux or Dakota) who lived in the upper Mississippi Valley. At the time of Nicolet's visit, the Dakota had an estimated population of thirty-eight thousand, a figure that correlates with the description of the great multitudes seen by Le Jeune's unnamed Algonquin. North of Lake Superior, around Lake Nipigon, lived the Assinipour (Assiniboines), also of Siouan stock. The Eriniouai (Illinois) were a confederacy of Algonquian speakers who likely lived in southern Michigan at the time of Nicolet's visit and later moved into northern Illinois and southern Wisconsin. The Rasaouakoueton (Mascoutens), an Algonquian group, lived in the southwest corner of the Lower Peninsula of Michigan and were closely related to the Sauk, Fox, and Kickapoos. The Algonquian-speaking Pouutouatami (Potawatomis) lived on the western shore of the Lower Peninsula to the north of the Mascoutens, just across Lake Michigan from the Puans and Menominees.[99]

Did Nicolet visit any of these tribes beyond the Green Bay area? The short answer is no, but as with other answers to the seemingly endless questions that surround Nicolet's journey, it requires examination. Several scholars, after reading Le Jeune's list and knowing many of these tribes lived well outside the Green Bay region, took considerable license with one of his statements. Le Jeune wrote, "I will say, by the way, that sieur Nicolet, interpreter of the Algonquin and Huron languages . . . has given me the names of these nations, which he himself has visited, for the most part in their own country."[100]

Shea was the first to argue Nicolet traveled beyond Green Bay, up the Fox River, and down the Wisconsin River to the Mississippi, although Shea discussed this fictional expedition only in the most general terms. Benjamin Sulte also embraced this conclusion; Henri Jouan, on the other hand, believed Nicolet went instead into southern Wisconsin and northern Illinois, a conclusion he largely built upon the fact Le Jeune had mentioned the Illinois Confederacy. All these scholars based their notion that Nicolet traveled beyond Green Bay on the fact he did not show up again in the historical record until he was serving as an interpreter at Trois-Rivières in December 1635 and thus had time to make an extended journey. They concluded Nicolet continued his explorations until July 1635, when he finally departed Green Bay for Huronia. This provided Nicolet with plenty of time to return to Trois-Rivières. Consul W. Butterfield developed this argument most fully, asserting Nicolet traveled among many of the southern tribes mentioned by Le Jeune, including the Mascoutens and Illinois Confederacy. As with so much about Nicolet, what began as speculation passed into incontrovertible truth to the point even the most careful scholars have accepted these arguments, particularly those of Butterfield, up to the present day.[101] Not everyone accepted this theory; Louise P. Kellogg (employing the royal "we") rightly noted, "We think that Nicolet did not explore far beyond his landfall on Green Bay."[102] Kellogg asserted the context of what Vimont wrote did not allow for such wild speculation. Indeed, Vimont stated in very direct language, "The peace was concluded; he [Nicolet] returned to the Hurons."[103]

There is no reason we should not take Vimont at his word. Yet, how did Nicolet acquire information concerning so many different Indian tribes in the region? Once again, Champlain's career provides the answer.

Following the advice of the English writer Edward Hayes, Champlain queried the Indians about the regions to the west and north of Lake Huron and the Indian societies in these areas. Several times, he asked his Indian allies to take him on journeys of exploration; when they did not, he settled for asking them what they knew about more distant regions. Champlain also considered his participation on the military expeditions of his Indian allies to be journeys of exploration; he even queried the Indians' prisoners. If he did not have access to the Indians and their knowledge, he settled for information received secondhand through people like Gabriel Sagard or his *truchements*, such as Étienne Brûlé. Clearly, Nicolet did the same. Le Jeune did not say Nicolet visited all the tribes on his list; he wrote instead that Nicolet visited them "for the most part in their own country."[104]

These words suggest Nicolet met some of the tribes on the list but not all of them. Given the fact three thousand to five thousand Native people gathered at Green Bay to catch their first glimpse of a European, many Indians from the immediate region must have come to the Grand Village of the Menominees. However, Nicolet learned about those tribes beyond Green Bay by doing exactly what Champlain did: querying the local Indians about what they knew. Moreover, there is the case of the unnamed Algonquin who told Le Jeune that he had been west of Green Bay, possibly to the headwaters of the Mississippi. He traveled many hundreds of miles from his own country, and perhaps as many as one thousand miles. It is safe to assume the Indians at Green Bay, like the unnamed Algonquin, had extensive knowledge of both the physical and human geography of the greater region in which they lived.[105]

What did Nicolet do after his council with the Puans and Menominees? Again, Vimont unambiguously stated Nicolet immediately departed for Huronia after concluding the peace and later traveled to Trois-Rivières, where he continued his employment as an agent and interpreter. As mentioned, the next time Nicolet appears in the historical record is at Trois-Rivières on December 9, 1635. Le Jeune wrote a *Relation* covering the events that occurred at Trois-Rivières from 1635 to 1636. From this we learn that, upon arriving at Trois-Rivières, Nicolet served in his previous role as an interpreter, this time for the Algonquins who came to trade at the new post. According to both Vimont and Le Jeune, he was quite diligent in his duties at Trois-Rivières and was a devout Roman Catholic as well. In December 1635, Nicolet visited the Jesuit fathers there to inform them about a sick Algonquin they should visit. According to Le Jeune, one of the Jesuits "instructed him [the Algonquin] . . . allowing the faith and Christian truths to flow . . . into the soul of this poor young man."[106] Vimont reinforced this image of Nicolet as a devout assistant to the Jesuits in their religious mission, noting Nicolet had endeared himself to "both the French and the Savages, by whom he was equally and singularly loved. In so far as his office allowed, he vigorously coöperated with our Fathers for the conversion of those peoples."[107]

Nicolet developed a rather close relationship with Vimont while he was at Trois-Rivières, for Vimont wrote the obituary in 1643 that recounted not only his mission to Green Bay but his career in New France. Vimont also noted the Indians called Nicolet *Achirra*, a Huron word that may have meant "strap" and thus symbolized Nicolet's ability to carry great burdens. Certainly, Nicolet's voyage to Huronia in 1634 and his subsequent journey to Green Bay demonstrated his courage and strength. While living earlier among the Algonquins, according to Vimont, Nicolet "often passed seven or eight days without food, and once, full seven weeks with no other nourishment than a little bark from the trees."[108] Thus, while we have no images of what Nicolet looked like, we can imagine him as strong, imposing, and physically and mentally robust.

We should again summarize what we know concerning Nicolet. During his visit to the Grand Village of the Menominees, Nicolet fired his pistols as part of a demonstration designed to show the Puans the powerful weapons the French could bring into battle in support of their allies. The feasts he attended were part of the diplomatic protocols common among the Indians of northeastern North America. Such feasts cemented peace treaties between former enemies and confirmed alliances between friends. Additionally, Nicolet took part in a calumet ceremony and distributed presents to his hosts as well. After concluding a successful peace, he returned to Huronia. He did not spend the winter at Green Bay and did no further exploring beyond the immediate region. After spending the winter in Huronia, he traveled to the St. Lawrence Valley, probably in the summer of 1635, and was definitely at Trois-Rivières by December 9, 1635. While there, he continued to act as an interpreter for the

Hundred Associates. He also assisted the Jesuits with their evangelization efforts and was respected among the Indians. While it is seemingly ten-uous to assert Nicolet did not spend the winter at Green Bay and did not explore beyond this region, no evidence proves he did so. The Indians who assembled at Green Bay could easily have provided Nicolet with the names of the distant tribes. Since we know Champlain obtained similar information in this manner, this conclusion is actually quite secure.

The only potentially problematic assertion is that Nicolet spent the winter in Huronia. Given how rapidly the Indians could travel in their canoes, it is very possible that he arrived back in Huronia sometime in September 1634, with two good months of travel time still available. He might have arrived at Trois-Rivières or possibly even Quebec in the late autumn of 1634. However, we know agents and interpreters who worked among the most distant tribes, such as the Hurons and Algonquins, tended to come down to the St. Lawrence once a year during the summer trading season, and that was probably what Nicolet did in July 1635.[109] However, even if he did depart for the St. Lawrence earlier than this, it is a relatively negligible point; it would not have impacted his mission to Green Bay.

How successful was his diplomatic mission to the Puans? Unfortu-nately, the Puans did not remain at peace with their neighbors. Jean de Brébeuf noted in his 1636 *Relation*, "On the eighth of June, the Captain of the Naiz percez, or Nation of the Beaver [Amikwas], which is three days journey from us, came to request one of our Frenchmen to spend the Summer with them, in a fort they had made from fear of the *Aweatsi-waenrrhonon* [the name of the Puans in Iroquoian], or stinking tribe, who have broken the treaty of peace, and have killed two of their men, of whom they made a feast."[110] Are we to fault Nicolet for this failure of di-plomacy? Again, if we use Champlain's career as a guide, we see making peace between Indian tribes was often a thankless task. Champlain began his efforts to broker a truce between those Indians allied to the French and the Five Nations League of the Iroquois in 1622 and confidently saw a treaty of peace concluded between them in 1624. Nevertheless, isolated incidents of violence occurred in 1627, and by 1633, the year Champlain returned from his four-year exile, the fighting had resumed. He decided diplomacy had failed, and a military campaign was required to break the strength of the Five Nations League.[111]

However, these small raids against New France's Indian allies were merely the first shots fired in what would become a much larger conflagration in the 1640s. In this decade began a series of wars that would be the gravest threat to the colony of New France in its short history as the Iroquois unleashed what amounted to an all-out offensive against their enemies, particularly the Hurons, who became virtually extinct. The Puans fared little better, for they became embroiled in a conflict with the Illinois Confederacy that almost led to the destruction of the entire tribe. What was once a very populous Indian nation of twenty thousand people or more became a mere shadow of what it had been. These conflicts in the St. Lawrence Valley and the eastern Great Lakes, as well the war between the Puans and the Illinois Confederacy in the western Great Lakes, prevented another Frenchman from following in Nicolet's steps for twenty years.

5

NICOLET, NEW FRANCE, AND THE PUANS

After 1634

Jean Nicolet's journey did not make any great impact on the larger community of New France. The fact Paul Le Jeune did not mention it until six years later and Barthélemy Vimont did not describe the broad contours of the visit until he penned Nicolet's obituary three years after that indicates the French did not consider it a significant event within the colony. Only one other source mentions Nicolet's expedition, the 1655–1656 *Relation* of Jean de Quen, published fourteen years after Nicolet's death and twenty-two years after the journey. Nicolet certainly had the opportunity to inform Samuel de Champlain of the expedition's results. Le Jeune wrote, "On the tenth [of July 1635], a bark which was ascending the [St. Lawrence] river brought us Father Pijart. At the same time, two of our Frenchmen, coming down from the Hurons, presented to us the letters of our Fathers who are in that country."[1] If Nicolet was one of the two Frenchmen whom Le Jeune recorded as arriving at Quebec, he would have been able to make a report to Champlain. If Nicolet was not present, he may have included a written report along with the letters written by the Jesuits. Of course, this is speculation; it is also somewhat irrelevant, for a few months later, Champlain suffered a stroke that left him debilitated, and he lost the ability to use his arms. The last document he composed was his will, and that was written by another person. On

December 25, 1635, Champlain, in the words of Le Jeune, was "reborn in Heaven."[2] Thus, whatever knowledge he had of Nicolet's voyage died with him on a cold winter's day in Quebec.

The seeming lack of interest in Nicolet's voyage may startle the modern reader, but it highlights the context in which his contemporaries put the event and the historical context in which we have tended to place it. Nicolet's mission was one of several actions taken to secure the colony, and it was not the most important, as it addressed a distant threat on the western frontier. The Iroquois presented a far more immediate danger than did the Puans. Champlain, for example, ordered the construction of fortifications and trading posts at Sainte-Croix about thirty-five miles upstream from Quebec in 1633 and at Trois-Rivières in 1634, thirty-five miles farther upstream from Sainte-Croix. Both posts figured prominently in the *Relations* of the Jesuits, and both were important bulwarks against the Iroquois. Moreover, while Nicolet was still on his mission, the Jesuits founded the Residence of the Conception in September 1634 at Trois-Rivières, a new and glorious mission to spread the Gospel. Nicolet's voyage was not insignificant, but neither was it the most important news in the colony between 1634 and 1635 or even in the following years. Le Jeune's list of the tribes Nicolet identified in the western Great Lakes was only one part of a much longer list that included those Indian societies at the eastern end of the Gulf of St. Lawrence, the present-day Canadian Maritime Provinces, the St. Lawrence River valley, the eastern shore of Lake Huron, and southern Ontario. Vimont included Nicolet's obituary in an extended narrative that discussed events at Quebec and the remainder of New France during 1642 and 1643. Everything Vimont wrote about Nicolet consumed a mere six pages in a *Relation* over three hundred pages in length.[3]

Had Champlain lived longer, he might have taken more interest in Nicolet's mission and the information it provided and acted on it so as to bring the tribes of the Lake Michigan region more firmly into the French sphere of influence during the 1630s. However, such a conclusion is worse than speculation; it is counterfactual history. The voyage appears to have been an important event in Nicolet's life, for he related details of it to Le Jeune, Vimont, and de Quen. However, by the time de Quen wrote of Nicolet's voyage in 1656, fourteen years after Nicolet's death, he did not even mention Nicolet's name. He only wrote, "A Frenchman once told me that he had seen, in the Country of the people of the Sea [Puans], three thousand men in an assembly held to form a treaty of peace."[4] Nicolet's voyage seemed to have almost vanished from the collective memory of the people of New France by the time de Quen penned his *Relation*.

The reason Nicolet's voyage looms so large today is rooted in the mythology we have built around it. Much of it is pure Eurocentric bias. He has been proclaimed the "first white man" to penetrate the western Great Lakes and set foot in what are today the Upper Peninsula of Michigan and Wisconsin. This is particularly the case with older historical works penned by historians eager to immortalize his accomplishment. In the first decade of the twentieth century, Publius V. Lawson and Arthur C. Neville fought tooth and nail to have historical markers placed at both Red Banks and Doty Island that proclaimed Nicolet's visit to those places. The various historical markers, statues, and artistic renderings that celebrate Nicolet's journey also have ensured later generations developed the belief his voyage had far greater significance than it really did.[5] Historians recently have become interested in the relationship between actual historical events and how subsequent generations remember those events. Often there are significant differences between the two. Moreover, powerful visual images such as paintings, sculptures, and historical markers tend to reinforce distortions that have crept into historical memory, and people in one generation find themselves imprisoned by inaccurate understandings of the past.[6] This is truly the case with our conception of Nicolet.

The perceptions later generations possessed of the Native peoples with whom Nicolet met have suffered even greater misrepresentations over time. Nicolet described the Indians' numbers as being in the thousands, but he did not name one person—not a chief, not a warrior, not a woman, not a child—at least not a specific Native person whom Le Jeune or Vimont recorded. Later scholars and artists saw these Indians not as individuals but as a throng of undifferentiated, primitive "savages." Of course, all the Indians present when Nicolet arrived at Green Bay had names and identities; they shared their lives—both the joys and sorrows—with wives, husbands, children, and networks of kith and kin. Vimont's description of Nicolet's initial meeting with the Indian people of Green Bay did much

George Peter's 1917 painting, *Nicolet's Landing*, like all renderings of Nicolet produced in the early twentieth century, depicts Nicolet wearing what was later determined to be a fictitious Chinese robe. The image also shows the Indians bowing down before him in reverence and fear, thus illustrating the often Eurocentric notions that early scholars and artists infused into the narrative of Nicolet's 1634 journey. COURTESY OF THE MILWAUKEE PUBLIC MUSEUM

to shape the negative images produced by later scholars and artists, for Vimont noted they called Nicolet "the wonderful man" in the Menominee language and fled in terror at the "thunder" produced by his pistols.[7]

Of course, we would be remiss if we did not place ourselves in the same situation as the Native people who encountered Nicolet almost four hundred years ago. Human beings, whether they live in the early twenty-first century or the early seventeenth, whether they are American Indians or members of another cultural tradition, would undoubtedly respond in a similar manner if they saw a human being with racial characteristics they had never seen before, wearing clothes they could never have imagined, and wielding technology they found inconceivable. Nevertheless, artists in particular have used this event not only to make Nicolet appear foolish in his mythical Chinese robe but also to depict Native peoples as lesser beings who supplicated themselves and literally bowed before

Nicolet. The most conspicuous example is that of George Peter, an artist who produced a mural for the Milwaukee Public Museum in 1917 that depicted the Puans and Menominees not only as inferior to Nicolet but subservient to him.[8] Indeed, the image drips with ethnocentrism if not outright racism.

An excellent counterpoint to Nicolet is the Algonquin whom Le Jeune mentioned in his 1640 *Relation*. According to Le Jeune, this man had journeyed westward beyond the land of the Puans where he saw thousands of Indians assembled. It is difficult to know exactly from where this Algonquin hailed and where he went. Le Jeune's description of his destination matches that of Prairie du Chien along the Mississippi, for a well-known eighteenth-century traveler, Jonathan Carver, described it as a "great mart, where all the adjacent tribes, and even those who inhabit the most remote branches of the Mississippi, annually assemble about the latter end of May."[9] If this Algonquin had departed from Allumette Island, where many of his people lived, and traveled to Prairie du Chien, he would have traveled more than nine hundred miles, almost twice the distance covered by Nicolet. This Indian's travels illustrate the fact a journey such as that of Nicolet was not uncommon for the Native peoples of northeastern North America in the early seventeenth century. We know from Gabriel Sagard that the Ottawas regularly traveled to the country of the Puans in the 1620s, and even earlier if Champlain's 1615–1616 interviews with the Indians along the eastern shore of Lake Huron are accurate.[10]

Thus, Nicolet's so-called accomplishment was one many Ottawas (and probably Hurons, Nipissings, and Algonquins) had achieved long before he did. Of course, Nicolet, having lived for many years among various groups of Indians prior to his 1634 voyage, undoubtedly knew this, so we cannot fault him for inflating his own reputation in the contemporary historical consciousness. That is a product of our desire to create heroes in our own image. If we knew from where his Algonquin counterpart hailed and where he traveled, we would be able to construct sculptures and historical markers in his honor. But ironically, doing so would only serve to distort his image in our minds, as it has Nicolet's.

—II—

Nicolet's life at Trois-Rivières differed significantly from his previous sixteen years among the Algonquins, Nipissings, and Hurons; he had the company of other Frenchmen, including family members. His brother Gilles, a secular priest, arrived in 1635 and remained in New France until 1647. His brother Pierre, a mariner, also spent time in the colony and left shortly after his brother's death in 1642. On May 23, 1637, the Hundred Associates granted Jean Nicolet 160 acres of land in the vicinity of Trois-Rivières that he owned in common with a fellow *truchement*, Olivier Letardif. On October 7, 1637, Nicolet married Marguerite Couillard, who descended from some of the earliest French settlers and whose godfather was Champlain. Like Champlain, Nicolet, who was about thirty-nine, was significantly older than his wife, who was only eleven years old on the day of her nuptials. Nicolet and Letardif became brothers-in-law as they both married daughters of the Couillard family. Jean's and Marguerite's names appear frequently in the church register at Trois-Rivières as having been godfather and godmother to several children and adults, all of them apparently Christian Indians. The couple had two children. The son, Ignace, died in 1640 at probably three years of age or younger. The daughter,

Marguerite, was baptized in April 1642, almost certainly a few days after her birth and only a few months before her father's death. In 1639, Jean Nicolet appeared as a witness for the marriage of Jean Jolliet, whose progeny, Louis Jolliet, embarked upon his own great voyage in 1673 that had as its purpose the discovery of a waterway to the Pacific Ocean.[11]

In his years at Trois-Rivières from 1635 until his death in 1642, Nicolet frequently assisted the Jesuits in their spiritual duties. The short passages written by the Jesuits in their *Relations* tell us a bit more about Nicolet and the cultural misunderstandings between the missionaries and Indians. According to Paul Le Jeune, one of the Jesuits told a young Algonquin girl who had just been baptized that "if she were a Christian, when she came to die her soul would go to Heaven to joys eternal. At this word, 'to die,' she was so frightened that she would no longer listen to the Father. Sieur Nicolet, the interpreter, who willingly performs such acts of charity, was sent to her, and she listened to him quietly."[12] About a week later, an Indian who had not yielded to the blandishments of the Jesuits found his son on "the verge of death" and "begged sieur Nicolet to do all he could to save this soul. So they went, Father Quentin and he, to his bark house, and strongly urged this Savage to consent to the baptism of his little son."[13] Nicolet also revealed a bit about his own religious maintenance when he explained his reason for returning to the St. Lawrence Valley and Trois-Rivières. Le Jeune wrote in April 1636 that Nicolet decided to depart from the Indians after many years of residence among them in order to "place his salvation in safety by the use of the Sacraments, without which there is great risk for the soul among the Savages."[14]

Nicolet also shared with the Jesuits interesting bits of information he had learned during his residence in New France. Le Jeune seemed particularly interested in the abundance of wildlife, and, like many Frenchmen of his era, he was amazed at the size and strength of the beaver dams he encountered. He wrote, "Sieur Olivier [Letardif] informed me that he crossed over one of these dams, which was more than two hundred steps long. Sieur Nicolet has seen another of almost a quarter of a league [half a mile], so strong and so well made that he was filled with astonishment."[15] According to Le Jeune, Nicolet even tried to impress upon the landscape some small tribute to himself. While traveling with Nicolet in the area of present-day Montreal, Le Jeune wrote:

At or near the middle of this Island [Laval Island north of Montreal Island], there are two rapids . . . one being in the River des Prairies, the other in the River St. Jean. By the way, I will mention the origin of the names of these rivers. The River St. Jean takes its name from sieur Jean Nicolet, interpreter and clerk of the store at the three Rivers [Trois-Rivières], who often passed through all these regions.[16]

This river that today flows between Laval Island and the mainland is Rivière des Mille Îles. However, Nicolet's countrymen conferred a similar honor upon him. On the southern bank of the St. Lawrence opposite Trois-Rivières was a tributary that the local colonists named the Nicolet River. This honor was certainly not because of Nicolet's 1634 voyage; it was likely because both the Indians and French at Trois-Rivières had great respect for him, according to the Jesuits' narratives. It is uncertain as to when the Nicolet River received its appellation, but documents as early as 1663 refer to it by this name. The river changed names several times as the land around it passed from one landowner to the next, but the locals continued to call it the Nicolet River. Eventually this name stuck and remains in use today. The river eventually lent its name to the village through which it flowed: Nicolet, Quebec. Benjamin Sulte did not think this tribute was enough. He wrote to a fellow Nicolet historian, Henri Jouan, in 1886 stating, "If Canada had entered the era of statues, it would be high time that Jean Nicolet had his bronze in the city of Nicolet."[17]

The bliss of domestic life and serving the Jesuits did not mean that Nicolet's life as a diplomat was over. Warfare between the Iroquois and New France's Indian allies continued into the early 1640s, and by 1641, the Five Nations League, particularly the Mohawks, sought peace with the French. By this time, the leader of the colony was Charles Huault de Montmagny, whose name in French meant "great mountain" and whom the Hurons and Iroquois called *Onontio*, an Iroquoian word with an identical meaning and a term the Indians used for the next century to describe the governors of New France. Unlike Champlain, Montmagny held the title of governor; like Champlain, he also saw the Iroquois as a grave threat, particularly after they began to receive firearms from the Dutch in 1639. On June 5, 1641, about 350 Mohawks arrived at Trois-Rivières. At these talks, Jean Nicolet reprised his role as a diplomat; his fluency in the Iroquoian languages made him indispensable. The Mohawks had two French prisoners they had taken earlier and promised to release as a sign of their sincere intent. Nicolet and the Jesuit Paul Ragueneau, who was also fluent in Iroquoian languages, met with the Mohawk delegation and conducted the initial talks. A few days later, Montmagny arrived at Trois-Rivières from Quebec accompanied by four armed shallops. He sent Nicolet and Ragueneau as his personal envoys to meet again with the Mohawks while he stayed across the river at Trois-Rivières. During the course of the talks, one of the Mohawk chiefs, Onagan, rose to speak. At one point, he touched Nicolet's and Ragueneau's faces, proclaiming, "Not only shall our customs be your customs, but we shall be so closely united that our chins shall be reclothed with hair, and with beards like yours."[18]

Champlain and the Jesuits had always expressed the hope the Indians would adopt the manners of the French, but Onagan inferred the French would become Iroquois. Nicolet and Ragueneau managed to secure the prisoners and made a report to Montmagny. However, Montmagny was in no mood to accept the peace proposal of the Mohawks, who had arrived at Trois-Rivières with thirty-six arquebuses of Dutch manufacture. They wanted thirty more from the French. They also wanted peace and an ongoing trade relationship with the colony. Montmagny gave them presents, but no firearms. He did not trust the Mohawks and doubted their promises to make peace with New France's Indian allies. Giving them firearms, he believed, would provide the Mohawks with powerful weapons to use against the Hurons, Algonquins, and Montagnais. The treaty conference ended in ruin with both the Mohawks and French exchanging fire. While French sources from the period paint the Five Nations League and its component tribes as the aggressors in the St. Lawrence, the reality was far different. Before 1641, those tribes allied with the French initiated considerably more raids against the Iroquois than the League initiated against them. Montmagny, like Champlain before him, believed maintaining the alliance with the Hurons, Algonquins, Montagnais, Nipissings, and Ottawas was the best policy for New France to pursue. After 1641, this objective revealed itself to be shortsighted. This year marked the ascendency of the Five Nations League of the Iroquois, which posed the greatest threat New France faced during its first century.[19]

Before that happened, Jean Nicolet had one more diplomatic mission to perform. In the late summer or early autumn of 1642, Nicolet went to Quebec to serve as the general superintendent of the Hundred Associates' operations there in place of Olivier Letardif, who had gone back to France for a short period. While at Quebec, Nicolet assumed the task of returning an Iroquois prisoner to Trois-Rivières on October 27. He sailed in a shallop owned and operated by François Berchereau de Chavigny, who traveled with three of his men to deliver goods to the post. Shortly after they left Quebec, a fierce storm caused the vessel to capsize near Sillery, a missionary village established by the Jesuits in 1638 for Montagnais converts and only a few miles upstream from Quebec. The cold, churning waters took the lives of the men on board, including Nicolet. Only de Chavigny survived. Upon reaching the nearby mission, he recounted his harrowing tale to the Jesuits. According to de Chavigny, Nicolet's last words were, "Sir, save yourself; you can swim. I cannot; as for me, I depart to God. I commend to you my wife and my daughter."[20]

Thus ended the life of the man who served New France as a diplomat and interpreter. Sadly, his body was never found; his family held a funeral two days later on October 29, 1642. As with so much that is written about Nicolet, we should read de Chavigny's tale with a bit of skepticism. While it seems incredible that a man who paddled almost five hundred miles over the open waters of Lakes Huron and Michigan could not swim, it was far more likely, given the cold water, that Nicolet and the others succumbed not to drowning but hypothermia. Moreover, how would de Chavigny have been able to hear his comrade make such a valiant final oration over the din of the churning waves and violent storm? Would Nicolet have been able to make so eloquent a speech as his core body temperature dropped and water filled his lungs? Indeed, de Chavigny's account appears to have been the first of many myths concocted about Nicolet over the centuries.[21]

Not surprisingly, Nicolet's wife, who was almost thirty years younger than her late husband, remarried. On November 12, 1646, at a ceremony that commenced at 5 a.m., Marguerite married Nicolas Macart, who hailed from the Champagne region of France. Jean Nicolet's old friend Barthélemy Vimont did not attend the wedding, possibly because of how early in the day it took place. According to one source, "Father Vimont escaped from the Annoyance of attending the nuptials, and so contrived that something for the wedding should be sent to the house."[22] In 1656, Nicolet's daughter Marguerite married Jean Baptiste le Gardeur, who later received land near Quebec. Jean Nicolet's widow and her new husband, his daughter Marguerite and her husband, and all their future progeny lived in a very different colony than the one Nicolet came to in 1619 when the total French population did not exceed one hundred persons. By 1666, the population of New France consisted of 4,219 French inhabitants. While still miniscule compared to Old France, the colony was far more populous and more securely French. By 1663, more than half the population had been born in the colony, and thus a new Frenchman was in the process of coming into being: the French Canadian. The Hundred Associates began to grant land in the form of a seigneury, held by a landlord or seigneur, similar to a fief under Europe's feudal system. Additional settlements emerged in New France in the years after Nicolet's death, including at Montreal.[23]

In addition to Nicolet's French wife and French daughter, he also had a daughter with a Nipissing woman. At some point in her life, this young woman came to the St. Lawrence Valley. Why or when she came down from the country of the Nipissings, or whether Nicolet's French wife and daughter knew her, are unknown. The daughter's name was Madeleine-Euphrosine, and she was one of the first members of New France's newest society, the Métis, a people of mixed French and Indian ancestry who often possessed intimate ties with both societies. As young Frenchmen and young Indian women engaged in relationships that ranged from casual sexual encounters to lifelong marriages, their progeny lived in a rich world of two races, two languages, and two cultures. The millions of Métis who eventually were born and lived in Canada were a physical fulfillment of a prophecy uttered by Champlain when he met with the Montagnais Indians in May 1633: "Our young men will marry your daughters, and we shall be one people."[24]

Madeleine-Euphrosine was approximately thirty-eight years of age in 1666 and thus was likely born in 1628. On January 18, 1642, she became the godmother of an Indian girl raised by the sisters of the Ursuline order at Quebec. She was able to sign her name, thus indicating she had received at least a rudimentary education, most likely from the Ursuline nuns as a young girl. Madeleine-Euphrosine continued her residence at Quebec, and on November 21, 1642, at about fourteen years of age, she married Jean LeBlanc, with whom she had at least five children. Her first husband's death most likely precipitated her second marriage to Elie Dusceau with whom she had four more children.[25] Thus, Jean Nicolet, a man who spent most of his adult life living among the Native peoples of North America, had children and grandchildren who were the descendants of two societies and produced a new syncretic culture that still graces the human geography of North America today.

—‖—

Montmagny's failed council with the Mohawks in 1641 was, in many ways, the end of an era; the council that summer began a new phase in the relationship between New France and her Indian allies and the Five Nations League of the Iroquois. In the wake of this failed diplomatic summit, the Mohawks began the process of leading a war against New France and her allies that lasted sixty years. Historians once thought this series of conflicts originated in the desire of the League to dominate the Great Lakes fur trade, and hence, they earned the rather benign sobriquet of the "Beaver Wars." Recent research confirms the Iroquois had more than enough fur-bearing animals in their own territories. The Wars of the Iroquois, a more accurate term, originated in part from diseases brought by Europeans, which began to take their toll on the Iroquois. Many Iroquois accused the Jesuits of spreading these epidemics through the practice of sorcery. The incessant warfare also led to significant population losses, and the traditional method by which the Iroquois solved this dilemma was by taking captives. In the wake of the failed peace talks, the Iroquois, under the leadership of the Mohawks, annunciated an ingenious solution to the dual problems of their Indian enemies and their population losses. They would launch a massive military offensive by which their enemies would cease to exist as independent communities. The Iroquois would then integrate the remnants of these communities into the five tribes that composed the League. This policy already appeared to be taking shape at the peace council of 1641. In addition to telling Nicolet and Ragueneau that they both easily could be transformed into Iroquois tribesmen, Onagan said of the two French prisoners he paroled, "These two young men whom you see, are Hiroquois [Iroquois], they are no longer Frenchmen, the right of war has made them ours. . . . At last, we have learned to change Frenchmen into Hiroquois."[26]

The Iroquois initiated a series of raids into the country of the Algonquins and Hurons from 1642 to 1645 and in 1646 began preparations for a major campaign. The assault began in earnest when the Iroquois, well supplied with firearms, destroyed the Huron village of Teanaostaiaé in July 1648, killing seven hundred. The remaining Huron villages fell over the next three years in rapid succession. In 1649, the Jesuit Jean de Brébeuf, with whom Nicolet had ascended the Ottawa River in 1634, was tortured to death along with another Jesuit, Gabriel Lalemant, by the Iroquois. By 1651, Huronia had been virtually depopulated. Refugees streamed into the western Great Lakes; many Christian Hurons migrated eastward to Quebec. The nearby Neutrals and Petuns ceased to exist. Later, the Iroquois extended their forays into the western Great Lakes, invading the region west of Lake Michigan and the Lake Superior basin in the 1650s and 1660s. There they suffered defeats at the hands of the Ojibwas, a tribal entity that emerged in the latter half of the seventeenth century as closely related Algonquian groups such as the Saulteurs, Amikwas, Achiligouans, and Maramegs constructed a new set of relationships and a new cultural configuration. By 1680, the Iroquois invaded the Illinois Country, but this would be the last year of their ascendency, as the League suffered reversals in subsequent years. By 1687, the Iroquois had abandoned the southern shore of Lake Ontario. By 1700, the League sued for peace, which the French and the Iroquois accomplished at Montreal in 1701.[27]

Far more documentation is available concerning the Wars of the Iroquois than the war between the Puans and the Illinois Confederacy. Only later Ho-Chunk oral traditions and scattered writings by French observers in the period afterward document the conflict. These limited sources are enough to indicate the Puans, like the Hurons, became embroiled in a war that almost led to their extinction. Brébeuf noted in 1636 that the Puans had renewed their attacks against their neighbors. Nicolas Perrot's description of events hints at the fact that, in the wake of Nicolet's visit, the Puans began to receive goods of French manufacture. The resumption of warfare led to civil wars among the Puans over the appropriateness of pursuing this policy. At the same time, other tribes in the immediate region formed an alliance to make war upon their Puans enemies. The Puans assembled in a single village. This may have been the palisaded fortification at Red Banks or a location in the area of the Middle Fox Passage to the west of Lake Winnebago. Archaeological evidence suggests the Illinois Confederacy made war against not only the Puans but also other related Chiwere-Siouans, and perhaps even Algonquian-speaking allies, in eastern Wisconsin and northern Illinois. If this is the case, it is possible, although quite speculative given the nature of the evidence, the remnants of these various communities later assembled at Red Banks and ultimately coalesced into a single polity that reconstituted itself in the generations afterward as the historic Ho-Chunk tribe.[28]

Disease took its toll within the confines of the Puans' overpopulated village into which they assembled during their war with the Illinois Confederacy. A tribe that once possessed four thousand to five thousand men declined to only fifteen hundred warriors. After the Puans lost five hundred men in a failed expedition against the Fox Indians, the Puans' enemies took pity, and a five-hundred-man delegation from the Illinois Confederacy brought the Puans provisions. During a feast that included the Illinois, the Puans descended on them, massacred them, and then consumed their flesh. The Illinois Confederacy responded by creating another alliance that attacked the Puans and virtually exterminated them. A few weary survivors took refuge in the Grand Village of the Menominees. The establishment of a Jesuit mission at Red Banks in 1670 indicates they later returned to this location, where, as mentioned, they likely began the process of becoming the historic Ho-Chunk people. By the time Perrot observed the Puans in the late 1660s, he reported they had only about 150 warriors, or a total population of no more than six hundred persons. Much of what Perrot reported is confirmed in other sources. The Jesuit *Relation* for 1657–1658 mentions the Menominees, Puans, and Noquets living in a single village along with refugees who went westward to escape the Iroquois. One Jesuit missionary, Claude Dablon, reported in 1670 that "the people named Puans . . . have been reduced to nothing from their very flourishing and populous state in the past, having been exterminated by the Illinois, their enemies"[29]

In fact, the entire area west of Lake Michigan became a vast refuge zone as the Indians in the Lower Peninsula of Michigan and Huronia fled westward to avoid the Iroquois onslaught. These refugees put additional pressure on the Puans, whose own population had been decimated by disease and their war with the Illinois Confederacy. The Menominees, who are not mentioned as participating in the war between the Puans and the Illinois, also suffered from the pestilence and famine caused by the presence of the refugee populations. Perrot put the Menominees' numbers at a mere forty men, or fewer than two hundred total tribal members. The first Frenchmen known to have visited the Green Bay region after Nicolet were Médard Chouart, sieur des Groseilliers, and another, unnamed Frenchman in 1654. Groseilliers's brother-in-law, Pierre-Esprit Radisson, claimed also to have made this voyage, but this is unlikely. While Radisson conducted many travels into the North American interior, recent research indicates he composed his narrative of this expedition primarily on the basis of the testimony of Groseilliers and his anonymous attendant.[30] Groseilliers and his companion were the first Europeans to witness the destruction and horrors caused by the Wars of the Iroquois and the aftermath of the Puans' war with the Illinois Confederacy. They did not mention the Puans specifically during this journey, but their comment, "We meet with severall [sic] nations all sedentary . . . amazed to see us, and weare very civil," appears to allude to the horticultural Puans.[31]

The Ho-Chunk elder Spoon Decorah in 1887 referred to Groseilliers and his companion when he stated that at Red Banks his ancestors "met at that place the first Frenchmen whom they ever saw."[32] The Ho-Chunks and Menominees related similar information to Charles C. Trowbridge in 1823. The details within these accounts indicate Trowbridge's informants also referred to Groseilliers and his companion rather than Nicolet, although these narratives also may have conflated elements of Nicolet's visit with those of Groseilliers.[33] Nevertheless, none of these oral traditions specifically mentions Nicolet. As occurred with the residents of New France, Nicolet's journey was ultimately forgotten among the later Ho-Chunks and the Menominees. The Puans' grave losses in their war with the Illinois Confederacy, and the precipitous decline of the

Menominees shortly thereafter, probably served to practically erase this episode from both groups' collective memories.

In the wake of Groseilliers came the Jesuits, who took advantage of the various lulls in fighting to establish new missions in what became known as the *pays d'en haut*, or the upper country west of Montreal. In 1665, the Jesuits established the mission of St. Esprit at Chequamegon Bay in present-day northern Wisconsin, a region that, like Green Bay, had become a haven for refugee Hurons and members of other tribes fleeing the Iroquois. In 1669, the Jesuit Claude Allouez established the mission of St. François Xavier on the western shore of Green Bay, most likely at a village of refugee Potawatomis and Sauks at the mouth of the Oconto River. In spring 1670, he shifted the mission to the vicinity of Red Banks. In 1671, he established yet another mission on the Fox River at present-day De Pere, about six miles south of Green Bay. By 1673, six Jesuits labored in the mission field of present-day Wisconsin and the Upper Peninsula of Michigan. Like Groseilliers, the Jesuit missionaries saw the devastation the various wars of the 1640s and 1650s had left behind. One Jesuit, Claude Dablon, confirmed what Nicolet undoubtedly learned about the name of the Puans: "The people living at the head of the Bay [are] commonly called des Puans. This name, which is the same as that given by the Savages to those who live near the sea, it bears perhaps because the odor of the marshes surrounding this Bay somewhat resembles that of the sea."[34]

The Jesuits finally figured out the geographic puzzle of the western Great Lakes, but this was not due to Nicolet's journey. Champlain believed Lakes Superior and Michigan were but one lake west of Lake Huron. In September 1641, the Jesuits Charles Raymbault and Isaac Jogues ascended the St. Mary's River, the "great river" mentioned by Nicolet, and became the first Frenchman definitely known to have seen the Sault Ste. Marie Rapids. Other Jesuits who worked along the shores of Georgian Bay of Lake Huron in the 1640s gained additional information about the western Great Lakes. The Catholic nun Mother Marie de l'Incarnation referenced correspondence received from these missionaries. A letter she wrote in September 1646 confirmed these Jesuits had learned two great bodies lay to the west, not one as Champlain had thought.[35]

The Jesuit Paul Ragueneau's writings leave no doubt that by 1648, the French knew of both Lakes Michigan and Superior and the Upper Peninsula of Michigan that separated them as

> the shores of another lake [Lake Superior] larger than the fresh-
> water sea [Lake Huron], into which it discharges by a very large
> and very rapid river [St. Mary's River]; the latter, before mingling
> its waters with those of our fresh-water sea, rolls over a fall [the
> Sault Ste. Marie Rapids]. . . . A Peninsula, or a rather narrow strip
> of land [the Upper Peninsula of Michigan] separates that superior
> Lake [Lake Superior] from a third Lake, which we call the Lake of the
> Puants [Lake Michigan], which also flows into our fresh-water sea by
> a mouth [the Strait of Mackinac] on the other side of the Peninsula,
> about ten leagues [twenty-one miles] farther West than the Sault.
> This third Lake extends between the West and Southwest . . . and
> is almost equal in size to our fresh-water sea [Lake Huron]. On its
> shores dwell other nations whose language is unknown,—that is, it
> is neither Algonquin nor Huron. These peoples are called Puants, not
> because of any bad odor that is peculiar to them; but, because they
> say that they come from the shores of a far distant sea toward the
> North, the water of which is salt, they are called "the people of the
> stinking water."[36]

The distance from the mouth of the southern channel of the St. Mary's River to the Strait of Mackinac is closer to forty miles rather than the twenty-one mentioned by Ragueneau, but other than that, his description of the region where all three lakes meet is accurate. However, we do not know how Ragueneau acquired this information. The same is true of the contents of l'Incarnation's 1646 letter. Ragueneau and l'Incarnation certainly did not receive what they knew from Nicolet. L'Incarnation's correspondence indicates letters sent by the Jesuits laboring on the shores of Georgian Bay were received at Quebec sometime in 1646, but unfortunately, these have been lost. Quite possibly, either the Jesuits or Groseilliers conducted additional journeys westward toward Lakes Michigan and Superior during the 1640s, for in his journal Radisson wrote of Groseilliers making "severall [sic] journeys when the fathers lived about the lake of the Hurons [Lake Huron]."[37] The Ottawas also may have supplied this information, for the Indians had always been an important source of geographical information.[38]

Regardless of whether the information came from unnamed Frenchmen or Native persons, it allows us to roughly date when the Puans became engaged in their war with the Illinois Confederacy. In her letter, l'Incarnation described the Puans in 1646—and in the present tense—as "numerous and sedentary"; later observers, such as Perrot and Dablon, also described the Puans as populous before their conflagration with the Illinois Confederacy. If l'Incarnation's statement is accurate, the Puans' war with the Illinois began after September 1646, about the same time as the commencement of the Wars of Iroquois.[39]

L'Incarnation also suggested the Great Lakes provided an outlet to the Pacific Ocean. She noted, "A new country has been discovered and its entrance found. It is the nation of *the gens de mer* [People of the Sea or Puans] . . . by which it is claimed that the road to China will be found."[40] Ragueneau, on the other hand, knew all three of the western Great Lakes—Lakes Huron, Superior, and Michigan—were freshwater bodies. L'Incarnation wrote her letter only twelve years after the journey of Nicolet, but neither she nor Ragueneau, who knew Nicolet, mentioned him. Again, this illustrates how inconsequential Nicolet's expedition was. He paddled into Lake Michigan and Green Bay and knew both were freshwater bodies. Why did l'Incarnation not know this? Nicolet must have known the water around Green Bay had a rather putrid smell and was the source of the Puans' name among their neighbors; why did he not tell Ragueneau that it had nothing to do with the Puans having a fictitious origin along a distant saltwater sea to the north?[41]

Clearly, Nicolet did not extensively disseminate what he had learned, and l'Incarnation's letter indicates much of the knowledge the French acquired about the western Great Lakes in the 1640s came from sources other than Nicolet. Even Paul Le Jeune, who possessed Nicolet's written report, had a rather confused understanding of the geography of the western Great Lakes. In his 1640 *Relation*, Le Jeune wrote of an Englishman who had entered the St. Lawrence River looking for a body of water that might provide the Northwest Passage. Le Jeune quoted this anonymous English explorer, who remarked:

For two years I have ranged the whole Southern coast, from Virginia to Quinebiqui [Kennebec River], seeking to find some great river or great lake that might lead me to peoples who had some knowledge of this sea which is to the North of Mexico. Not having found any, I came to this country [the St. Lawrence Valley] to . . . penetrate, if I could . . . to the North sea.[42]

The story of this hapless Englishman (who was escorted under guard by the French from the St. Lawrence and thus did not complete his journey) prompted Le Jeune to write that Nicolet had already penetrated these areas and had related to him information about the "great river" that led to the "sea" of which the Englishman spoke. Le Jeune went on to write, "It is highly probable one can descend through the second great lake of the Hurons [Lake Michigan] . . . into this sea [Lake Superior] that he was seeking. . . . Now I have strong suspicions that this is the sea which answers to that North of new Mexico, and that from this sea there would be an outlet towards Japan and China."[43] In summary, Le Jeune believed that to travel to Lake Superior, one first had to enter Lake Michigan, make a three-day journey up the St. Mary's River (which he believed flowed out of Lake Michigan, not Lake Superior), and then enter Lake Superior. Of course, this is not the case, as the St. Mary's River connects Lakes Superior and Huron. Moreover, Le Jeune made no mention of the Strait of Mackinac, while Ragueneau did. It is evident after reading Le Jeune's *Relation* that Ragueneau, writing eight years later, had a much more accurate understanding of the basic geography of the western Great Lakes. Astonishingly, we know Le Jeune received his information from the first Frenchman to have traveled in this region: Jean Nicolet![44]

Had Le Jeune confused what Nicolet told him? Did Nicolet not emphasize Lake Huron was connected to Lake Superior by the St. Mary's River and not Lake Michigan? The answers are not obvious, but the questions confirm that Nicolet did not see himself as an explorer, and he was certainly no geographer. Le Jeune's and Vimont's narratives affirm Nicolet saw himself instead as a diplomat. He seems not to have passed on to Le Jeune or anyone else detailed information concerning the lands and lakes through which he traveled; if he did, it was in a rather incoherent manner. He did relate detailed knowledge concerning the new tribes of which he learned, which in his mind was of greater significance. Information concerning these tribes was also more important to missionaries such as Le Jeune, as the Jesuits constantly sought new Indian societies to which they could bring the Gospel. Moreover, Champlain does not appear to have widely disseminated his theories concerning the Great Lakes upon his return to Quebec in 1633, probably because he was consumed with securing New France from the dangers it faced. Even then, exploration in his mind, especially later in his career, was more important for extending French influence to new Indian tribes than it was for finding the Northwest Passage. Nicolet probably knew learning about these tribes would have been Champlain's priority as well. Given these two considerations, we should not be surprised Nicolet focused his attention on the human geography of the western Great Lakes rather than on the physical geography. For these reasons, Frenchmen in the years after Nicolet's voyage still clung to incorrect theories about the Great Lakes and continued to believe they might find access to the Pacific Ocean by sailing through them.

Solving the puzzle of the Great Lakes proceeded through fits and starts for the French, particularly the Jesuits who, in their zeal to minister to the various refugee Indians in the western Great Lakes, continued to gather geographic information. By the 1640s, many Frenchmen eschewed the earlier dual drainage theory of the Great Lakes that Champlain, Gabriel Sagard, and Marc Lescarbot had championed from about 1600 to the 1620s. This is evident in the writings of Le Jeune (1640) and Ragueneau (1648), who described Lakes Huron, Michigan, and Superior as freshwater bodies. As mentioned, Champlain had abandoned this idea, most likely in 1624. However, l'Incarnation's 1646 letter suggests some residents of New France continued to believe these bodies of water might provide direct access to the Pacific. However, like Champlain later in his career and Le Jeune in 1640, she may have assumed instead that the rivers of the western Great Lakes simply provided portages to other watersheds that flowed westward toward the Pacific.[45] Like many documentary sources produced in early New France, her letter is too vague to draw any firm conclusions on this point.

Regardless, by the 1660s, any theories about the Great Lakes flowing into both the Atlantic and Pacific Oceans were finally put to rest. In 1660, a Jesuit, most likely Gabriel Druillettes, interviewed a Christian Nipissing named Michel Awatanik. In June 1658, Awatanik departed Green Bay, a place where he and many of his people sought refuge during the Wars of the Iroquois. He wanted to travel to the St. Lawrence River by a course other than the familiar Ottawa River route, which at the time was blocked by the Mohawks. In the process, he traveled to James Bay of Hudson Bay and, by means of various portages, arrived at Tadoussac on the St. Lawrence River in 1660. On the basis of this interview, Druillettes wrote Lake Michigan was "only a large bay in lake Huron" and thus was a freshwater body.[46] Clearly, Lake Michigan offered no route to the Pacific. Also significant is the fact an Indian, Michel Awatanik, and not a Frenchman, provided the crucial information.

Claude Allouez became the first Frenchman known to have traveled throughout Lake Superior and Lake Nipigon during a journey that lasted from August 1665 until his return to Quebec in August 1667. Thus, by the late 1660s, it was evident that Lake Superior also offered no direct passage westward. This did not stop Frenchmen from hoping a new body of water of which they learned—the Mississippi River—might flow to the Pacific. The Jesuit Claude Dablon first advanced this theory in his 1659–1660 *Relation*, but Louis Jolliet and the Jesuit Jacques Marquette confirmed this was not so in 1673. They traveled as far south as present-day Arkansas and concluded the Mississippi drained into the Gulf of Mexico. During the course of their expedition, Marquette and Jolliet set their eyes upon another great river that fed into the Mississippi. Marquette wrote that the "Pekitanouï [Missouri River] is a river of Considerable size, coming from the Northwest, from a great Distance; and it discharges into the Missisipi. . . . I hope by its means to discover the vermillion or California sea [the Pacific Ocean]."[47] The adventurer René-Robert Cavelier, sieur de La Salle, followed up on their voyage. La Salle, who had a trading post near the Lachine Rapids, also sought a route to China via the Mississippi. His feckless efforts to locate the Northwest Passage caused the local settlers, in a condescending manner, to bestow upon the rapids where he had his post the Lachine (or the China) Rapids when he made an abortive exploration attempt in 1669. Later, he descended the entire length of the Mississippi and on April 9, 1682, claimed Louisiana for France.[48]

While the Mississippi River failed to be the long-sought-after North-west Passage, Gabriel Druillettes proffered a theory that yet another body of saltwater might exist westward beyond the Great Lakes. Thus was born the idea of the Mer de l'Ouest, or the Western Sea:

> For we learn from these peoples [the Indians of the Lake Superior
> basin] that they find the Sea on three sides, toward the South, to-
> ward the West, and toward the North . . . these three Seas . . . form
> in reality but one Sea, which is that of China . . . that of the South,
> which is the Pacific sea and is well enough known, being connected
> with the North sea [Hudson Bay], which is equally well known, by
> a third Sea, the one about which we are in doubt . . . from this same
> lake Superior, following a River toward the North, we arrive, after
> eight or ten days' journey, at Hudson bay. . . . These two Seas, then,
> of the South and of the North, being known, there remains only
> that of the West, which joins them, to make only one from the
> three . . . and that it only remains now . . . to enter nothing less
> than the Japan sea.[49]

This description indicates that Druillettes had been influenced by a map made in 1650 by Nicolas Sanson that had Hudson Bay linking with a hypothetical western sea that plunged deep into the western half of North America.

Other Frenchmen also embraced the idea of a western sea beyond the Great Lakes. Claude Dablon gave credence to this notion in his 1670–1671 *Relation* when he wrote "Two hundred leagues [420 miles] from the Mission of saint Esprit [at Chequamegon Bay of Lake Superior] . . . toward the West, is the Western Sea."[50] Dablon was, in many ways, the Champlain of his age. He was deeply interested in North American geography and zealously sought the Northwest Passage in the lands beyond the Great Lakes basin. However, what Dablon's Indian infor-mants described was not a great western sea that was a saltwater bay of the Pacific Ocean; they referred instead to Canada's Lake Winnipeg, which, like Green Bay, also has brackish, undrinkable water. In fact, the word *Winnipeg*, like the word *Winnebago*, is derived from *ouinipeg*, or "stinking water." Once again, many years after Champlain, Frenchmen

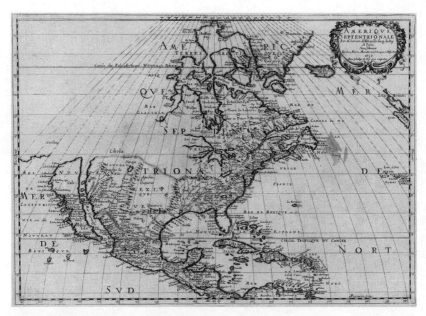

Nicolas Sanson's 1650 map, *Amerique Septentrionale*, kept alive the notion that the Northwest Passage might be found through North America and provide a relatively easy water route to the Pacific Ocean. COURTESY OF THE JOHN CARTER BROWN LIBRARY AT BROWN UNIVERSITY

listened to the Indians' descriptions of Lake Winnipeg, a closed freshwater lake that is about as large as Lake Erie. They mistook the Indians to mean a saltwater adjunct to the Pacific lay just a few hundred miles west of the Great Lakes that might be accessed by portages from Lake Superior into another watershed.[51]

Of course, Mer de l'Ouest did not exist. It was a later version of the ambiguous bay Samuel de Champlain placed on his 1616 map a century earlier, or Lake Tadouac on Edward Wright's 1599 map. It kept alive the dream of the Northwest Passage for later generations eager to acquire the riches of Asia. Even after the French realized Lake Winnipeg was not the Western Sea, they simply pushed the boundaries of this elusive body of water farther west. On maps such as that those of Guillaume Delisle, it stretched as far inland as present-day Saskatchewan and North and South Dakota. Even by the 1730s, when it had become common knowledge that Lake Winnipeg was not Mer de l'Ouest, new bodies of water lured Frenchmen deeper into the continent. Pierre Gaultier de Varennes,

This 1750 map by Philippe Buache shows Mer de l'Ouest. Buache's rendition was based on an earlier map by Guillaume Delisle. Like Nicolas Sanson's 1650 map, it also suggests that the Northwest Passage to the Pacific Ocean might be found by navigating the various rivers and waterways of North America to Mer de l'Ouest. COURTESY OF THE JOHN CARTER BROWN LIBRARY AT BROWN UNIVERSITY

sieur de la Vérendrye, after hearing stories from the Cree Indians around Lake Superior of a great river farther west, sought to find this yet-to-be-discovered River of the West in the hope that it led to the equally enigmatic Mer de l'Ouest. La Vérendrye began his explorations in 1731 and over the course of the next decade slowly pushed westward into the region of Lakes Winnipeg and Manitoba. In 1742–1743, he sent his sons to the south and west, where they explored the upper Missouri River and traveled as far as the Black Hills in present-day South Dakota or possibly the Big Horn Mountains in Wyoming. But, alas, the Missouri River and its tributaries flowed to the south and east; the la Vérendryes had not located the mythical River of West.[52]

Jacques Legardeur de Saint-Pierre (interestingly, a great-grandson of Jean Nicolet) built upon the la Vérendryes' explorations by navigating westward on another river, the Saskatchewan. Saint-Pierre himself did not extensively explore the river; that task was left to a young ensign and nine men who managed in 1750 to journey westward on the Saskatchewan River and establish Fort La Jonquière near present-day Nipawin, Saskatchewan. Warfare between the tribes of the northern Great Plains stymied further efforts to penetrate the great mountain range to the west known as the Rockies, and Saint-Pierre returned eastward in 1753. Saint-Pierre blamed his failure to find Mer de l'Ouest on his troubles with the Indians and their allegiance to the English traders at Hudson Bay. He was not particularly eager to conduct further explorations. He expressed more interest in a military campaign to conqueror the English posts at Hudson Bay. He also undoubtedly realized the Rocky Mountains, which lay about five hundred miles farther westward of Fort La Jonquière, had to be crossed to reach the Pacific.[53]

The Scottish-Canadian fur trader Alexander Mackenzie managed to overcome this obstacle. Departing his post of Fort Chipewyan on the western end of Lake Athabasca in June 1789, Mackenzie led an expedition by way of the Great Slave Lake and the Mackenzie River that bears his name. However, he was disappointed to discover the Mackenzie emptied into the ice-covered waters of the Arctic Ocean rather than the Cook Inlet of present-day Alaska and the Pacific Ocean. After a round trip of almost three thousand miles, he returned to Fort Chipewyan, discouraged but not daunted. The Peace River, he determined, would be a more feasible route, and in May 1793, he departed Fort Fork in present-day Alberta with nine men. The Peace River, Mackenzie soon learned, required numerous, exhausting portages. The mountains presented an even more formidable obstacle. He and his men crossed the Continental Divide on June 12 and later reached the Fraser River, which Mackenzie learned had many rapids and other obstacles. He decided to strike out overland. After reaching a Nuxalk Indian village, he secured guides and canoes and descended the

Bella Coola River. On July 22, 1793, he recorded his accomplishment upon a rock along the shore of the present-day Dean Channel, an estuary of the Pacific Ocean, with makeshift paint. Mackenzie and his men thus became the first Europeans to traverse North America from east to west. However, Mackenzie was again disappointed. He had not located a commercially viable route to the Pacific Ocean, as the Rocky Mountains and their impassable rivers provided no such means by which to achieve this goal.[54]

The Royal Navy fared no better. In 1776, the British Admiralty dispatched Captain James Cook to find a passage by plying the waters of the northern Pacific beyond the Bering Strait. The stories of Spanish mariners who had explored the western coast of North America had lured the British into this project of the "Northeast Passage." The first, Juan de Fuca, had allegedly sailed from Acapulco in 1592 and discovered an inlet that flowed to the northeast. In 1640, another Spaniard, Bartholomew de Fonte, reportedly sailed north of de Fuca's inlet and discovered a river he named Los Reyes that also flowed eastward into Hudson Bay and ultimately the Atlantic. Yet alas, like so many other oft-repeated tales about supposed water routes through and around North America, the so-called "discoveries" of de Fuca and de Fonte turned out to be mere fables. The two Spanish sea captains likely were also fictional. Cook was dubious of these accounts; nevertheless, he held high hopes as he passed through the Bering Strait that the waters of the frigid Arctic might afford a passage eastward. He abandoned all such notions on August 17, 1778, when he spied a massive wall of ice that stretched east and west as far as the eye could see at the latitude of 70 degrees 41 minutes north. Natives killed Cook in February 1779 while he was wintering in the Hawaiian Islands. His ships' crews continued their explorations of the seas north of the Bering Strait that year. The great barrier of the polar ice cap once again stopped them. Cook's ships returned to Great Britain in October 1780 after an absence of more than four years.[55] The Northwest Passage remained as elusive as ever.

Captain George Vancouver, who had sailed on Cook's voyage from 1776 to 1780, laid to rest the myths of Juan de Fuca and Bartholomew de Fonte. Over the course of two years, from 1792 to 1794, Vancouver meticulously surveyed the Pacific coast from the Columbia River northward toward Alaska. At one point, he missed meeting up with Alexander

Mackenzie's expedition by only forty-seven days. Vancouver had been skeptical of the various Spanish accounts from the beginning. He believed the ultimate purpose of his explorations was to put an end to such speculations, particularly since critics in his country, in Vancouver's opinion, had wrongly faulted Cook for failing to find the waterway. Indeed, Vancouver was unique in that he was probably the only explorer over the course of three centuries who was eager to disprove the existence of the Northwest Passage! As his men finished their final surveys in August 1794, Vancouver took great pride in having refuted the "numerous train of hypothetical navigators" who had given credence to the outlandish claims of de Fuca and de Fonte. He went on to write with great confidence that his explorations would "remove every doubt, and set aside every opinion of *a north-west passage*, or any water communication navigable for shipping, existing between the north pacific, and the interior of the American continent."[56]

Vancouver's statement proved to be accurate. Over the course of the next century, other explorers continued to investigate the vast Canadian Arctic Archipelago north of Hudson Bay, although these voyages were purely scientific in their objectives. The British naval officer Robert McClure and his crew were the first to accomplish the task of negotiating the Northwest Passage between 1850 and 1854 by pushing eastward from the Pacific through the many islands and channels of the archipelago. McClure went in search of the earlier expedition led by Sir John Franklin from 1845 to 1848, during which the entire crew succumbed to disease, starvation, and death after their ships became trapped in the ice. McClure's expedition almost suffered this same fate. Pack ice forced McClure's men to abandon their ship in 1853 and complete much of their expedition by sledge over the snowpack until they made contact with ships from another expedition that traveled from the east. About fifty years later, from 1903 to 1906, the intrepid Norwegian Roald Amundsen made his way through the archipelago using a sailing vessel for the entire journey over the course of three difficult years. The voyages of McClure and Amundsen confirmed what had been clear by the dawn of the nineteenth century: the waterways north of Hudson Bay—with short seasons for navigation and treacherous ice fields—did not offer a commercially viable route that would serve as the Northwest Passage.[57] However, hope persisted that the great rivers of the West in the interior of North America might offer an accessible means that linked the Atlantic and Pacific Oceans. The French and their Canadian descendants had been engaged in this project for more than two centuries and had had no luck; their American successors fared no better.

When did the dream of the Northwest Passage die? A decade after Alexander Mackenzie had reached the Pacific Ocean, two American army officers, Meriwether Lewis and William Clark, led an expedition between 1803 and 1806, as per the orders of President Thomas Jefferson, to explore the western districts of the United States' newest territorial acquisition, the Louisiana Purchase. Inspired by Mackenzie's earlier expedition as well as the passage in Marquette's writings that declared the Missouri River as the gateway to the Pacific Ocean, Jefferson hoped that when Lewis and Clark reached the headwaters of the Missouri, they might find a relatively short passage through the mountains that offered access to the Columbia River and the Pacific. On August 12, 1805, Lewis finally crossed the Continental Divide. He no doubt believed Jefferson's theory was correct. As he ascended a valley between the mountains that lay to west of the Missouri headwaters, Lewis noted with anticipation, "I therefore did not despair of shortly finding a passage over the mountains and taisting [sic] the waters of the great Columbia this evening."[58] What he saw was not what Jefferson had hoped. Lewis did not look down on a broad, blue ribbon of water that boldly made its way to the Pacific. He spied only mountains as far as the eye could see: "We proceeded to the top of the dividing ridge from which I discovered immence [sic] ranges of mountains still to the West of us with their tops covered partially with snow."[59] He had to content himself with a cool drink of water from one of the small streams that ultimately fed into the Columbia River.[60] Thus ended the centuries' long project to find a natural waterway that bridged the Atlantic and Pacific Oceans in the interior of North America.

Would such a route ever be realized? Yes, but only by the hand of man. In 1904, President Teddy Roosevelt ordered the construction of the Panama Canal after the French had abandoned the project in 1889. Through the expenditure of great amounts of money; with the use of powerful machines to move the earth; and at the cost of many thousands of lives lost due to yellow fever, malaria, and dysentery, the Panama Canal opened on August 15, 1914.[61]

That Jean Nicolet was not one of the brave explorers who sought the Northwest Passage should not bother us today. In fact, dismissing the notion allows us to finally put to rest the many myths that have made him look naive and perhaps even a little foolish. This includes the idea that he thought he had sojourned to the far reaches of China when he actually knew he was simply going deeper into the heart of North America, and especially the ridiculous myth that he wore a flamboyant Chinese robe when he arrived. His journey westward still required tremendous courage, both physical and moral. He braved the cold, turbulent waters of the western Great Lakes and negotiated peace with a tribe whose power and aggressiveness were well known among the Indians of New France with whom he lived. He did not see himself as an explorer, as some sort of "inland Columbus" who, like his predecessors such as Verrazano and Cartier, searched in vain for the Northwest Passage. Instead, we have an image of him as an ambassador—as a diplomat—who served the commander of New France, Samuel de Champlain, with courage, tenacity, loyalty, and perseverance. It is a far more accurate portrait of the man and a far greater one to appreciate.

ACKNOWLEDGMENTS

Many people deserve high praise for their assistance in writing this book. The library staff at the Milwaukee School of Engineering has been a constant source of support since I started working there in 2003, particularly the interlibrary loan specialists, Denise Gergetz, Karen Bolton, and Sarah Rowell, who have never failed to fulfill my numerous requests for the occasional obscure book or arcane article. The staffs at the John P. Raynor Library at Marquette University in Milwaukee and the Golda Meir Library and the American Geographical Society Library at the University of Wisconsin–Milwaukee also have been indispensable throughout this project. I also want to thank the staffs at the Cartographic Branch of the National Archives, the Burton Historical Collection of the Detroit Public Library, and the Wisconsin Historical Society for their assistance in locating maps and textual information concerning the site known as Red Banks along the shores of Green Bay.

Conrad E. Heidenreich provided many valuable observations and suggestions for the first book I wrote about Jean Nicolet with my co-author, the late Nancy Oestreich Lurie, several years ago, and I found much of what he suggested for that earlier work was equally valuable for this book. The late K. Janet Ritch, who worked with Dr. Heidenreich on a recent biography of Samuel de Champlain, read an earlier draft of this book and must be thanked for her insightful suggestions. My good friend and colleague Carma M. Stahkne also read successive drafts of this book and smoothed the rough edges of the original prose. Kathy Borkowski, Kate Thompson, Erika Wittekind, Elizabeth Boone, and the staff of the Wisconsin Historical Society Press receive my sincere thanks for assisting in the publication of this work.

Many archaeologists assisted me in navigating the rich body of archeological literature needed to understand the Native communities residing in the western Great Lakes at the time of Nicolet's journey. David E. Overstreet, Dale R. Henning, Carol I. Mason, John Richards, Patricia Richards, Seth Schneider, Amy Rosebrough, Thomas E. Emerson, Robert F. Mazrim, John F. Swenson, and Janet M. Speth assisted me with finding relevant books, articles, and reports that detail the recent archaeological work in this region. As a historian who has never turned a trowel of earth in search of artifacts, I found their guidance essential to my research. David E. Overstreet is to be particularly thanked for reading successive drafts of this book. Alice Beck Kehoe, an anthropologist who has devoted her career to the study of American Indian culture and history, also read an earlier draft of this book and offered many insightful comments. Additionally, I want to thank Ives Goddard, Craig Kopris, and Susan Rita Ruel for their efforts in deciphering the elusive meaning of Nicolet's Indian name, *Achirra*, which comes from the Iroquoian language of the Hurons. Leslie Weidensee, Helen Johnson, and the late Martine Meyer must be thanked for their assistance in translating many of the seventeenth-century French texts that are essential for understanding the story of Jean Nicolet.

Most of all, I want to thank the late Nancy Oestreich Lurie for her years of friendship, mentorship, and scholarly comradery. This book would not have been possible without her.

NOTES

Abbreviations

Short-form references are used in the endnotes to cite all sources, and full entries can be found in the bibliography. Many of the cited sources come from various manuscript and document collections, and the abbreviations that follow are used to reference these collections in the endnotes.

Bloomfield MSS	Leonard Bloomfield Papers, National Anthropological Archives, Smithsonian Institution, Washington, DC.
Brown MSS	Charles E. Brown Papers, Wisconsin Historical Society, Madison, WI.
CWMF	Civil Works Map File, Record Group 77, Records of the Office of the Chief of Engineers, National Archives, Washington, DC. (Individual file numbers are provided in the citations.)
Gale MSS	George Gale Papers, Wisconsin Historical Society, Madison, WI.
Iowa Series 20	Crawford and Iowa County Criminal Case Files for the Additional Circuit Court of Michigan Territory, 1824–1836, Iowa Series 20, Records of the Iowa County Clerk of Court, University of Wisconsin–Platteville Area Research Center, Platteville, WI.
NASR	Alfred J. Hill and Theodore H. Lewis, Northwestern Archaeological Survey Records, 1880–1895, Minnesota Historical Society, St. Paul, MN.
T-907	United States Weather Bureau, Climatological Records, 1819–1892, Microfilm Publication T-907, Record Group 27, Records of the United States Weather Bureau, National Archives, Washington, DC.
Trowbridge MSS	Charles C. Trowbridge Papers, Burton Historical Colection, Detroit Public Library, Detroit, MI.

Introduction

1. Two excellent introductions to transnational history are Bayly et al., "AHR Conversation: On Transnational History," 1441–1464; and Iriye, "Transnational History," 211–213 (qtd. 213).
2. Greer, "National, Transnational, and Hypernational Historiographies," 695–742 (qtd. 701).
3. Lurie and Jung, *Nicolet Corrigenda*, passim.
4. Butterfield, *History of the Discovery*, 39, 58–60 (qtd. 39, 58–59).
5. I located a copy of my fourth-grade textbook and immediately recognized the picture of Nicolet meeting the Indians that I saw as a child. See Romano and Georgiady, *Exploring Wisconsin*, 12–13. For a discussion of the artistic depictions of Nicolet and the various historical markers that celebrate his landfall, see Lurie and Jung, *Nicolet Corrigenda*, frontispiece, 14–15, 59, 62, 124.
6. Charlevoix, *Journal of a Voyage to North-America*, 1:286, 2:61; Lurie and Jung, *Nicolet Corrigenda*, 2, 7; Thwaites, *Jesuit Relations*, 18:231; Hodge, *Handbook*, 2:958, 961; Radin, "Winnebago Tribe," 53; Hall, "Relating the Big Fish and the Big Stone," 19; Lurie, "Winnebago Protohistory," 793; Lurie, "Winnebago," 692–695.
7. Trigger, *Children of Aataentsic*, 1:xxiii; Pendergast, "Identity of Stadacona and Hochelaga," 68–72.

Chapter 1

1. Hamelin, "Nicollet de Belleborne, Jean," 516; Sulte, *Mélanges*, 436; Trudel, "Jean Nicollet," 185; Butterfield, *History of the Discovery*, 27, 27n1, 88–89; Thwaites, *Jesuit Relations*, 9: 215–217;

Kamen, *Early Modern European Society*, 95–99, 104–107; Maza, "Bourgeoisie," 127–140; Jouan, "Jean Nicolet, Interpreter," 6–9.

2. For Le Jeune's and Vimont's accounts, see Thwaites, *Jesuit Relations*, 18:231–233, 237, 23:275–283. For other references, see Thwaites, *Jesuit Relations*, 8:99, 247, 257–259, 267, 9:125, 131, 215, 11:145, 12:41–43, 135, 151, 163, 177–179, 203, 253, 20:291, 21:39, 43–51, 24:57, 28:183, 42:223.

3. For a recent study that arrives at a very different set of conclusions from those presented here, see Mason, "Where Nicolet and the Winnebagoes First Met," 65–74.

4. Fritze, *New Worlds*, 92–119, 127–157, 171.

5. Fritze, *New Worlds*, 157–158, 167–173; Allen, "Indrawing Sea," 26–30; Allen, "From Cabot to Cartier," 512–514; Trudel, *Atlas of New France*, 28–37.

6. Fritze, *New Worlds*, 173–174; Allen, "From Cabot to Cartier," 514–516.

7. Morison, *European Discovery*, 339–371; Gordon, *Hero and the Historians*, 12–15, 191.

8. Morison, *European Discovery*, 371–375; Trudel, "Cartier, Jacques," 166; Parmenter, *Edge of the Woods*, 10. Historians have debated whether or not Cartier sought to establish sovereignty by erecting the cross. For works that argue establishing sovereignty was his intent, see Green and Dickason, *Law of Nations*, 8–10, 220; and Seed, "Taking Possession," 192–193, 192n35, 193n37. For a contrary view, see Slattery, "French Claims in North America," 147–149.

9. Morison, *European Discovery*, 375–395; Trudel, "Cartier, Jacques," 167; Gordon, *Hero and the Historians*, 18–19; Trudel, *Atlas of New France*, 40–41; Cartier, *Voyages*, 105–106 (qtd. 105–106).

10. Morison, *European Discovery*, 401–405; Cartier, *Voyages*, 119 (qtd. 119).

11. Morison, *European Discovery*, 405–407, 429; Trudel, "Cartier, Jacques," 167.

12. Morison, *European Discovery*, 407–417; Gordon, *Hero and the Historians*, 20; Cartier, *Voyages*, 170–171.

13. Morison, *European Discovery*, 415–419; Delâge, *Bitter Feast*, 94–95; Cartier, *Voyages*, 201, 221–222 (qtd. 221).

14. Morison, *European Discovery*, 419–424; Heidenreich and Ritch, "Champlain and His Times to 1604," 43; Trudel, "Cartier, Jacques," 168.

15. Morison, *European Discovery*, 430–434, 455; Lescarbot, *History of New France*, 2:182–187.

16. Baxter, *Memoir of Jacques Cartier*, 315–322; Morison, *European Discovery*, 434–436; Slattery, "French Claims in North America," 158–162.

17. Trudel, "Cartier, Jacques," 168–169; Cartier, *Voyages*, 252 (qtd. 252).

18. Morison, *European Discovery*, 434–439; Trudel, "Cartier, Jacques," 169; Cartier, *Voyages*, 252–255; Roquebrune, "La Rocque de Roberval," 424 (qtd. 424).

19. Morison, *European Discovery*, 439–441.

20. Morison, *European Discovery*, 441–443; Roquebrune, "La Roque de Roberval," 423.

21. Morison, *European Discovery*, 448–451; Cartier, *Voyages*, 293.

22. Morison, *European Discovery*, 454, 470; Trudel, *Atlas of New France*, 58–59.

23. Delâge, *Bitter Feast*, 32–33; Morison, *European Discovery*, 480–481; Quinn, "Bellenger, Etienne," 87–88; Lanctôt, "La Roche de Mesgouez, Troilus de," 421; Biggar, *Early Trading Companies*, 34–37; Trudel, "New France," 27; Fischer, *Champlain's Dream*, 604–608.

24. Morison, *European Discovery*, 480–481; Lanctôt, "La Roche de Mesgouez, Troilus de," 421–422; Biggar, *Early Trading Companies*, 38–41.

25. Trudel, "New France," 27; Morely, "Chauvin de Tonnetuit," 209; Biggar, *Early Trading Companies*, 41–44.

26. Champlain, *Works*, 2:219–221; Slattery, "French Claims in North America," 159–169; Morison, *European Discovery*, 458–463.

27. Winsor, *Cartier to Frontenac*, 64–70; Kellogg, *French Régime*, 35–42; Heidenreich and Ritch, "Champlain's Des Sauvages," 457–461; Trudel, *Atlas of New France*, 66–67.

28. Heidenreich, "History of the St. Lawrence-Great Lakes Area," 482; Trigger and Pendergast, "Saint Lawrence Iroquoians," 359–361; Chapdelaine, "Review of the Latest Developments in St. Lawrence Iroquoian Archaeology," 67–68; Pendergast, "Identity of Stadacona and

Hochelaga," 53–73; Parmenter *Edge of the Woods*, 14; Delâge, *Bitter Feast*, 49; Champlain, *Works*, 1:129; Bishop, *Champlain*, 49–52; Trigger and Swagerty, "Entertaining Strangers," 327.

29. Richter, *Ordeal of the Longhouse*, 15; Parmenter *Edge of the Woods*, 14, 16, 18; Engelbrecht, "New York Iroquois Political Development," 175–177; Kuhn and Sempowski, "New Approach to Dating the League of the Iroquois," 301–314; Eccles, *Canadian Frontier*, 6, 30–31; Heidenreich, *Huronia*, 81–85; Trigger, "French Presence in Huronia," 109–111; Trigger, "Original Iroquoians," 41; Tooker, *Ethnography of the Huron*, 9–19; Delâge, *Bitter Feast*, 49; Trigger and Swagerty, "Entertaining Strangers," 327.

30. Lawson, "Habitat of the Winnebago," 165 (qtd. 165).

31. Excellent examinations of this topic are Echo-Hawk, "Ancient History in the New World," 267–290; and Whiteley, "Archaeology and Oral Tradition," 405–415. For a similar application of this methodology, see Wonderley, "Effigy Pipes, Diplomacy, and Myth," 225–228.

32. Charles C. Trowbridge, "Comparison of the manners, Customs and international laws of the Win-nee-baá-goa nation of Indians with those of their neighbors, the Munnoáminnees [1823]," pp 120, 124–125 (qtd. 120, 124), Trowbridge MSS, box 15, folder I4Me. For information concerning Trowbridge, see Campbell, "Biographical Sketch," 483–485.

33. La Potherie, "History of the Savage Peoples," 1:293; Kay, "Fur Trade," 266–277; Mason, "Historic Identification and Lake Winnebago Focus Oneota," 345; Nicolas Boilvin, Depositions in the Methode Murder, 18 July 1826–4 August 1826, p. 14 (qtd. 14), Iowa Series 20, box 1, folder 84.

34. Decorah, "Narrative," 457–458 (qtd. 457).

35. Schoolcraft, *Information Respecting the History*, 227–228, 236 (qtd. 227, 228, 236).

36. Assikinack, "Social and Warlike Customs," 307.

37. Lurie and Jung, *Nicolet Corrigenda*, 92; Hall, "Red Banks, Oneota, and the Winnebago," 33; Radin, *Social Organization of the Winnebago Indians*, 18–19; Radin, "Winnebago Tribe," 50, 52, 65, 207–208, 213, 217, 229, 241, 245, 250 (qtd. 229). Also see Radin, "Winnebago Tales," 309.

38. George Gale, "Creation Myth of the Winnebago Indians," pp 5–6, Gale MSS, box 1, folder 3 (qtd. 5). Also see Gale, *Upper Mississippi*, 184.

39. La Potherie, "History of the Savage Peoples," 1:15, 26–27, 293, 2:250 (qtd. 1:293).

40. La Potherie, "History of the Savage Peoples," 1:293; Thwaites, *Jesuit Relations*, 55:183 (qtd. 183).

41. For examinations of this problem, see Mason, "Ethnicity and Archaeology in the Upper Great Lakes," 349–361; Emerson and Brown, "Late Prehistory and Protohistory of Illinois," 104–106; and Overstreet, "Overview of Theoretical Frameworks," 24–25.

42. For works that argue the Oneota were the ancestors of Chiwere-Siouan peoples, see McKern, "Preliminary Report," 172–173; Griffin, "Hypothesis for the Prehistory of the Winnebago," 808–862; Quimby, *Indian Life*, 105; Hall, *Archaeology of Carcajou Point*, 1:102–103, 150–154; Springer and Witkowski, "Siouan Historical Linguistics," 75–81; Hall, "Red Banks, Oneota, and the Winnebago," 34–66; Richards, "Winnebago Subsistence," 275–279; and Mason, "Oneota and Winnebago Ethnogenesis," 400–421. Nancy Oestreich Lurie proposed the residents of Aztalan in southern Wisconsin (who possessed Middle Mississippian culture as opposed to the Upper Mississippian culture of the Oneota) were the ancestors of the Puans and the later Ho-Chunks, but this theory has not been widely accepted. See Lurie, "Aztalan-Winnebago Hypothesis," 1–27; and Lurie and Jung, *Nicolet Corrigenda*, 71–93.

43. La Potherie, "History of the Savage Peoples," 1:293; Kay, "Fur Trade," 272; Schoolcraft, *Information Respecting the History*, 228 (qtd. 228).

44. Radin, "Winnebago Tribe," 50; Hall, *Archaeology of Carcajou Point*, 1:154; Gibbon, "Cultural Dynamics," 166–185; Spector, "Winnebago Indians," 34; Overstreet, "Oneota Prehistory and History," 254, 287–291; Richards, "I Should Have Dug Red Banks," 248–249; Mazrim, *Protohistory at the Grand Village of the Kaskaskia*, 45–47, 114, 131–133, 145; Brown, "Ethnohistoric Connections," 159; Hall, "Rethinking Jean Nicolet's Route," 249.

45. For the Hanson and Astor sites, see Rosebrough et al., "On the Edge of History," iii, 1, 31–85, 131–135; and Overstreet, "McCauley, Astor, and Hanson," 142–156, 180–188. For works that

examine Sawyer Harbor and other sites on the Door Peninsula, see Lurie and Jung, *Nicolet Corrigenda*, 4–5, 58, 71–93; Radin, "Winnebago Tales," 309; Hall, "Relating the Big Fish and the Big Stone," 23; Hall, "Rethinking Jean Nicolet's Route," 249; Freeman, "Analysis of the Point Sauble and Beaumier Farm," 13–39; Gibbon, "Mississippian Tradition," 331–334; and Brown, "Wisconsin Garden Beds," 97–105.

46. Newbigging, "History of the French-Ottawa Alliance," 1, 6, 40–47, 78, 90–94, 113–114, 120; Smith, "Systems of Subsistence and Networks of Exchange," 78–97; Heidenreich, *Explorations and Mapping*, 23; Feest and Feest, "Ottawa," 772; Garrad, "Champlain and the Odawa," 62; Champlain, *Works*, 3:44, 105, 119–120; Sagard, *Le Grand Voyage*, [xx]; Sagard, *Long Journey*, 9; Sagard, *Historie du Canada*, 200–201; Thwaites, *Jesuit Relations*, 16:253 (qtd. 253).

47. Theler and Boszhardt, *Twelve Millennia*, 158–159; Schneider, "Oneota Ceramic Production," 363–370.

48. Robinson, "Legend of Red Banks," 491–492; Neville, "Some Historic Sites About Green Bay," 144–149; Lurie and Jung, *Nicolet Corrigenda*, 5–7, 73–83; *Green Bay Intelligencer* (Green Bay, WI), 8 January 1834; Trowbridge, "Comparison of the manners, Customs and international laws of the Win-nee-baá-goa nation," p. 125, Trowbridge MSS, box 15, folder I4Me; Sketch of the Head of Green Bay, n.d., CWMF 0-128-9; W.G. Williams and J.W. Gunnison, Chart of Green Bay, 1844, CWMF 0-128-2; Alfred J. Hill and Theodore H. Lewis, 15 June 1892, Supplementary Notebook No. 4, p. 47, NASR. An existing embankment near Red Banks might be a remnant of the parapet, but the evidence is inconclusive. See Speth, "Site Complex at Red Banks," 14–15.

49. Schoolcraft, *Information Respecting the History*, 231 (qtd. 231).

50. Carol I. Mason and David Overstreet must be thanked for assisting in the development of this hypothesis. See David Overstreet, personal communications, 8 February 2015, 11 November 2015, 12 September 2017; Carol I. Mason, personal communication, 29 January 2016; Trowbridge, "Comparison of the manners, Customs and international laws of the Win-nee-baá-goa nation," pp 120–125, Trowbridge MSS, box 15, folder I4Me; Lurie and Jung, *Nicolet Corrigenda*, 108–109; Lurie, "Winnebago Protohistory," 802; Hauser, "Illinois Indian Tribe," 128; Mazrim and Esarey, "Rethinking the Dawn of History," 174–186; La Potherie, "History of the Savage Peoples," 1:293–300; Williams and Gunnison, Chart of Green Bay, 1844, CWMF 0-128-2; and Stevenson, "Chronological and Settlement Aspects," 243–244, 285–288.

51. La Potherie, "History of the Savage Peoples," 1:300; Thwaites, *Jesuit Relations*, 55:183; Trowbridge, "Comparison of the manners, Customs and international laws of the Win-nee-baá-goa nation," pp 124–125, Trowbridge MSS, box 15, folder I4Me; Decorah, "Narrative," 457–458; Schoolcraft, *Information Respecting the History*, 227; Theler and Boszhardt, *Twelve Millennia*, 171–181.

52. Overstreet, "Lake Winnebago Phase," 136–138, 195; David Overstreet, personal communications, 19 April 2017, 22 April 2017, 3 May 2017; La Potherie, "History of the Savage Peoples," 1:293 (qtd. 293).

53. Overstreet, "Lake Winnebago Phase," 170–172; Charles Richter to A. F. Laue, 4 May 1903, Brown MSS, part 1, box 47, folder 1863–1916; H. P. Hamilton to Charles E. Brown, 12 January 1912, Brown MSS, part 1, box 47, folder 1863–1916.

54. Trowbridge, "Comparison of the manners, Customs and international laws of the Win-nee-baá-goa nation," p. 120, Trowbridge MSS, box 15, folder I4Me; Radin, "Winnebago Tribe," 229; Gale, "Creation Myth of the Winnebago Indians," p. 5, Gale MSS, box 1, folder 3.

55. Ronald J. Mason argues, on the basis of the writings of the Jesuit Claude Dablon, the Menominees' residence at Green Bay occurred after Nicolet's visit and was due to the migrations of Central Algonquian societies westward during the Iroquois Wars in the 1640s and 1650s. However, Dablon's testimony in this instance is suspect; he lived only two years (1669–1671) in the western Great Lakes and spent most of that time at Sault Ste. Marie organizing the western missions. He stayed only about a week at Green Bay and, unlike many of his contemporaries, never acquired a fluency in the regional Indian languages. Nicolas Perrot's works are more credible,

as he lived among the Indians of the western Great Lakes for over thirty years, made many visits to the tribes at Green Bay, and acquired a fluency in Algonquian languages. Perrot's writings indicate the Menominees' residence at Green Bay preceded the Iroquois Wars. See Mason, "Archaeoethnicity and the Elusive Menominis," 85; Thwaites, *Jesuit Relations*, 55:103, 185, 199; Delanglez "Claude Dablon," 98–100; La Potherie, "History of the Savage Peoples," 1:26–27, 217–220, 293, 2:250.

56. La Potherie, "History of the Savage Peoples," 1:15, 293; Charles C. Trowbridge, "Traditions, Manners, and Customs of the Mun-oá-min-nee Nation of Indians," p. 9 (qtd. 9; emphasis in original), Trowbridge MSS, box 15, folder I4Me. For a typescript of this document, see Charles C. Trowbridge, "Account of the Menominee Taken at Green Bay, Summer of 1823," Bloomfield MSS, box 1.

57. Hoffman, "Mythology of the Menomoni Indians," 243 (qtd. 243). This and other myths that relate the origin of the Menominee people are also in Hoffman, "Menomini Indians," 20, 39, 41.

58. Skinner, *Social Life*, 8, 16. Also see Keesing, *Menomini Indians*, 6; and Beck, *Siege and Survival*, 11, 25–26.

59. Grignon, "Seventy-Two Years' Recollections," 195, 265 (qtd. 265). Also see Hodge, *Handbook*, 2:82–83; and Bellfy, *Three Fires Unity*, 3.

60. Charlevoix, *Journal of a Voyage to North-America*, 2:61 (qtd. 61).

61. Trowbridge, "Traditions, Manners, and Customs of the Mun-oá-min-nee Nation," p. 1, Trowbridge MSS, box 15, folder I4Me; Beck, *Siege and Survival*, 26.

62. For the dearth of archaeological evidence concerning the location of the Grand Village as well as the inability of archaeologists to definitively link the Menominees with various prehistoric and protohistoric archaeological assemblages in the Green Bay region, see Mason, "Archaeoethnicity and the Elusive Menominis," 81–85; and Richards, "I Should Have Dug Red Banks," 243–249. For archaeological studies of the sites along the Peshtigo, Oconto, and Big Suamico Rivers as well as other sites in northeastern Wisconsin that support the case, at least tentatively, for the Menominees' residence along the western shore of Green Bay at the time of Nicolet's visit, see Overstreet, "Overview of Theoretical Frameworks," 41–47, 57–58, 64–71; Overstreet, "Mero Complex," 180–192, 213–216; Overstreet, "Elusive Menominee," 50–51; and Dirst, "Reconsidering the Prehistory of Northeastern Wisconsin," 113, 117–120.

Chapter 2

1. Vaugeois, "Seeking Champlain," 22–35; Bishop, *Champlain*, 5; Fischer, *Champlain's Dream*, 20–22; Heidenreich and Ritch, "Champlain and His Times to 1604," 3–6; Ritch, "Discovery of the Baptismal Certificate of Samuel du Champlain," para. 1, 7, 16; Champlain, *Works*, 1:209–210 (qtd. 209–210).

2. Fischer, *Champlain's Dream*, 22, 45; Trudel, "Champlain, Samuel de," 186–187, 190–191; Delâge, *Bitter Feast*, 29; Kamen, *Early Modern European Society*, 97–107; Heidenreich and Ritch, "Champlain's Signature and Titles," 438–439.

3. Ritch, "Discovery of the Baptismal Certificate of Samuel du Champlain," para. 1, 4; Thwaites, *Jesuit Relations*, 6:103; Bishop, *Champlain*, 5–6; Trudel, "Champlain, Samuel de," 186; Champlain, *Works*, 3:3–24, 6:73; Fischer, *Champlain's Dream*, 23–24, 639n.

4. Bishop, *Champlain*, 7; Heidenreich and Ritch, "Champlain and His Times to 1604," 8–13.

5. Fischer, *Champlain's Dream*, 42–46.

6. Fischer, *Champlain's Dream*, 55–57, 82, 340, 362.

7. Fischer, *Champlain's Dream*, 47–56, 60; Deslandres, "Samuel de Champlain and Religion," 191–204.

8. Fischer, *Champlain's Dream*, 61–67.

9. Fischer, *Champlain's Dream*, 74–98; Champlain, *Works*, 1:41 (qtd. 41). Much controversy surrounds Champlain's memoir of his travels with the Spanish fleet, a document titled *Brief Discours*. The three extant manuscript copies of this document are not in Champlain's

handwriting. This fact has led some scholars to suspect he never wrote the document and possibly did not travel to the West Indies and Mexico. Today, most historians who have investigated these issues conclude Champlain traveled with the Spanish fleet. They also argue the various manuscript versions of *Brief Discours* contain discrepancies because others composed them on the basis of notes written by Champlain or from an oral report he provided. He did not keep any kind of log or journal during his travels, and the various discrepancies arise from the fact he composed his narrative after he concluded his journey. For examinations of this topic, see Fischer, *Champlain's Dream*, 586–593; Heidenreich and Ritch, "Champlain and His Times to 1604," 32–33; Giraudo, "Manuscripts of the *Brief Discours*," 63–82; and Gagnon, "Is the *Brief Discours* by Champlain," 83–97.

10. Fischer, *Champlain's Dream*, 94, 108; Heidenreich and Ritch, "Champlain and His Times to 1604," 24–31; Champlain, *Works*, 1:43, 63–66.

11. Fischer, *Champlain's Dream*, 105–125; Bishop, *Champlain*, 37; Heidenreich and Ritch, "Champlain and His Times to 1604," 40, 437–438; Biggar, *Early Trading Companies*, 45–47; Champlain, *Works*, 3:321–322 (qtd. 321–322).

12. Heidenreich and Ritch, "Champlain and His Times to 1604," 52–55; Heidenreich and Ritch, "Of the French Who Have Become Accustomed to Being in Canada," 368–369; Cayet, "Of the French Who Have Become Accustomed to Being in Canada," 371–373 (qtd. 371).

13. Heidenreich and Ritch, "Champlain and His Times to 1604," 53–55; Trudel, "Noël (Nouel), Jacques," 520; Heidenreich and Ritch, "Champlain's *Des Sauvages*," 457–461; D'Abate, "On the Meaning of a Name," 66–69. Hayes's treatise and the quotation in the text are in Brereton, *Briefe and True Relation*, 15–24 (qtd. 21). For a work that argues Jacques Noël or his sons penetrated the St. Lawrence to Lake Ontario, see Quinn and Quinn, *English New England Voyages*, 177.

14. Heidenreich and Ritch, "Champlain and His Times to 1604," 53–55; Brereton, *Briefe and True Relation*, 22.

15. Heidenreich and Ritch, "Champlain and His Times to 1604," 55–58; Winsor, *Cartier to Frontenac*, 64–70; Seaver, "Norumbega and 'Harmonia Mundi,'" 39–40. Wright's map was published in the well-known work by Richard Hakluyt, *Principal Navigations* (1599). Wright's map is also found in later reprints of Hakluyt's works. See Hakluyt, *Principal Navigations* (1903).

16. Heidenreich and Ritch, "Champlain's *Des Sauvages*," 459–460; Heidenreich and Ritch, "Champlain and His Times to 1604," 55–58; Hunter, "Was New France Born in England," 39–44; Barbiche, "Henry IV and the World Overseas," 24–32; Fischer, *Champlain's Dream*, 126–127.

17. Fischer, *Champlain's Dream*, 126–133, 575; Heidenreich and Ritch, "Champlain and His Times to 1604," 59–66; Beaulieu, "Birth of the Franco-American Alliance," 154; Champlain, *Works*, 1:98–110 (qtd. 108).

18. Fischer, *Champlain's Dream*, 575.

19. Champlain, *Works*, 1:121–124 (qtd. 124).

20. Winsor, *Cartier to Frontenac*, 64–70; Fischer, *Champlain's Dream*, 137–138; Champlain, *Works*, 1:123–124, 2:19.

21. Brereton, *Briefe and True Relation*, 21; Fischer, *Champlain's Dream*, 139–140, 575; Heidenreich, "Beginning of French Exploration," 238–239; Heidenreich and Ritch, "Champlain and His Times to 1604," 67–70; Champlain, *Works*, 1:137–143 (qtd. 141, 143).

22. Turgeon, "French in New England," 102; Champlain, *Works*, 2:94.

23. The most popular version of Champlain's writings is the six-volume set published by the Champlain Society from 1922 to 1936, with a seventh volume of maps published in 1956. Unfortunately, the editors and translators made several errors of translation, particularly with Champlain's 1603 work *Des Sauvages*. One error in particular was using an earlier English translation written by Richard Hakluyt and edited by Samuel Purchas that translated the French word *salubre* (which means "wholesome" or "fresh") as "brackish," which means "slightly salty water." Hakluyt, like Edward Hayes in his treatise, may well have done this intentionally in order to lend support to the idea the Great Lakes provided access to the Pacific Ocean. See

Heidenreich and Ritch, "Textual Introduction to *Des Sauvages*," 94, 106; Heidenreich and Ritch, "Preface," xi–xiii; Champlain, *Works*, 1:155; Purchas, *Hakluytus Posthumus*, 4:1614; and Heidenreich and Ritch, "Champlain's *Des Sauvages* and Edward Hayes's Treatise," 459. The Champlain Society's edited volumes are used throughout this book, but for any discussion of Champlain's activities in the St. Lawrence River valley in 1603, it is crucial to use the most recent version of *Des Sauvages* edited by Conrad E. Heidenreich and K. Janet Ritch that provides a more accurate translation. For the information and quotations in the text, see Champlain, "Des Sauvages," 317–325 (qtd. 325). Also see Heidenreich and Ritch, "Champlain and His Times to 1604," 70–71.

24. Heidenreich, *Explorations and Mapping*, 45–50; Champlain, "Des Sauvages," 325, 327 (qtd. 327).

25. Champlain, "Des Sauvages," 327 (qtd. 327).

26. Champlain, "Des Sauvages," 327 (qtd. 327).

27. Champlain, "Des Sauvages," 327, 329 (qtd. 329).

28. Heidenreich and Ritch, "Champlain and His Times to 1604," 71–75; Champlain, "Des Sauvages," 331 (qtd. 331).

29. Heidenreich and Ritch, "Champlain and His Times to 1604," 71–75; Champlain, "Des Sauvages," 331, 333 (qtd. 331, 333).

30. Heidenreich and Ritch, "Champlain and His Times to 1604," 74; Champlain, "Des Sauvages," 325, 335, 337 (qtd. 335, 337).

31. Champlain, "Des Sauvages," 337 (qtd. 337).

32. Heidenreich and Ritch, "Champlain and His Times to 1604," 74–75 (qtd. 74–75).

33. Heidenreich and Ritch, "Champlain and His Times to 1604," 74 (qtd. 74).

34. Cabot, "Dual Drainage Anomalies," 474–482; Brereton, *Briefe and True Relation*, 21; Lescarbot, *History of New France*, 2:317; Sagard, *Long Journey*, 43; Kellogg, *French Régime*, 36–37.

35. Heidenreich and Ritch, "Champlain and His Times to 1604," 71; Cuoq, *Lexique de la Langue Algonquine*, 439–440 (qtd. 439, 440).

36. Crouse, *Contributions of the Canadian Jesuits*, 35–36; Crouse, *In Quest of the Western Ocean*, 237–239; Champlain, "Des Sauvages," 323, 335. For another work that advances this interpretation, see Butterfield, *History of Brulé's Discoveries*, 100–101.

37. Crouse, *Contributions of the Canadian Jesuits*, 36 (qtd. 36).

38. Thwaites, *Jesuit Relations*, 45:219 (qtd. 219).

39. Thwaites, *Jesuit Relations*, 59:97–99 (qtd. 97, 99).

40. Quoted from William Beaumont, Fort Howard Quarterly Weather Return, January–March, 1827, T-907, reel 546.

41. Martin, *History of Brown County*, 8; *Milwaukee Sentinel* (Milwaukee, WI), 24 June 1872.

42. Lurie, "Winnebago Protohistory," 793.

43. Champlain, "Des Sauvages," 327 (qtd. 327).

44. Champlain, "Des Sauvages," 335 (qtd. 335).

45. Heidenreich and Ritch, "Champlain and His Times to 1604," 75–77; Morissonneau, "Champlain's Dream," 261–264; Champlain, "Des Sauvages," 339–345 (qtd. 345).

46. Champlain, *Works*, 1:231 (qtd. 231).

47. Heidenreich and Ritch, "Champlain and His Times to 1604," 77–82; Arseneault, "Acadia in Champlain's New France," 115; Champlain, *Works*, 3:321–322.

48. Fischer, *Champlain's Dream*, 151, 160–182; Arseneault, "Acadia in Champlain's New France," 120; Morison, *Samuel de Champlain*, 52; Morison, *European Discovery*, 464–470; D'Abate, "On the Meaning of a Name," 75; Champlain, *Works*, 1:226, 284–285, 370, 377 (qtd. 370).

49. Fischer, *Champlain's Dream*, 171–173; Champlain, *Works*, 1:294–295.

50. Fischer, *Champlain's Dream*, 182–223; Arseneault, "Acadia in Champlain's New France," 120.

51. Fischer, *Champlain's Dream*, 227–245; Champlain, *Works*, 2:24, 4:31–32; Jurgens, "Brûlé, Étienne," 130–131; Vachon, "Marsolet, de Saint–Aignan, Nicolas," 493.

52. Dionne, *Samuel Champlain*, 421; Trudel, "Continent on which Champlain Set Foot," 62; Champlain, *Works*, 2:63–71, 135; Fischer, *Champlain's Dream*, 244–260.

53. Fischer, *Champlain's Dream*, 260–270, 577, 614–615; Champlain, *Works*, 2:79–80, 89–101 (qtd. 99–100).

54. Fischer, *Champlain's Dream*, 270–271, 577, 614–615; Purchas, *Hakluytus Posthumus*, 3:581–595; Champlain, *Works*, 2:79–80, 89–102 (qtd. 102).

55. Champlain, *Works*, 2:102–104 (qtd. 103–104).

56. Richter, *Ordeal of the Longhouse*, 32–38; Eid, "'National' War," 125–154; Edmunds, "Indian-White Warfare," 35–45; Jaenen, "Amerindian views of French Culture," 289; Starkey, *European and Native American Warfare*, 17–56; Hadlock, "War among the Northeastern Woodland Indians," 210–219.

57. Wallace, *Death and Rebirth of the Seneca*, 102–107; Axtell and Sturtevant, "Unkindest Cut," 451–472; Knowles, "Torture of Captives," 151–153, 190–220; Ball, "Grim Commerce," 13–50; Williamson, "'Otinontsiskiaj ondaon,'" 193–194, 216; Delâge, *Bitter Feast*, 63–66, 211–212 (qtd. 65, 66).

58. Fischer, *Champlain's Dream*, 280; Champlain, *Works*, 2:85, 118, 203–204, 254, 285, 3:74, 5:73–75, 216–226 (qtd. 5:216).

59. Fischer, *Champlain's Dream*, 254–255, 274–299, 577–578; Champlain, *Works*, 2:118–134.

60. Fischer, *Champlain's Dream*, 294–299, 578–580; Heidenreich, *Explorations and Mapping*, 16; Champlain, *Works*, 2:186–194 (qtd. 191–192).

61. Heidenreich, *Explorations and Mapping*, 11–13, 79–83; Heidenreich and Dahl, "Samuel de Champlain's Cartography," 317–318; Trudel, *Atlas of New France*, 78–85.

62. Fischer, *Champlain's Dream*, 301–303; Biggar, *Early Trading Companies*, 195–196; Champlain, *Works*, 2:118–134, 211–212, 256–258, 4:151, 153–157 (qtd. 4:155).

63. Fischer, *Champlain's Dream*, 303–305; Trudel, "Vignau, Nicolas de," 662; Champlain, *Works*, 2:256, 4:155.

64. Fischer, *Champlain's Dream*, 303–305, 578–579; Heidenreich, *Explorations and Mapping*, 17–19; Champlain, *Works*, 2:253–286 (qtd. 286).

65. Fischer, *Champlain's Dream*, 303–305, 578–579; Heidenreich, *Explorations and Mapping*, 17–19; Champlain, *Works*, 2: 253–291 (qtd. 289).

66. Trudel, "Vignau, Nicolas de," 662–663; Fischer, *Champlain's Dream*, 305–310; Champlain, *Works*, 2:291–309.

67. Mancall, *Fatal Journey*, 5–16, 120–133; Crouse, *In Quest of the Western Ocean*, 165–178; Kenyon and Turnbull, *Battle for James Bay*, 41–65; Campeau, "La Route commerciale," 29–30; Heidenreich, "Early French Exploration," 125–126, 143.

68. Trudel, "Vignau, Nicolas de," 663; Heidenreich, *Explorations and Mapping*, 18–19; Delâge, *Bitter Feast*, 94–95; Campeau, "La Route commerciale," 34–37.

69. Fischer, *Champlain's Dream*, 310–313, 317–323, 580; Carpin, "Migrations to New France in Champlain's Time," 170; Heidenreich, *Explorations and Mapping*, 12; Champlain, *Works*, 3:31–32 (qtd. 32).

70. Newbigging, "History of the French-Ottawa Alliance," 1, 6, 40–47, 78, 90–94, 113–114, 120; Smith, "Systems of Subsistence and Networks of Exchange," 78–97; Heidenreich, *Explorations and Mapping*, 23; Feest and Feest, "Ottawa," 772; Garrad, "Champlain and the Odawa," 62; Champlain, *Works*, 3:34–44 (qtd. 44).

71. Heidenreich, "Early French Exploration," 86; Heidenreich, *Huronia*, 28–31, 91–103; Tooker, *Ethnography of the Huron*, 11, 125–127; Delâge, *Bitter Feast*, 53–57, 59, 121–122; Campeau, "La Route commercial," 34; Fischer, *Champlain's Dream*, 322–327; Heidenreich, "Huron," 383–385; Champlain, *Works*, 2:188, 3:45–54, 122 (qtd. 3:47).

72. Fischer, *Champlain's Dream*, 328–330, 615–616; Starkey, *European and Native American Warfare*, 24–26; Keener, "Ethnohistorical Analysis of Iroquois Assault Tactics," 780–786; Champlain, *Works*, 3:56–67.

73. Fischer, *Champlain's Dream*, 330–333; Champlain, *Works*, 3:67–79.

74. Heidenreich, *Explorations and Mapping*, 24–26; Champlain, *Works*, 3:104–105 (qtd. 104–105).

75. Champlain, *Works*, 3:105 (qtd. 105).
76. Champlain, *Works*, 3:119–120 (qtd. 119–120).
77. La Potherie, "History of the Savage Peoples," 1:293; Sagard, *Histoire du Canada*, 201.
78. Heidenreich, "Huron," 385; Ray, "Northern Interior," 265; Eccles, "French Exploration," 160, 183–184; McLaird, "Welsh, Vikings, and the Lost Tribes of Israel," 245–273; Newman, "Blond Mandan," 255–272.
79. See Butterfield, *History of the Discovery*, 37; Kellogg, *French Régime*, 78; Parkman, *La Salle*, xxiii; Heidenreich, *Explorations and Mapping*, 26.
80. Champlain, *Works*, 3:120 (qtd. 120).
81. Wroth, "Unknown Champlain Map," 85–94.
82. For works that identify this lake as Lake Superior and the peninsula as the Keweenaw Peninsula, see Stiebe, *Mystery People of the Cove*, 59; Hayes, *Historical Atlas of Canada*, 54, 56; Trudel, "Jean Nicollet," 189–190; and Mason, "Where Nicolet and the Winnebagoes First Met," 67–70. For Conrad E. Heidenreich's analysis, see Heidenreich, *Explorations and Mapping*, 23–26, 85–89.
83. Champlain, "Des Sauvages," 327, 329, 337; Heidenreich, *Explorations and Mapping*, 86, 89.
84. Heidenreich, *Explorations and Mapping*, 26–27; Fischer, *Champlain's Dream*, 349, 353–354; Champlain, *Works*, 2:344–345 (qtd. 345).
85. Fischer, *Champlain's Dream*, 354–355; Champlain, *Works*, 2:326 (qtd. 326).
86. Champlain, *Works*, 2:330 (qtd. 330).
87. Fischer, *Champlain's Dream*, 581–584.

Chapter 3

1. Champlain, *Works*, 3:207–211, 226–228.
2. Butterfield, *History of Brulé's Discoveries*, 66–67; Cranston, *Étienne Brûlé*, 83–84; Champlain, *Works*, 3:57–58, 213–218 (qtd. 218).
3. Butterfield, *History of Brulé's Discoveries*, 66–67; Cranston, *Étienne Brûlé*, 84–88.
4. Champlain, *Works*, 3:224–225 (qtd. 225).
5. Champlain, *Works*, 3:225–226 (qtd. 226).
6. Fischer, *Champlain's Dream*, 362, 371–384; Dickinson, "Champlain, Administrator," 211–217.
7. Fischer, *Champlain's Dream*, 384–385, 582; Dionne, *Samuel Champlain*, 425–433; Trudel, "New France," 28–29; Champlain, *Works*, 2:35, 39.
8. Heidenreich, *Explorations and Mapping*, 28–31; Champlain, *Works*, 4:209–216 (qtd. 213).
9. Champlain, *Works*, 5:142–149 (qtd. 146).
10. Heidenreich, *Explorations and Mapping*, 29–31.
11. Heidenreich, *Explorations and Mapping*, 29–31; Trigger, *Natives and Newcomers*, 186–195; Trudel, "Jean Nicollet," 185; Thwaites, *Jesuit Relations*, 4:209, 269; Lanctôt, *History of Canada*, 124; Fischer, *Champlain's Dream*, 632–633.
12. Thwaites, *Jesuit Relations*, 23:277; Delâge, *Bitter Feast*, 59, 77, 125, 203–204; Champlain, *Works*, 5:132 (qtd. 132).
13. Thwaites, *Jesuit Relations*, 23:281; Hamelin, "Nicollet de Belleborne, Jean," 517–518.
14. Dionne, *Samuel Champlain*, 423–429; Jaenen, "Problems of Assimilation," 269–274; Delâge, *Bitter Feast*, 118–119; Trigger, *Natives and Newcomers*, 200–203; Codignola, "Competing Networks," 544–545.
15. Daillon's report dated July 18, 1627 is published in Le Clercq, *First Establishment of the Faith*, 1:264–272. Also see Trigger, *Natives and Newcomers*, 200–203; Delâge, *Bitter Feast*, 53–54; Jurgens, "Brûlé, Étienne," 132; Campeau, "Bruslé, Etienne," 809; Thwaites, *Jesuit Relations*, 21:203–205; Heidenreich, *Explorations and Mapping*, 31–32; and Champlain, *Works*, 6:43–44.
16. Trudel, "Champlain, Samuel de," 195 (qtd. 195).
17. Many works overemphasize Champlain's interest in the Northwest Passage, particularly after 1620, and ignore his other interests, such expanding the French trade network. Not surprisingly,

Nicolet's 1634 expedition is often the principal piece of evidence for arguing Champlain remained fixated on finding the Northwest Passage in the later years of his career. For examples, see Butterfield, *History of the Discovery*, 33–39; Kellogg, *French Régime*, 78; Bishop, *Champlain*, 338; Morissonneau, "Champlain's Dream," 258–265; and Gervais, "Champlain and Ontario," 180.

18. Champlain, *Works*, 2:254, 3:104–105, 4:285–287, 5:58–59, 132, 6:45 (qtd. 6:45).

19. Heidenreich, *Explorations and Mapping*, 32–33.

20. For scholars who argue Brûlé entered and explored Lake Superior, see Butterfield, *History of Brûlé's Discoveries*, 99–108; Sulte, "Étienne Brûlé," 97, 111–114; Cranston, *Étienne Brûlé*, 1–2, 85, 89–92; and Wilson, "Étienne Brulé," 43. Lucien Campeau's research indicates Brûlé was in France from 1622 to 1623, and thus a journey to Lake Superior could have happened only after 1623. This corrects Consul W. Butterfield's earlier claim that Brûlé journeyed to Lake Superior between 1621 and 1623. See Campeau, "Bruslé, Etienne," 809. For works that cast doubt on whether Brûlé journeyed to Lake Superior or the Sault Ste. Marie Rapids, see Crouse, *Contributions of the Canadian Jesuits*, 124–128; Quaife, "Discovery of Lake Superior," 198; and Heidenreich, *Explorations and Mapping*, 32.

21. Sagard, *Historie du Canada*, 644; Jurgens, "Brûlé, Étienne," 132; Lurie and Jung, *Nicolet Corrigenda*, 126.

22. Sagard, *Historie du Canada*, 222, 358, 788; Sagard, *Long Journey*, 242. For arguments concerning whether or not the ingot of copper was additional proof of Brûlé penetrating Lake Superior beyond the Sault Ste. Marie Rapids, see Butterfield, *History of Brûlé's Discoveries*, 104–106; and Crouse, *Contributions of the Canadian Jesuits*, 125–126. For information on the copper mines in the Lake Huron basin, see *Descriptive Catalog*, 26–27. For examples of works that assert Brûlé was the first European in present-day Wisconsin, see Wyman, *Wisconsin Frontier*, 10; Wisconsin Cartographers' Guild, *Wisconsin's Past and Present*, 4–5; and Bogue, *Around the Shores of Lake Superior*, 3.

23. Sagard, *Historie du Canada*, 200–201 (qtd. 201). The English translation in the text is taken from Lurie and Jung, *Nicolet Corrigenda*, 126 (qtd. 126).

24. Sagard, *Le Grand Voyage*, [xx] (qtd. xx). The English translation in the text is taken from Sagard, *Long Journey*, 9 (qtd. 9).

25. Champlain, *Works*, 5:131–132 (qtd. 131–132).

26. Fischer, *Champlain's Dream*, 423–427; Champlain, *Works*, 6:99–100 (qtd. 99–100).

27. Heidenreich, *Explorations and Mapping*, 28–29, 89–90; Champlain, *Works*, 6:234 (qtd. 234).

28. Sagard, *Historie du Canada*, 644 (qtd. 644). The English translation in the text is taken from Jurgens, "Brûlé, Étienne," 132 (qtd. 132); and Lurie and Jung, *Nicolet Corrigenda*, 126 (qtd. 126).

29. Sagard, *Historie du Canada*, 644; Champlain, "Des Sauvages," 335; Champlain, *Works*, 2:330, 3:116–119, 331, 362, 5:131–132, 6:234.

30. Champlain, *Works*, 6:234 (qtd. 234).

31. Heidenreich, *Explorations and Mapping*, 94–96 (qtd. 95–96).

32. For an analysis of the evolution of the unnamed body of water west of Lake Huron in Champlain's 1616 map into the Grand lac on Champlain's 1632 map, see Heidenreich, *Explorations and Mapping*, 85–97. For the word *lac*, see Wilson, *French and English Dictionary*, 301.

33. Champlain, *Works*, 6:362–363 (qtd. 362–363). The English translation in the text is taken from Lurie and Jung, *Nicolet Corrigenda*, 137–138 (qtd. 137–138).

34. Champlain, *Works*, 3:298–301, 6:363; Trudel, "Champlain, Samuel de," 196; Rioux, "Sagard, Gabriel," 590–591.

35. Berthiaume, "From Champlain's Voyage Accounts," 291–297; Champlain, *Works*, 3:300–301 (qtd. 301).

36. Champlain, *Works*, 1:231, 3:316–318; Berthiaume, "From Champlain's Voyage Accounts," 293.

37. Heidenreich, "Early French Exploration," 94, 113; Delanglez, "Mirage: The Sea of the West (Part I)," 356, 381; Thwaites, *Jesuit Relations*, 18:237 (qtd. 237).

38. Thwaites, *Jesuit Relations*, 33:149–151.

39. Thwaites, *Jesuit Relations*, 45:16, 221–225.

40. Champlain, *Works*, 3:44, 119, 4:282, 6:234; Heidenreich, *Explorations and Mapping*, 23, 26, 31, 87–97.

41. Trudel, "Jean Nicollet," 185; Thwaites, *Jesuit Relations*, 23:277; Goddard, "Central Algonquian Languages," 583; Lurie, "Winnebago," 690; Sagard, *Historie du Canada*, 200–201, 644; Lurie and Jung, *Nicolet Corrigenda*, 126; Sagard, *Long Journey*, 9; Champlain, *Works*, 3:34–44; Heidenreich, *Explorations and Mapping*, 23, 85–89; Jurgens, "Brûlé, Étienne," 132.

42. Fenton, *Great Law and the Longhouse*, 243–245; Trigger, *Natives and Newcomers*, 255, 262, 309; Richter, "War and Culture," 538; Richter, *Ordeal of the Longhouse*, 88–89; Delâge, *Bitter Feast*, 134–135; Thwaites, *Jesuit Relations*, 6:309, 23:277; Trigger, *Children of Aataentsic*, 1:382–385, 390, 417–418; Hunt, *Wars of the Iroquois*, 25, 69–70, 167–175; Worcester and Schilz, "Spread of Firearms," 104; Champlain, *Works*, 5:73–80, 117–119, 130–133; Goldstein, *French-Iroquois Diplomatic and Military Relations*, 57–59; Fischer, *Champlain's Dream*, 382–383. Jon Parmenter asserts Nicolet accompanied the Algonquins on their diplomatic journey to Iroquoia in 1620, but nothing in the primary sources supports the assertion it occurred in this year. See Parmenter, *Edge of the Woods*, 28.

43. Champlain, *Works*, 3:101–105, 5:60–65, 78, 107–108, 134; Fischer, *Champlain's Dream*, 382–387.

44. Treasure, *Cardinal Richelieu*, 207–211; Tapié, *France in the Age of Louis XIII*, 254–263; Rule, "Old Regime in America," 577–578; Fischer, *Champlain's Dream*, 392–398.

45. Fischer, *Champlain's Dream*, 401–402; Champlain, *Works*, 5:240–246, 312.

46. Starna and Brandão, "From the Mohawk-Mahican War to the Beaver Wars," 734–738; Parmenter, *Edge of the Woods*, 32–33; Tessier, "Boullé, Eustache," 109–110; Trudel, "Caën, Emery de," 159; Champlain, *Works*, 5:214–221 (qtd. 221).

47. Parmenter, *Edge of the Woods*, 33; Champlain, *Works*, 5:221–226 (qtd. 226).

48. Parmenter, *Edge of the Woods*, 33–34; Champlain, *Works*, 5:221–231, 308–312.

49. Brandão, *Your fyre shall burn no more*, table D.1; Fischer, *Champlain's Dream*, 402–405, 409–410, 604–607; Trudel, "New France," 29; Dionne, *Samuel Champlain*, 430–431.

50. Fischer, *Champlain's Dream*, 402–406, 409–413; Moir, "Kirke, Sir David," 405; Allaire, "Occupation of Quebec," 247–248, 252; Champlain, *Works*, 5:277–285 (qtd. 284).

51. Fischer, *Champlain's Dream*, 409–416; Champlain, *Works*, 6:1–2.

52. Fischer, *Champlain's Dream*, 416–425; Allaire, "Occupation of Quebec," 246–248; Dionne, *Samuel Champlain*, 432–433; Champlain, *Works*, 6:101 (qtd. 101).

53. Fischer, *Champlain's Dream*, 425–441; Champlain, *Works*, 6:145–147.

54. Fischer, *Champlain's Dream*, 445–449; Allaire, "Occupation of Quebec," 249–251; Jouan, "Jean Nicolet, Interpreter," 1, 10 (qtd. 10). For a contemporary work that supports Jouan's statement, despite the lack of firm evidence for such an assertion, see Parmenter, *Edge of the Woods*, 35.

55. Hamelin, "Nicolet," 517; Gosselin, *Jean Nicolet et Le Canada*, 177–178; Trudel, "Jean Nicollet," 185; Thwaites, *Jesuit Relations*, 5:239, 23:277; Sagard, *Histoire du Canada*, 467; Trigger, *Children of Aataentsic*, 1:74–75, 2:473–476; Richter, *Ordeal of the Longhouse*, 35–36, 303–304n12; Abler, "Iroquois Cannibalism," 309–316; Butterfield, *History of Brulé's Discoveries*, 467.

56. Fischer, *Champlain's Dream*, 450–462; Blackburn, *Harvest of Souls*, 81–82; Brandão, *Your fyre shall burn no more*, table D. 1; Parmenter, *Edge of the Woods*, 36–37; Thwaites, *Jesuit Relations*, 5:93, 107, 211–215, 251, 6:145, 7:213–215.

57. Fischer, *Champlain's Dream*, 518–519; Champlain, *Works*, 6:375–377 (qtd. 376). An English translation of this document is found in Lurie and Jung, *Nicolet Corrigenda*, 138–139 (qtd. 139).

58. Champlain, *Works*, 6:378–379 (qtd. 379). An English translation of this document is found in Lurie and Jung, *Nicolet Corrigenda*, 139–140 (qtd. 140).

59. For the original text, see [Champlain], "Relation du voyage," *Mercure François*, 803–867. A more recent, edited version is [Champlain], "Relation du Voyage," *Monumenta Novae Franciae II*, 350–397. For scholars who believe this narrative was penned by Champlain, see Campeau, "Le

dernier voyage de Champlain," 81–101; and Fischer, *Champlain's Dream*, 503, 722, 753. Samuel Morison, on the other hand, suggests the author may have been the Jesuit Paul Le Jeune. See Morison, *Samuel de Champlain*, 288. I agree with Lucien Campeau and David Hackett Fischer that Champlain was likely the author of this document.

60. [Champlain], "Relation du voyage,"*Mercure François*, 841–844; [Champlain], "Relation du Voyage," *Monumenta Novae Franciae II*, 380–382. An English gloss of the relevant text can be found in Morison, *Samuel de Champlain*, 288–289.

61. Trigger, *Natives and Newcomers*, 284.

62. Sagard, *Histoire du Canada*, 200–201; Radin, "Winnebago Tribe," 63, 219–220; Champlain, *Works*, 3:119–120, 4:282; Lurie and Jung, *Nicolet Corrigenda*, 99, 111–112; Thwaites, *Jesuit Relations*, 16:253, 23:277; La Potherie, "History of the Savage Peoples," 1:293 (qtd. 293).

63. Thwaites, *Jesuit Relations*, 23:277.

64. Thwaites, *Jesuit Relations*, 18:231–233; 23:277; Heidenreich, *Explorations and Mapping*, 33; Fischer, *Champlain's Dream*, 513, 518–519.

Chapter 4

1. Vimont is listed as the author for both *Relations* mentioned in the text, but many parts of the various *Relations* were authored by a variety of people. Vimont's role was that of editor for the 1640 *Relation* in which Le Jeune described Nicolet's journey. The 1642–1643 *Relation* was lost during an Iroquois attack, and Vimont penned a new draft by his own hand in the autumn of 1643. See Thwaites, *Jesuit Relations*, 18:2, 23:15. For the original editions of these *Relations* and the passages that refer to Nicolet, see Vimont, *Relation* (1641), 131–133, 137; and Vimont, *Relation* (1644), 9–10. Unless otherwise noted, the translated edition of the *Relations* will be used. See Thwaites, *Jesuit Relations*, 18:231–233, 23:275–279.

2. Greer, *Jesuit Relations*, 14–16; Cohen and Warkentin, "Things Not Easily Believed," 9–15.

3. Thwaites, *Jesuit Relations*, 23:277 (qtd. 277).

4. Gervais, "Champlain and Ontario," 189; Fischer, *Champlain's Dream*, 449; Trudel, "Caën, Emery de," 159; Trudel, "Caën, Guillaume de," 161.

5. Fischer, *Champlain's Dream*, 409, 425–426; Allaire, "Occupation of Quebec," 249–251.

6. Trudel, "Jean Nicollet," 187–188. For the document cited by Trudel, see Champlain, *Oeuvres*, 5:1434. For other sources cited in text, see Champlain, *Works*, 6:108; Jouan, "Jean Nicolet, Interpreter," 7–8; Allaire, "Occupation of Quebec," 249–251; Thwaites, *Jesuit Relations*, 23:277 (qtd. 277).

7. Trudel, "Jean Nicollet," 185, 187. For other scholars who also suggest Nicolet was at Quebec in 1633, see Sulte, "Notes on Jean Nicolet," (1879), 190–191; Sulte, "Notes on Jean Nicolet," (1880), 158–159; and Butterfield, *History of the Discovery*, 32–33.

8. Thwaites, *Jesuit Relations*, 5:239.

9. [Champlain], "Relation du voyage,"*Mercure François*, 825–826; [Champlain], "Relation du voyage," *Monumenta Novae Franciae II*, 370–371; Fischer, *Champlain's Dream*, 454, 503, 586, 722. Leslie Weidensee is to be thanked for her assistance in translating the relevant text.

10. Thwaites, *Jesuit Relations*, 8:69, 71, 99, 23:277.

11. The itinerary for the three parties that traveled to Huronia and Nicolet's departure from Huronia to conduct his journey to the Puans can be found in Thwaites, *Jesuit Relations*, 8:67–99, 23:277. Several scholars have suggested Nicolet departed on July 1 or 2 from Quebec with Brébeuf and then went to Trois-Rivières. While this is possible, no primary sources attest to this. See Sulte, "Notes on Jean Nicolet," (1879), 191; Sulte, *Mélanges*, 426; and Jouan, "Jean Nicolet, Interpreter," 11–12. For the location of Ihonatiria, see Thwaites, *Jesuit Relations*, 5:293n61–294n61; and Heidenreich, *Huronia*, 31–32.

12. Fischer, *Champlain's Dream*, 494–496; Thwaites, *Jesuit Relations*, 8:67, 71, 99, 7:225. Henri Jouan stated Nicolet traveled with the second party, but definite evidence is lacking. See Jouan, "Jean Nicolet, Interpreter," 12.

13. Trudel, "Jean Nicollet," 186–187; Thwaites, *Jesuit Relations*, 7:225–227, 8:99 (qtd. 8:99).

14. Thwaites, *Jesuit Relations*, 8:71–99, 7:225–227. For Trudel's argument, see Trudel, "Jean Nicollet," 186–187.

15. Champlain,. *Works*, 6:151–152 (qtd. 152).

16. Champlain, *Works*, 2:80–81, 118–134, 254, 285, 3:34–74, 207–211, 226–229, 298–301, 5:73–
78, 130–132, 214–226, 240–246, 308–312, 6:234, 362–363, 375–377; Lurie and Jung, *Nicolet
Corrigenda*, 137–139; Heidenreich, *Explorations and Mapping*, 85–97; Berthiaume, "From
Champlain's Voyage Accounts," 293; Thwaites, *Jesuit Relations*, 23:277; Fischer, *Champlain's
Dream*, 280, 383–387, 450–462, 518–519.

17. Thwaites, *Jesuit Relations*, 23:277 (qtd. 277).

18. Sagard, *Historie du Canada*, 200–201; Thwaites, *Jesuit Relations*, 15:153–155; La Potherie, "History of the Savage Peoples," 1:293; Trigger, *Children of Aataentsic*, 1:62–66, 354–356; Trigger,
"French Presence in Huronia," 113; Delâge, *Bitter Feast*, 53–56; Lurie, "Winnebago Protohistory," 793–794.

19. Hodge, *Handbook*, 1:49, 277–280, 2:909–910; Bellfy, *Three Fires Unity*, 1–5; Thwaites, *Jesuit
Relations*, 18:229, 231 (qtd. 231).

20. Thwaites, *Jesuit Relations*, 18:231 (qtd. 231).

21. Wilson, "Where Did Nicolet Go," 216–217; Dever, "Nicolet Myth," 319; Trudel, "Jean Nicollet,"
189; Campeau, *La mission des Jésuites*, 73; Mason, "Where Did Nicolet Land," 39; Gagnon, "Jean
Nicolet," 95; Stiebe, *Mystery People of the Cove*, 81; McCafferty, "Where did Jean Nicollet Meet
the Winnebago," 171; Mason, "Where Nicolet and the Winnebagoes First Met," 70. A detailed
critique of these arguments can be found in Lurie and Jung, *Nicolet Corrigenda*, 49–69; and
Lurie and Jung, "Jean Nicolet (Again)," 303–307.

22. Cotgrave, *Dictionarie of the French and English Tongues*, n.p. (see entry Delà); Wilson, *French
and English Dictionary*, 57, 376 (qtd. 376); Thwaites, *Jesuit Relations*, 18:230, 231 (qtd. 230, 231).
For the inaccurate translations found in the *Jesuit Relations* edited by Thwaites, see Codignola,
"Battle is Over," 3–5. The late Martine Meyer, emerita professor of French at the University of
Wisconsin–Milwaukee, and Helen Johnson, emerita professor of French at the University of
Wisconsin–Stevens Point, are to be thanked for assisting in unraveling the multiple meanings
of the phrase *au delá*.

23. Thwaites, *Jesuit Relations*, 18:229, 231 (qtd. 231). For historians who assert the "little lake" is
Whitefish Bay or some other bay of Lake Superior, see Wilson, "Where Did Nicolet Go," 217;
Dever, "Nicolet Myth," 319; Mason, "Where Did Nicolet Land," 39; and McCafferty, "Where
did Jean Nicolet Meet the Winnebago," 173.

24. Thwaites, *Jesuit Relations*, 18:237 (qtd. 237).

25. Shea, *Discovery and Exploration*, xxi; Butterfield, *History of the Discovery*, 64–67.

26. Kellogg, *French Régime*, 81–82; Hall, "Relating the Big Fish and the Big Stone," 20–21; Mason,
"Where Nicolet and the Winnebagoes First Met," 71.

27. Mason, "Where Nicolet and the Winnebagoes First Met," 71 (qtd. 71).

28. Thwaites, *Jesuit Relations*, 18:237 (qtd. 237).

29. Carey and Lea, *Geography, History, and Statistics*, 318; Thwaites, *Jesuit Relations*, 54:127–129
(qtd. 129).

30. Carey and Lea, *Geography, History, and Statistics*, 318; Bremer, "Henry Rowe Schoolcraft," 40–
59; Schoolcraft, *Narrative Journal of Travels*, 125–145.

31. Mason, "Where Nicolet and the Winnebagoes First Met," 66–69; Thwaites, *Jesuit Relations*,
18:231 (qtd. 231). For other works that make this argument, see Wilson, "Where Did Nicolet Go,"
217; Dever, "Nicolet Myth," 319; Mason, "Where Did Nicolet Land," 39; Stiebe, *Mystery People
of the Cove*, 81–85; and McCafferty, "Where did Jean Nicollet Meet the Winnebago," 171.

32. Mason, "Where Nicolet and the Winnebagoes First Met," 66 (qtd. 66). For the original text, see
Thwaites, *Jesuit Relations*, 18:231.

33. I have based this observation on my own travels through and around the Strait of Mackinac by boat in the summer of 2015.

34. Thwaites, *Jesuit Relations*, 45:219; Chapman and Bolen, *Ecology of North America*, 280.

35. Heidenreich, "Early French Exploration," 94–96; Heidenreich, *Explorations and Mapping*, 94–96.

36. Thwaites, *Jesuit Relations*, 9:215, 217 (qtd. 215, 217).

37. Trudel, "Jean Nicollet," 190; Dever, "Nicolet Myth," 320. Also see Wilson, "Where Did Nicolet Go," 219; Stiebe, *Mystery People of the Cove*, 77–78; and Morissonneau, *Le rêve américain de Champlain*, 150–151. For a work that supports Trudel's theory, see Gervais, "Champlain and Ontario," 189. For Mason's argument and works that refute it, see Mason, "Where Nicolet and the Winnebagoes First Met," 66–70; Heidenreich, *Explorations and Mapping*, 23–26, 85–89, 94–96; Heidenreich, "Analysis of the Map 17th-Century Map 'Novvelle France,'" 74, 107; Heidenreich, "Early French Exploration," 94–96; Steckley, "Early Map 'Novvelle France,'" 18, 21; and Lurie and Jung, "Jean Nicolet (Again)," 304–305.

38. For works that argue the term *Winnebago* referred to an Algonquian-speaking group, see Dever, "Nicolet Myth," 321; Wilson, "Where Did Nicolet Go," 219; Stiebe, *Mystery People of the Cove*, 77–79, 84–87; and Mason, "Where Nicolet and Winnebagoes First Met," 69–71. For French sources that demonstrate this was not the case, see Thwaites, *Jesuit Relations*, 16:253, 18:233, 33:151. A more detailed discussion and refutation of these arguments is found in Lurie and Jung, *Nicolet Corrigenda*, 50–69, 113–124.

39. Kellogg, *French Régime*, 81n34 (qtd. 81n34; emphasis in the original).

40. Butterfield, *History of the Discovery*, 54–55, 63 (qtd. 55, 63).

41. Kellogg, *French Régime*, 79 (qtd. 79).

42. Thwaites, *Jesuit Relations*, 18:233, 23:277; Cranston, *Étienne Brûlé*, 83–84.

43. Sulte, "Notes on Nicolet," (1879), 192; Thwaites, *Jesuit Relations*, 23:279.

44. Thwaites, *Jesuit Relations*, 8:77–79 (qtd. 77).

45. Thwaites, *Jesuit Relations*, 8:79–81, 85, 89; Delâge, *Bitter Feast*, 54, 67; Little, "Inland Waterways in the Northeast," 58–59.

46. Champlain, *Works*, 2:52–53; Thwaites, *Jesuit Relations*, 4:193, 5:105, 123, 125, 13:145, 245, 13:249; Trigger, *Children of Aataentsic*, 1:41–43; Newbigging, "History of the French-Ottawa Alliance," 55, 61, 81.

47. Thwaites, *Jesuit Relations*, 8:71–99.

48. Champlain, *Works*, 2:105 (qtd. 105).

49. Thwaites, *Jesuit Relations*, 23:279 (qtd. 279).

50. Thwaites, *Jesuit Relations*, 8:247.

51. Champlain, *Works*, 3:62–63 (qtd. 62–63).

52. Champlain, *Works*, 3:79 (qtd. 79).

53. Thwaites, *Jesuit Relations*, 23:277 (qtd. 277).

54. Hodge, *Handbook*, 1:192; Mason, "Where Did Nicolet Land," 39–40; Thwaites, *Jesuit Relations*, 23:277 (qtd. 277).

55. Thwaites, *Jesuit Relations*, 23:277, 279 (qtd. 277, 279).

56. Stiebe, *Mystery People of the Cove*, 57–184. For works that refute Stiebe's claims, see Cremin, "Sand Point (20 BG 14)," 7–90; Wykoff, "Physical Anthropology of the Sand Point Site (20 BG 14)," 24; and Heidenreich, *Explorations and Mapping*, 83–99.

57. Hall, "Relating the Big Fish and the Big Stone," 19–32; Hall, "Rethinking Jean Nicolet's Route," 238–251; Hall, "Red Banks, Oneota, and the Winnebago," 22–23; Charles E. Brown, "Red Banks Enclosure, 1909" Brown MSS, part 1, box 17, folder 1879–1944; Champlain, *Works*, 3:44; Assikinack, "Social and Warlike Customs," 307; Charles C. Trowbridge, "Comparison of the manners, Customs and international laws of the Win-nee-baá-goa nation of Indians with those of their neighbors, the Munnoáminnees [1823]," pp 119–125, 140 (qtd. 140), Trowbridge MSS, box 15,

folder I4Me. For works that support Hall's contention the Puans or other Chiwere-Siouans resided in the Calumet River drainage, see Brown, "Ethnohistoric Connections," 159; and Brown and Sasso, "Prelude to History," 213–215. A more detailed refutation of Hall's arguments is in Lurie and Jung, *Nicolet Corrigenda*, 63–69, 73, 77–83.

58. Shea, *Discovery and Exploration*, xx–xxi. For other scholars who have supported this position, see Kellogg, *French Régime*, 82; and Hodge, *Handbook*, 1:842.

59. Neville, "Some Historic Sites About Green Bay," 144–145. For works that support Neville's theory Nicolet went to Red Banks, see Quaife, "Landing Place of Jean Nicolet," 201–202; and Thwaites, *Wisconsin*, 29.

60. Lawson, "Outagamie Village," 206; Lawson, "Habitat of the Winnebago," 146–147; Lawson, *Winnebago Village on Doty Island*, 2; Lawson, "Winnebago Tribe," 87.

61. Lawson, "Habitat of the Winnebago," 145–146; Mason and Mason, "Doty Island Village Site (47 Wn 30)," 251–252; David Overstreet, personal communication, 4 April 2016; Radin, "Winnebago Tribe," 80, 87.

62. Thwaites, *Jesuit Relations*, 23:277, 279 (qtd. 277, 279).

63. For examples, see Trudel, "Jean Nicollet," 192; Dever, "Nicolet Myth," 320; Gagnon, "Jean Nicolet," 100; and Campeau, *La mission des Jésuites*, 73. Ronald Stiebe, on the other hand, insists the Puans were Chiwere-Siouan speakers but offers no explain for why they would have used an Algonquian word. See Stiebe, *Mystery People of the Cove*, 97.

64. Haefeli, "On First Contact and Apotheosis," 419–422; Bloomfield, *Menominee Lexicon*, 111 (qtd. 111).

65. La Potherie, "History of the Savage Peoples," 1:293 (qtd. 293).

66. Butterfield, *History of the Discovery*, 56–57; Hodge, *Handbook*, 2:958; Thwaites, *Jesuit Relations*, 23:277 (qtd. 277).

67. La Potherie, "History of the Savage Peoples," 1:293; Champlain, *Works*, 2: 101,175, 3:64; Furse, *Art of Marching*, 82–99, 216–220; Thwaites, *Jesuit Relations*, 8:79–81, 85, 89, 18:231.

68. La Potherie, "History of the Savage Peoples," 1:293; Thwaites, *Jesuit Relations*, 23:279 (qtd. 23:279).

69. Thwaites, *Jesuit Relations*, 23:279 (qtd. 279).

70. Feltwell, *Story of Silk*, 100; Leggett, *Story of Silk*, 198; Varron, "Origins and Rise of Silk," 351–353; Weibel, *Two Thousand Years of Textiles*, 22, 26, 68–69; Waugh, *Cut of Men's Clothes*, 16; Tortora, *Fairchild's Dictionary of Textiles*, 112–113, 161–162, 518 (qtd.161).

71. Giafferri, *History of French Masculine Costume*, 26 (qtd. 26).

72. Thwaites, *Jesuit Relations*, 23:279 (qtd. 279).

73. *Development of Various Decorative and Upholstery Fabrics*, 1–4; Chaiklin, "Silk," 1021–1024; Ferreira, "Chinese Textiles," 46–55.

74. Cotgrave, *Dictionarie of the French and English Tongues*, n.p. (see entry Robbe); Kelly and Schwabe, *Historic Costume*, 126–127; Giafferri, *History of French Masculine Costume*, 28; Gorsline, *What People Wore*, 74; Bradley, *Western World Costume*, 182; Bruhn and Tilke, *Pictorial History of Costume*, 37; Payne, *History of Costume*, 332–336; Boucher, *20,000 Years of Fashion*, 254; Hill and Bucknell, *Evolution of Fashion*, 94; Waugh, *Cut of Men Clothes*, 14, 6–17, 28–29 (qtd. 16).

75. Cotgrave, *Dictionarie of the French and English Tongues*, n.p. (see entry Grand); Wilson, *French and English Dictionary*, 302; Jouan, "Jean Nicolet, Interpreter," 7; Thwaites, *Jesuit Relations*, 23:278, 279 (qtd. 278, 279).

76. Sulte, *Mélanges*, 430 (qtd. 430). The English translation in the text is taken from Lurie and Jung, *Nicolet Corrigenda*, 10 (qtd. 10).

77. Butterfield, *History of the Discovery*, 39, 58–59 (qtd. 58–59).

78. Jouan, "Jean Nicolet (de Cherbourg)," 76; Jouan, "Jean Nicolet, Interpreter," 14 (qtd. 14).

79. Kellogg, *The French Régime*, 78n29 (qtd. 78n29).

80. Lurie and Jung, *Nicolet Corrigenda*, 12–15. For sources that provide published depictions of the art works mentioned in the text, see Kellogg, *French Régime*, 78; Martin, *History of Brown*

County, 14; Elliott, *History of the Nicolet National Forest*, 1; Romano and Georgiady, *Exploring Wisconsin*, 12–13; Heos, *Wisconsin*, 15; Hintz, *Wisconsin Portraits*, 3; Capua, *Menominee*, 7; Rodesch, "Jean Nicolet," 6; Risjord, "Jean Nicolet's Search," 34, 42–43; and Fischer, *Champlain's Dream*, 505. Bedore's statue was moved in 2009 from Red Banks to a new site two miles to the south at Wequiock Falls County Park in Door County, Wisconsin. See *Green Bay Press-Gazette* (Green Bay, WI), 8 April 2009, 18 August 2009.

81. Jung, "Forge, Destroy, and Preserve the Bonds of Empire," 36. For additional examples, see Lurie, "Winnebago Protohistory," 793–794; Heidenreich, *Explorations and Mapping*, 33; Clifton, *Prairie People*, 12; Eccles, *Essays on New France*, 96; and Marchand, *Ghost Empire*, 247–251.

82. Radin, "Winnebago Tribe," 53; Lurie, "Winnebago Protohistory," 793; Hall, "Red Banks, One-ota, and the Winnebago," 13–14; Thwaites, *Jesuit Relations*, 18:231 (qtd. 231).

83. For works that have reinforced the idea Nicolet sought the Northwest Passage because he was looking for the People of the Sea, see Butterfield, *History of the Discovery*, 37–39; Jouan, "Jean Nicolet, Interpreter," 14; Kellogg, *French Régime*, 79; Peterson, "Nicolet and the Winnebagos," 327; Rodesch, "Jean Nicolet," 6; Risjord, "Jean Nicolet's Search," 42; Stiebe, *Mystery People of the Cove*, 114; and Morissonneau, *Le rêve américain de Champlain*, 151.

84. Clifton, *Prairie People*, 12; Stiebe, *Mystery People of the Cove*, 92 (qtd. 92).

85. Berthiaume, "From Champlain's Voyage Accounts," 291, 293, 297. For those whom the Chinese robe has cast lingering suspicions, see Heidenreich, *Explorations and Mapping*, 33; Kellogg, *French Régime*, 78; and Delanglez, "Mirage: The Sea of the West (Part I)," 354–355, 381.

86. Champlain, *Works*, 3:119–120 (qtd. 120). For scholars who have cited the passage written by Champlain of fair-skinned people as the impetus for Nicolet's journey, see Butterfield, *History of the Discovery*, 37; Kellogg, *French Régime*, 75; and Heidenreich, *Explorations and Mapping*, 26, 33.

87. Champlain, *Works*, 1:226, 284–285.

88. Lawson, *Winnebago Village on Doty Island*, 2 (qtd. 2). Also see Sulte, *Mélanges*, 413–415, 430.

89. Fritze, *New Worlds*, 157–158, 167–173; Winsor, *Cartier to Frontenac*, 21–22; Allen, "From Cabot to Cartier," 512–514; Heidenreich, *Explorations and Mapping*, 31; Champlain, *Works*, 1:165, 3:248, 260.

90. Twitchett and Mote, *Cambridge History of China*, 336–337.

91. Thwaites, *Jesuit Relations*, 23:279 (qtd. 279).

92. Champlain, *Works*, 2:89–100.

93. Trigger, *Natives and Newcomers*, 255; Champlain, *Works*, 5:73–80 (qtd. 80). For the importance of presents as a diplomatic protocol, see Jaenen, "Role of Presents in French-Amerindian Trade," 231–250.

94. Delâge, *Bitter Feast*, 96–103, 110–113; Champlain, *Works*, 2:209, 211, 255, 259, 286, 298, 4:144, 158, 186, 197, 279, 330, 335–337, 5:226, 6:3, 8; [Champlain], "Relation du Voyage," *Monumenta Novae Franciae II*, 387.

95. Thwaites, *Jesuit Relations*, 23:279 (qtd. 279).

96. Beaulieu, "Birth of the Franco-American Alliance," 157–160; Champlain, *Works*, 1:99–106 (qtd. 99).

97. Champlain, *Works*, 1:107–110, 2:72, 100, 120, 198–199, 253, 281, 4:70, 99, 180, 233, 279, 282, 330–331 (qtd. 2:120, 4:146).

98. Thwaites, *Jesuit Relations*, 18:233, 23:279, 42:223 (qtd. 18:233).

99. Thwaites, *Jesuit Relations*, 18:231, 233; Hodge, *Handbook*, 1:102, 597; Anderson, *Kinsmen of Another Kind*, 2, 19; Hauser, "Illinois Indian Tribe," 128; Goddard, "Mascouten," 668–671; Clifton, *Prairie People*, 11; O'Gorman and Lovis, "Before Removal," 43.

100. Thwaites, *Jesuit Relations*, 18:233 (qtd. 233).

101. Shea, *Discovery and Exploration*, xx–xxi; Sulte, "Notes on Jean Nicolet," (1879), 193; Jouan, "Jean Nicolet, Interpreter," 15; Thwaites, *Jesuit Relations*, 8:247; Butterfield, *History of the Discovery*,

63–70; Peterson, "Nicolet and the Winnebagos," 329; Blémus, *Jean Nicollet*, 66–68; Wisconsin Cartographers' Guild, *Wisconsin's Past and Present*, 4–5; Fischer, *Champlain's Dream*, 497, 505.

102. Kellogg, *French Régime*, 82n36 (qtd. 82n36).

103. Kellogg, *French Régime*, 82; Thwaites, *Jesuit Relations*, 23:279 (qtd. 279).

104. Heidenreich, "Beginning of French Exploration," 238–242; Brereton, *Briefe and True Relation*, 21; Champlain, "Des Sauvages," 323–337; Champlain, *Works*, 2:79–80, 89–101, 118–134, 186–194, 253–286, 3:31–32, 34–45, 104–105, 118–120, 217–226, 4:282, 5:131–132, 6:43–44; Sagard, *Historie du Canada*, 200–201; Thwaites, *Jesuit Relations*, 18:233 (qtd. 233).

105. Sagard, *Historie du Canada*, 200–201; Thwaites, *Jesuit Relations*, 18:233.

106. Thwaites, *Jesuit Relations*, 8:247–249, 23:279 (qtd. 8:249).

107. Thwaites, *Jesuit Relations*, 23:279 (qtd. 279).

108. Hodge, *Handbook*, 1:924, 2:1026; Zeisberger, *Zeisberger's Indian Dictionary*, 108; Cuoq, *Lexique de la Langue Iroquoise*, 2, 79–80, 212; Thwaites, *Jesuit Relations*, 23:275–283, 28:14, 183 (qtd. 23:277).

109. Thwaites, *Jesuit Relations*, 5:239, 8:45.

110. Thwaites, *Jesuit Relations*, 10:83 (qtd. 83; emphasis in original). For the name of the Winnebagos in Iroquoian languages, see Steckley, "Early Map 'Novvelle France,'" 22.

111. Brandão, *"Your fyre shall burn no more,"* 101; Champlain, *Works*, 3:101–105, 5:73–80, 107–119, 130–133, 214–231, 308–312, 6:375–379; Lurie and Jung, *Nicolet Corrigenda*, 137–140.

Chapter 5

1. Thwaites, *Jesuit Relations*, 8:45 (qtd. 45).

2. Fischer, *Champlain's Dream*, 513–518; Thwaites, *Jesuit Relations*, 9:207–209 (qtd. 207). For Champlain's will, see La Blant, "Le Testament de Samuel de Champlain," 269–286.

3. Thwaites, *Jesuit Relations*, 8:18–19, 18:227–235; Champlain, *Works*, 6:378; Fischer, *Champlain's Dream*, 454–455, 495–496. For the original version of Vimont's *Relation* with the original pagination, see Vimont, *Relation* (1644), 8–13, and passim.

4. Thwaites, *Jesuit Relations*, 18:23, 1–233, 23:275–283, 42:223 (qtd. 42:223).

5. For works that celebrate the fact Nicolet was the first European in the western Great Lakes, see Butterfield, *History of the Discovery*, 49, 90–91 (qtd. 91); Michigan Historical Commission, *John Nicolet*, 17 (qtd. 17); "Michigan Historical Commission Places Tablet," 346–347 (qtd. 347); Poetker, "Jean Nicolet," 304–315 (qtd. 305, 308); and Shannon, "Green Bay Homecoming," 145 (qtd. 145). For the Lawson and Neville dispute, the various historical markers, and the artistic depictions of Nicolet, see Lurie and Jung, *Nicolet Corrigenda*, 13–16, 58–63.

6. For excellent introductions to this topic, see Nora, *Realms of Memory*, ix–20; Radstone and Hodgkin, *Regimes of Memory*, 1–21; Le Goff, *History and Memory*, ix–20; and Trouillot, *Silencing the Past*, xvii–30.

7. Thwaites, *Jesuit Relations*, 23:279 (qtd. 279).

8. Lurie and Jung, *Nicolet Corrigenda*, 15–16.

9. Thwaites, *Jesuit Relations*, 18:233, 23:279, 42:223; Carver, *Travels*, 50 (qtd. 50).

10. Sagard, *Historie du Canada*, 200–201; Champlain, *Works*, 3:119–120.

11. Ferland, *Cours d'Histoire*, 276–277; Ferland, *Notes sur les Registres*, 27, 30–33; Blémus, *Jean Nicollet*, 130–132; Jouan, "Jean Nicolet (de Cherbourg)," 77–83; Sulte, "Notes on Jean Nicolet," (1879), 193; Butterfield, *History of the Discovery*, 93–99; Thwaites, *Jesuit Relations*, 8:295; Hamelin, "Nicollet de Belleborne, Jean," 517; Trudel, "Letardif, Olivier," 473; Vachon, "Jolliet, Louis," 394–395.

12. Thwaites, *Jesuit Relations*, 8:257 (qtd. 257).

13. Thwaites, *Jesuit Relations*, 8:257–259 (qtd. 257, 259).

14. Thwaites, *Jesuit Relations*, 9:215–217, 11:145, 12:41–43, 135, 20:290 (qtd. 9:215, 217).

15. Thwaites, *Jesuit Relations*, 9:131 (qtd. 131).

16. Thwaites, *Jesuit Relations*, 12:135 (qtd. 135).

17. Thwaites, *Jesuit Relations*, 23:275–283, 28:14, 183; Geographic Board of Canada, *Ninth Report of the Geographic Board*, 196; Sulte, "Le nom de Nicolet," 21–23; Butterfield, *History of the Discovery*, 89–90; Jouan, "Jean Nicolet, Interpreter," 4–5 (qtd. 4).

18. Dubé, *Chevalier de Montmagny*, 121–122, 134, 143, 159–165; Goldstein, *French-Iroquois Diplomatic and Military Relations*, 64–65; Brandão, "*Your fyre shall burn no more*," 95–97, 100, table D.1; Parmenter, *Edge of the Woods*, 53–54; Thwaites, *Jesuit Relations*, 21:33–47 (qtd. 45, 47).

19. Thwaites, *Jesuit Relations*, 5:211, 21:47–67; Brandão, "*Your fyre shall burn no more*," 95–98; Parmenter, *Edge of the Woods*, 54; Carpenter, "Making War More Lethal," 44.

20. Ronda, "Sillery Experiment,"1–8; Gagnon, "Jean Nicolet," 100; Ferland, *Cours d'Histoire*, 325–326; Butterfield, *History of the Discovery*, 82–83, 104; Lurie and Jung, *Nicolet Corrigenda*, 123; Thwaites, *Jesuit Relations*, 23:279–281 (qtd. 281).

21. Ferland, *Notes sur les Registres*, 32; Lurie and Jung, *Nicolet Corrigenda*, 123–124.

22. Thwaites, *Jesuit Relations*, 28:243, 320n34 (qtd. 243).

23. Thwaites, *Jesuit Relations*, 8:296, 9:314; Trudel, *Population de Canada*, 58; Trudel, *Beginnings of New France*, 246–256.

24. Sulte, "Jean Nicolet," 420; Trudel, "Jean Nicollet," 186; Thwaites, *Jesuit Relations*, 5:211 (qtd. 211). There is a vast body of literature concerning the Métis of Canada and the Great Lakes region. For excellent introductions, see Ray, "Reflections on Fur Trade Social History," 91–107; Peterson, "Prelude to Red River," 41–67; and Peterson and Brown, *The New People*, passim.

25. Sulte, "Jean Nicolet," 420; Trudel, "Jean Nicollet," 186; Trudel, "New France," 30. René Blémus asserts Madeleine-Euphrosine was a niece of Jean Nicolet and the daughter of his brother Pierre, who definitely spent time in Canada. Blémus bases this assertion on a baptismal record in Cherbourg, France, for one Euphrasie Madeleine Nicollet dated 1626. However, the 1666 census for New France explicitly states Madeleine-Euphrosine hailed from the country of the Nipissings, not France. See Blémus, *Jean Nicollet*, 123; and Trudel, *Population de Canada*, 131.

26. Brandão, "*Your fyre shall burn no more*," 5–18, 77–91; Richter, *Ordeal of the Longhouse*, 57–66; Richter, "War and Culture," 537–541; Schlesier, "Epidemics and Indian Middlemen," 129–145; Jaenen, *Friend and Foe*, 63–64; Thwaites, *Jesuit Relations*, 21:43–45 (qtd. 43, 45).

27. Hunt, *Wars of the Iroquois*, 75–88; Jennings, *Ambiguous Iroquois Empire*, 98–102; Delâge, *Bitter Feast*, 134–135, 144–154; Trigger, *Children of Aataentsic*, 2:723–788; Hickerson, "Sociohistorical Significance of Two Chippewa Ceremonials," 67–85; Schenck, *Voice of the Crane*, 37–54; Eid, "Ojibwa-Iroquois War," 297–324; Fixico, "Alliance of the Three Fires," 17; Schmalz, "Role of the Ojibwa," 326–351; White, *Middle Ground*, 3, 19; Tanner, *Atlas of Great Lakes Indian History*, 29–35.

28. Thwaites, *Jesuit Relations*, 10:83; La Potherie, "History of the Savage Peoples," 1:293; Radin, "Winnebago Tribe," 57–58. For archaeological studies that lend credence to this interpretation, see Brown and Sasso, "Prelude to History," 213–215; Mazrim and Esarey, "Rethinking the Dawn of History," 157–164, 185–186; Mazrim, *Protohistory at the Grand Village of the Kaskaskia*, 131–133; and Richards, "I Should Have Dug Red Banks," 245.

29. La Potherie, "History of the Savage Peoples," 1:293–300; Lurie, "Winnebago Protohistory," 801–803; Kellogg, *French Régime*, 163; Thwaites, *Jesuit Relations*, 44:247, 55:183 (qtd. 55:183).

30. Germaine Warkentin argues convincingly that Radisson did not accompany Groseilliers on his journey to Lake Michigan from 1654 to 1656. See Radisson, *Collected Writings*, 14, 35–36, 42–46. Historians have long grappled with the incongruities in the chronology of Radisson's journeys, particularly Arthur T. Adams, whose earlier edition of Radisson's journals offers a rather improbable, though elegantly reasoned, alternative to Warkentin's argument. For Adam's chronology, see Radisson, *Explorations*, ii–xiii, 41, 239–258.

31. White, *Middle Ground*, 1–16; La Potherie, "History of the Savage Peoples," 303; Thwaites, *Jesuit Relations*, 54:235; Radisson, *Collected Writings*, 224 (qtd. 224).

32. Decorah, "Narrative," 457–458 (qtd. 457).

33. Charles C. Trowbridge, "Comparison of the manners, Customs and international laws of the Win-nee-baá-goa nation of Indians with those of their neighbors, the Munnoáminnees [1823],"

p. 125, Trowbridge MSS, box 15, folder I4Me; Charles C. Trowbridge, "Traditions, Manners, and Customs of the Mun-oá-min-nee Nation of Indians," p. 7, Trowbridge MSS, box 15, folder I4Me.

34. White, *Middle Ground*, 1–16; Kellogg, *French Régime*, 159–164; Thwaites, *Jesuit Relations*, 50:249–299, 54:227–235, 55:183 (qtd. 55:183).

35. Heidenreich, "Early French Exploration," 100; L'Incarnation, *Selected Letters*, 159.

36. Thwaites, *Jesuit Relations*, 23:221–227, 33:149–151 (qtd. 33:149–151).

37. Heidenreich, "Early French Exploration," 100–101; Thwaites, *Jesuit Relations*, 23:22, 1–227; L'Incarnation, *Selected Letters*, 159; Radisson, *Collected Writings*, 209 (qtd. 209).

38. Heidenreich, "Changing Role of Natives," 28–40.

39. La Potherie, "History of the Savage Peoples," 1:293; Thwaites, *Jesuit Relations*, 55:183; L'Incarnation, *Selected Letters*, 159 (qtd. 159). Robert L. Hall speculates the war took place around 1640, although he bases this speculation on a much less precise estimate taken from the Jesuit Claude Allouez in 1670. See Hall, "Red Banks, Oneota, and the Winnebago," 19.

40. L'Incarnation, *Selected Letters*, 159–160 (qtd. 159–160).

41. Thwaites, *Jesuit Relations*, 33:149–151.

42. Thwaites, *Jesuit Relations*, 18:235–237 (qtd. 237).

43. Thwaites, *Jesuit Relations*, 18:237 (qtd. 237).

44. Heidenreich, "Early French Exploration," 100–101; Thwaites, *Jesuit Relations*, 18:237, 33:149–151.

45. Champlain, *Works*, 1:165–170, 6:234; Lescarbot, *History of New France*, 2:317; Sagard, *Long Journey*, 43; Thwaites, *Jesuit Relations*, 18:231–237, 33:149–151; L'Incarnation, *Selected Letters*, 159–160.

46. Heidenreich, "Early French Exploration," 112–113; Heidenreich, "Analysis of the 17th-Century Map Nouvelle France," 96; Thwaites, *Jesuit Relations*, 45:219 (qtd. 219).

47. Heidenreich, "Early French Exploration," 117–118, 122, 127–128; Delanglez, "Mirage: The Sea of the West (Part I)," 358–359, 363–364; Thwaites, *Jesuit Relations*, 54:137, 189–191, 59:141 (qtd. 59:141).

48. Delanglez, "Mirage: The Sea of the West (Part I)," 374–375; Dupré, "Cavelier de la Salle, Réne-Robert," 173, 175–179; Heidenreich, "Early French Exploration," 122–123, 131–139, 143; Hennepin, *Nouveau voyage*, preface; Douglas, *Meaning of Canadian City Names*, 17.

49. Thwaites, *Jesuit Relations*, 45:221–225 (qtd. 221, 223, 225).

50. Delanglez, "Mirage: The Sea of the West (Part I)," 355–356; Crouse, *In Quest of the Western Ocean*, 258–260; Thwaites, *Jesuit Relations*, 45:221–225, 54:137 (qtd. 54:137).

51. Delanglez, "Mirage: The Sea of the West (Part I)," 358–359, 376–378, 381; Thwaites, *Jesuit Relations*, 45:221–223; O'Sullivan and Reynolds, *Lakes Handbook*, 67–68.

52. Delanglez, "Mirage: The Sea of the West (Part II)," 541–568; Eccles, "French Exploration," 160, 181–189; Smith, *Explorations of the La Vérendryes*, 2, 13–23, 32–40, 103–131; Wrong, *Conquest of New France*, 130–133; Trudel, *Atlas of New France*, 126–129.

53. Delanglez, "Mirage: The Sea of the West (Part II)," 541–568; Eccles, "French Exploration," 189–194; Wrong, *Conquest of New France*, 133–135; Peyser, *Jacques Legardeur de Saint-Pierre*, xxiv, 152, 163–192, 197n25–198n25.

54. Delanglez, "Mirage: The Sea of the West (Part II)," 541–568; Gough, *First Across the Continent*, 78–97, 123–162; Eccles, "French Exploration," 160, 181–194; Ambrose, *Undaunted Courage*, 73–74.

55. Crouse, *Search for the Northwest Passage*, 3–24; Williams, *Voyages of Delusion*, 132–136, 311–327, 333–334.

56. Williams, *Voyages of Delusion*, 366–367, 396–197, 386–405; Gough, *First Across the Continent*, 151; Vancouver, *Voyage of Discovery to the North Pacific Ocean*, 285, 295 (qtd. 285, 295; emphasis in original).

57. Crouse, *Search for the Northwest Passage*, 24, 419–454, 481–510; Savours, *Search for the North West Passage*, 219–230, 304–309.

58. Ambrose, *Undaunted Courage*, 75, 208–209, 230, 263, 331–333, 349; Nicandri, "Lewis and Clark," 171–173; Allen, "Indrawing Sea," 7–8; Moulton, *Journals of the Lewis & Clark Expedition*, 74 (qtd. 74).

59. Moulton, *Journals of the Lewis & Clark Expedition*, 74 (qtd. 74).

60. Moulton, *Journals of the Lewis & Clark Expedition*, 74.

61. Maurer and Yu, *Big Ditch*, 57–98.

BIBLIOGRAPHY

Manuscript Sources

Bloomfield, Leonard. Papers. National Anthropological Archives. Smithsonian Institution, Washington, DC.

Brown, Charles E. Papers. Wisconsin Historical Society, Madison, WI.

Gale, George. Papers. Wisconsin Historical Society, Madison, WI.

Hill, Alfred J., and Theodore H. Lewis. Northwestern Archaeological Survey Records, 1880–1895. Minnesota Historical Society, St. Paul, MN.

Iowa County Clerk of Court. Iowa Series 20, Crawford and Iowa County Criminal Case Files for the Additional Circuit Court of Michigan Territory, 1824–1836. Records of the Iowa County Clerk of Court. University of Wisconsin–Platteville Area Research Center, Platteville, WI.

Trowbridge, Charles C. Papers. Burton Historical Collection. Detroit Public Library, Detroit, MI.

United States Chief of Engineers. Civil Works Map File. Record Group 77, Records of the Office of the Chief of Engineers. National Archives, Washington, DC.

United States Weather Bureau. Climatological Records, 1819–1892, Microfilm Publication T-907. Record Group 27, Records of the United States Weather Bureau. National Archives, Washington, DC.

Newspapers

Green Bay Intelligencer. Green Bay, WI, 1833.

Green Bay Press-Gazette. Green Bay, WI, 2009.

Milwaukee Sentinel, Milwaukee, WI, 1872.

Published Sources, Papers, and Theses

Abler, Thomas S. "Iroquois Cannibalism: Fact Not Fiction," *Ethnohistory* 27 (Autumn 1980): 309–316.

Allaire, Bernard. "The Occupation of Quebec by the Kirke Brothers." In *Champlain: The Birth of French America*, pp 245–257. Raymond Litalien and Denis Vaugeois, eds., Käthe Roth, trans. Toronto: McGill–Queens University Press, 2004.

Allen, John L. "From Cabot to Cartier: The Early Exploration of Eastern North America, 1497–1543." *Annals of the Association of American Geographers* 82 (September 1992): 501–521.

———. "The Indrawing Sea: Imagination and Experience in the Search for the Northwest Passage, 1497–1632." In *American Beginnings: Exploration, Culture, and Cartography in the Land of Norumbega*, pp 7–35. Emerson W. Baker, et al., eds. Lincoln: University of Nebraska Press, 1994.

Ambrose, Stephen E. *Undaunted Courage: Meriwether Lewis, Thomas Jefferson, and the Opening of the American West.* New York: Simon and Schuster, 1996.

Anderson, Gary. *Kinsmen of Another Kind: Dakota-White Relations in the Upper Mississippi Valley, 1650–1862.* Lincoln: University of Nebraska Press, 1984.

Arseneault, Pauline. "Acadia in Champlain's New France: From Arcadia to China." In *Champlain: The Birth of French America*, pp 115–120. Raymonde Litalien and Denis Vaugeois, eds., Käthe Roth, trans. Toronto: McGill-Queens University Press, 2004.

Assikinack, Francis. "Social and Warlike Customs of the Odahwah Indians." *Canadian Journal of Industry, Science, and Art* 3 (July 1858): 297–309.

Axtell, James, and William C. Sturtevant. "The Unkindest Cut, or Who Invented Scalping?" *William and Mary Quarterly* 37 (July 1980): 451–472.

Ball, Margaret. "Grim Commerce: Scalps, Bounties, and the Transformation of Trophy-Taking in the Early American Northeast, 1450–1770." Ph.D. diss., University of Colorado, 2013.

Barbiche, Bernard. "Henry IV and the World Overseas: A Decisive Time in the History of New France." In *Champlain: The Birth of French America*, pp 24–32. Raymonde Litalien and Denis Vaugeois, eds., Käthe Roth, trans. Toronto: McGill-Queens University Press, 2004.

Baxter, James P. *A Memoir of Jacques Cartier, Sieur de Limoilou*. New York: Dodd, Mead, and Company, 1906.

Bayly, C. A., et al. "AHR Conversation: On Transnational History." *American Historical Review* 111 (December 2006): 1441–1464.

Beaulieu, Alain. "The Birth of the Franco-American Alliance." In *Champlain: The Birth of French America*, pp 153–162. Raymonde Litalien and Denis Vaugeois, eds., Käthe Roth, trans. Toronto: McGill-Queens University Press, 2004.

Beck, David R. M. *Siege and Survival: History of the Menominee Indians, 1634–1856*. Lincoln: University of Nebraska Press, 2002.

Bellfy, Phil. *Three Fires Unity: The Anishnaabeg of the Lake Huron Borderlands*. Lincoln: University of Nebraska Press, 2011.

Berthiaume, Pierre. "From Champlain's Voyage Accounts to His 1632 Report." In *Champlain: The Birth of French America*, pp 284–301. Raymonde Litalien and Denis Vaugeois, eds., Käthe Roth, trans. Toronto: McGill-Queens University Press, 2004.

Biggar, H. P. *The Early Trading Companies of New France*. Toronto: University of Toronto Press, 1901.

Bishop, Maurice. *Champlain: The Life of Fortitude*. New York: Alfred A. Knopf, 1948.

Blackburn, Carole. *Harvest of Souls: The Jesuit Missions and Colonialism in North America, 1632–1650*. Montreal: McGill-Queen's University Press, 2000.

Blémus, René. *Jean Nicollet en Nouvelle France: Un Normand à la découverte des Grand Lacs canadiens (1598–1642)*. Cherbourg, France: Editions Isoète, 1988.

Bloomfield, Leonard. *Menominee Lexicon*. Charles F. Hockett, ed. Publications in Anthropology and History, No. 3. Milwaukee: Milwaukee Public Museum, 1975.

Bogue, Margaret Beattie. *Around the Shores of Lake Superior: A Guide to Historic Sites*. Madison: University of Wisconsin Press, 2007.

Boucher, Francois. *20,000 Years of Fashion*. New York: Harry N. Abrams, 1966.

Bradley, Carolyn G. *Western World Costume: An Outline of History*. New York: Appleton Century-Crofts, 1954.

Brandão, José A. *"Your fyre shall burn no more": Iroquois Policy toward New France and Its Native Allies to 1701*. Lincoln: University of Nebraska Press, 1997.

Bremer, Richard G. "Henry Rowe Schoolcraft: Explorer in the Mississippi Valley, 1818–1832." *Wisconsin Magazine of History* 66 (Autumn 1982): 40–59.

Brereton, John. *A Briefe and True Relation of the Discoverie of the North Part of Virginia*. London: George Bishop, 1602.

Brown, Charles E. "Wisconsin Garden Beds." *Wisconsin Archeologist* 8 (August–October 1909): 97–105.

Brown, James A. "Ethnohistoric Connections." In *At the Edge of Prehistory: Huber Phase Archaeology in the Chicago Area*, pp 155–160. James A. Brown and Patricia J. O'Brien, eds. Kampsville, IL: Illinois Department of Transportation, 1990.

Brown, James A., and Robert F. Sasso. "Prelude to History on the Eastern Prairies." In *Societies in Eclipse: Archaeology of the Eastern Woodlands Indians, A.D. 1400–1700*, pp 205–228. David S. Brose and C. Wesley Cowan, eds. Washington, DC: Smithsonian Institution Press, 2001.

Bruhn, Wolfgang, and Max Tilke. *A Pictorial History of Costume*. London: A. Zwemmer, 1955.

Buache, Philippe. *Cartes des nouvelles découvertes au nord de la Mer du Sud: tant à l'est de la Sibérie et du Kamtchatka, qu'à l'ouest del a Nouvelle France*. Paris: Dezauche, Rue, des Noyers, près la Rue des Anglois, 1750.

Butterfield, Consul W. *History of Brulé's Discoveries and Explorations, 1610–1626*. Cleveland: Helman-Taylor Company, 1898.

———. *History of the Discovery of the Northwest by John Nicolet in 1634 with a Sketch of His Life*. Cincinnati: Robert Clarke & Co., 1881.

Cabot, Edward C. "Dual Drainage Anomalies in the Far North." *Geographic Review* 36 (July 1946): 474–482.

Campbell, James V. "Biographical Sketch of Charles Christopher Trowbridge." In *Collections of the Pioneer Society of the State of Michigan*. Vol. 6, pp 478–491. H. S. Bartholomew, ed. Lansing: Pioneer Society of the State of Michigan, 1907.

Campeau, Lucien. "Bruslé, Etienne, interpréte en huron." In *Monumenta Novae Franciae II: Établissement à Québec (1616–1634)*, pp 808–809. Lucien Campeau, ed. Quebec: Les Presses de l'Université Laval, 1979.

————. "Le dernier voyage de Champlain, 1633." *Délibérations et mémoires de la Société royale du Canada* 10 (1972): 81–101.

————. *La mission des Jésuites chez les Hurons, 1634–1650*. Montreal: Editions Bellarmin, 1987.

————. "La Route commerciale de l'Ouest au dix-septième siècle." *Les Cahiers des dix* 49 (1994): 21–49.

Capua, Sarah de. *The Menominee*. Tarrytown, NY: Marshall Cavendish Benchmark, 2010.

Carey, H. C., and J. Lea. *The Geography, History, and Statistics, of America, and the West Indies*. London: Sherwood Jones & Co., 1823.

Carpenter, Roger. "Making War More Lethal: Iroquois vs. Huron in the Great Lakes Region, 1609 to 1650." *Michigan Historical Review* 27 (Fall 2001): 33–51.

Carpin, Gervais. "Migrations to New France in Champlain's Time." In *Champlain: The Birth of French America*, pp 163–179. Raymonde Litalien and Denis Vaugeois, eds., Käthe Roth, trans. Toronto: McGill-Queen's University Press, 2004.

Cartier, Jacques. *The Voyages of Jacques Cartier*. H. P. Biggar, ed. and trans. Ottawa: F. A. Acland, 1924.

Carver, Jonathan. *Travels through the Interior Parts of North America in the Years 1766, 1767, and 1769*. London: J. Walter and S. Crowder, 1778.

Cayet, Pierre-Victor. "Of the French Who Have Become Accustomed to Being in Canada." In *Samuel de Champlain before 1604: Des Sauvages and Other Documents Related to the Period*, pp 371–399. Conrad E. Heidenreich and K. Janet Ritch, eds. Toronto: The Champlain Society, 2010.

Chaiklin, Martha. "Silk." In *The Encyclopedia of Western Colonialism since 1450*. Vol. 3, pp 1021–1024. Thomas Benjamin, ed. Farmington Hills, MI.: Macmillan Reference, 2006.

Champlain, Samuel de. "Des Sauvages, or Voyage of Samuel Champlain, [1603], 1604 / Des Sauvages, ou, Voyage de Samuel Champlain, [1603], 1604." In *Samuel de Champlain before 1604: Des Sauvages and Other Documents Related to the Period*, pp 232–365. Conrad E. Heidenreich and K. Janet Ritch, eds. Toronto: The Champlain Society, 2010.

————. *Oeuvres de Champlain*. 5 Vols. C. H. Laverdière, ed. Quebec: Geo. E. Desbarats, 1870.

[————]. "Relation du voyage du Sieur de Champlain en Canada." *Mercure François* (Paris) 19 (1636): 803–867.

[————]. "Relation du Voyage du Sieur de Champlain en Canada." In *Monumenta Novae Franciae II: Établissement à Québec (1616–1634)*, pp 350–397. Lucien Campeau, ed. Quebec: Les Presses de l'Université Laval, 1979.

————. *Les voyages de la Nouvelle France occidentale, dicte Canada, faits par le Sr de Champlain*. Paris: Chez Claude Collet, 1632.

————. *Les voyages du sieur de Champlain, xaintongeois, capitaine ordinaire pour le roy, en la marine*. Paris: Chez Jean Berjon, 1613.

————. *The Works of Samuel De Champlain*. 7 Vols. H. P. Biggar, ed., H. H. Langton and W. F. Ganong, trans. Toronto: The Champlain Society, 1922–1956.

Chapdelaine, Claude. "A Review of the Latest Developments in St. Lawrence Iroquoian Archaeology." In *A Passion for the Past: Papers in Honour of James F. Pendergast*, pp 63–75. James V. Wright and Jean-Luc Pilon, eds. Mercury Series Archaeological Paper 164. Gatineau, Quebec: Canadian Museum of Civilization, 2004.

Chapman, Brian R., and Eric G. Bolen. *Ecology of North America*. 2nd ed. Chichester, United Kingdom: Wiley Blackwell, 2015.

Charlevoix, Pierre-François-Xavier de. *History and General Description of New France*. Vol. 2. John Gilmary Shea, ed. and trans. New York: John Gilmary Shea, 1866.

———. *Journal of a Voyage to North-America*. 2 Vols. London: R. and J. Dodsley, 1761.

Clifton, James A. *The Prairie People: Continuity and Change in Potawatomi Indian Culture, 1665–1965*. Iowa City: University of Iowa Press, 1977.

Codignola, Luca. "The Battle is Over: Campeau's *Monumenta* vs. Thwaites's *Jesuit Relations*, 1602– 1650." *European Review of Native American Studies* 10 (1996): 3–10.

———. "Competing Networks: Roman Catholic Ecclesiastics in French North America, 1610–1658." *Canadian Historical Review* 80 (December 1999): 539–584.

Cohen, Thomas V., and Germaine Warkentin. "Things Not Easily Believed: Introducing the Early Modern Relation." *Renaissance and Reformation* 34 (Winter–Spring 2011): 7–23.

Cotgrave, Randle. *A Dictionarie of the French and English Tongues*. London: Adam Islip, 1611.

Cranston, J. Herbert. *Etienne Brûlé: Immortal Scoundrel*. Toronto: Ryerson Press, 1949.

Cremin, William M. "Sand Point (20 BG 14): A Lakes Phase Site on the Keweenaw Peninsula, Baraga County, Michigan." *Michigan Archaeologist* 26 (September–December 1980): 7–90.

Crouse, Nellis. *Contributions of the Canadian Jesuits to the Geographical Knowledge of New France, 1632–1675*. Ithaca, NY: Cornell Publications Printing Company, 1924.

———. *In Quest of the Western Ocean*. New York: William Morrow & Co., 1928.

———. *The Search for the Northwest Passage*. New York: Columbia University Press, 1934.

Cuoq, J. A. *Lexique de la Langue Algonquine*. Montreal: J. Chapleau et Fils, 1886.

———. *Lexique de la Langue Iroquoise avec Notes et Appendices*. Montreal: J. Chapleau et Fils, 1882.

D'Abate, Richard. "On the Meaning of a Name: 'Norumbega' and the Representation of North America." In *American Beginnings: Exploration, Culture, and Cartography in the Land of Norumbega*, pp 61–88. Emerson W. Baker et al., eds. Lincoln: University of Nebraska Press, 1994.

Decorah, Spoon. "Narrative of Spoon Decorah." In *Collections of the State Historical Society of Wisconsin*. Vol. 13, pp 448–462. Reuben G. Thwaites, ed. Madison: State Historical Society of Wisconsin, 1895.

Delâge, Denys. *Bitter Feast: Amerindians and Europeans in Northeastern North America, 1600–64*. Jane Brierley, trans. Vancouver: University of British Columbia Press, 1993.

Delanglez, Jean. "Claude Dablon, S.J. (1619–1697)." *Mid-America* 26 (April 1944): 91–110.

———. "A Mirage: The Sea of the West (Part I)." *Revue d'histoire de l'Amérique française* 1 (December 1947): 346–381.

———. "A Mirage: The Sea of the West (Part II)." *Revue d'histoire de l'Amérique française* 1 (March 1948): 541–568.

Descriptive Catalog of a Collection of the Economic Minerals of Canada. Montreal: Lovell Printing and Publishing Company, 1876.

Deslandres, Dominique. "Samuel de Champlain and Religion." In *Champlain: The Birth of French America*, pp 191–204. Raymonde Litalien and Denis Vaugeois, eds., Käthe Roth, trans. Toronto: McGill-Queens University Press, 2004.

The Development of Various Decorative and Upholstery Fabrics. New York: F. Schumacher & Co., 1924.

Dever, Larry. "The Nicolet Myth." *Minnesota History* 50 (December 1966): 318–322.

Dickinson, John A. "Champlain, Administrator." In *Champlain: The Birth of French America*, pp 211– 217. Raymonde Litalien and Denis Vaugeois, eds., Käthe Roth, trans. Toronto: McGill-Queens University Press, 2004.

Dionne, N.E. *Samuel Champlain: Fondateur de Québec et Père de la Nouvelle France*. Vol. 2. Quebec: A. Coté et cie Imprimeurs-Editeurs, 1906.

Dirst, Victoria. "Reconsidering the Prehistory of Northeastern Wisconsin." *Wisconsin Archeologist* 79 (January–June 1998): 113–121.

Douglas, Robert. *Meaning of Canadian City Names*. Ottawa: F. A. Acland, 1922.

Dubé, Jean-Claude. *The Chevalier de Montmagny (1601–1657): First Governor of New France*. Elizabeth Rapley, trans. Ottawa: University of Ottawa Press, 2005.

Dupré, Céline. "Cavelier de la Salle, Réne-Robert." In *Dictionary of Canadian Biography*. Vol. 1, pp 172–184. George W. Brown, ed. Toronto: University of Toronto Press, 1966.

Eccles, W. J. *The Canadian Frontier, 1534–1760*. New York: Holt, Rinehart and Winston, 1969.

————. *Essays on New France*. Toronto: Oxford University Press, 1987.

————. "French Exploration of North America, 1700–1800." In *North American Exploration*. Vol. 2, *A Continent Defined*, pp 149–202. John Logan Allen, ed. Lincoln: University of Nebraska Press, 1997.

Echo-Hawk, Roger C. "Ancient History in the New World: Integrating Oral Traditions and the Archaeological Record in Deep Time." *American Antiquity* 65 (April 2000): 267–290.

Edmunds, R. David. "Indian-White Warfare: A Look at Both Sides." *Northwest Ohio Quarterly* 61 (Spring–Autumn 1989): 35–45.

Eid, Leroy. "'National' War among Indians of Northeastern North America." *Canadian Review of American Studies* 16 (Summer 1985): 125–154.

————. "The Ojibwa-Iroquois War: The War the Five Nations Did Not Win." *Ethnohistory* 26 (Fall 1979): 297–324.

Elliott, Kennell M. *History of the Nicolet National Forest, 1928–1976*. Two Rivers, WI: Forest History Association of Wisconsin, 1977.

Emerson, Thomas E., and James A. Brown. "The Late Prehistory and Protohistory of Illinois." In *Calumet & Fleur-des-lys: Archaeology of Indian and French Contact in the Midcontinent*, pp 77–128. John A. Walthall and Thomas E. Emerson, eds. Washington, DC: Smithsonian Institution Press, 1992.

Engelbrecht, William. "New York Iroquois Political Development." In *Cultures in Contact: The European Impact on Native Cultural Institutions in Eastern North America, A.D. 1000–1800*, pp 163–183. William W. Fitzhugh, ed. Washington, DC: Smithsonian Institution Press, 1985.

Feest, Johanna E., and Christian F. Feest. "Ottawa." In *Handbook of North American Indians*. Vol. 15, *Northeast*, pp 772–786. Bruce G. Trigger, ed. Washington, DC: Smithsonian Institution, 1978.

Feltwell, John. *The Story of Silk*. New York: St. Martin's Press, 1990.

Fenton, William N. *The Great Law and the Longhouse: A Political History of the Iroquois Confederacy*. Norman: University of Oklahoma Press, 1998.

Ferland, J. B. A. *Cours d'Histoire du Canada*. Vol. 1. Quebec: N.S. Hardy, Libraire-Éditeur, 1861.

————. *Notes sur les Registres de Notre-Dame de Québec*. Quebec: G. et G. E. Desbarats, 1863.

Ferreira, Maria João Pacheco. "Chinese Textiles for Portuguese Tastes." In *Interwoven Globe: The Worldwide Textile Trade, 1500–1800*, pp 46–55. Amelia Peck, ed. New York: Metropolitan Museum of Art, 2013.

Fischer, David Hackett. *Champlain's Dream*. New York: Simon and Schuster, 2008.

Fixico, Donald. "The Alliance of the Three Fires in Trade and War, 1630–1812." *Michigan Historical Review* 20 (Fall 1994): 1–23.

Freeman, Joan E. "An Analysis of the Point Sauble and Beaumier Farm Sites." Master's thesis, University of Wisconsin–Madison, 1956.

Fritze, Ronald H. *New Worlds: The Great Voyages of Discovery, 1400–1600*. Phoenix Mill, United Kingdom: Sutton Publishing, 2002.

Furse, George A. *The Art of Marching*. London: William Clowes and Sons Limited, 1901.

Gagnon, François-Marc. "Is the *Brief Discours* by Champlain?" In *Champlain: The Birth of French America*, pp 83–92. Raymonde Litalien and Denis Vaugeois, eds., Käthe Roth, trans. Toronto: McGill-Queens University Press, 2004.

Gagnon, Jacques. "Jean Nicolet au lac Michigan: histoire d'une erreur historique." *Revue D'histoire de l'Amérique française* 50 (Summer 1996): 95–101.

Gale, George. *Upper Mississippi: Or, Historical Sketches of the Mound Builders, the Indian Tribes, and the Progress of Civilization in the North-West; From A.D. 1600 to the Present Time*. Chicago: Clark and Company, 1867.

Garrad, Charles. "Champlain and the Odawa." *Midcontinental Journal of Archaeology* 24 (Spring, 1999): 57–77.

Geographic Board of Canada. *Ninth Report of the Geographic Board of Canada for the Year Ending June 30, 1910.* Ottawa: C. H. Parmelee, 1911.

Gervais, Gaétan. "Champlain and Ontario (1603–35)." In *Champlain: The Birth of French America,* pp 180–190. Raymonde Litalien and Denis Vaugeois, eds., Käthe Roth, trans. Toronto: McGill–Queens University Press, 2004.

Giafferri, Paul Louis Victor de. *The History of French Masculine Costume.* New York: Foreign Publications, 1927.

Gibbon, Guy E. "Cultural Dynamics and the Development of the Oneota Life-Way in Wisconsin." *American Antiquity* 37 (April 1972): 166–185.

———. "The Mississippian Tradition: Oneota Culture." *Wisconsin Archeologist* 67 (September–December 1986): 314–338.

Giraudo, Laura. "The Manuscripts of the *Brief Discours.*" In *Champlain: The Birth of French America,* pp 63–82. Raymonde Litalien and Denis Vaugeois, eds., Käthe Roth, trans. Toronto: McGill–Queens University Press, 2004.

Goddard, Ives. "Central Algonquian Languages." In *Handbook of North American Indians.* Vol. 15, *Northeast,* pp 583–587. Bruce G. Trigger, ed. Washington, DC: Smithsonian Institution, 1978.

———. "Mascouten." In *Handbook of North American Indians.* Vol. 15, *Northeast,* pp 668–672. Bruce G. Trigger, ed. Washington, DC: Smithsonian Institution, 1978.

Goldstein, Robert A. *French-Iroquois Diplomatic and Military Relations, 1609–1701.* The Hague, the Netherlands: Mouton, 1969.

Gordon, Alan. *The Hero and the Historians: Historiography and the Uses of Jacques Cartier.* Vancouver: University of British Columbia Press, 2010.

Gorsline, Douglas. *What People Wore: A Visual History of Dress from Ancient Times to Twentieth Century America.* New York: Bonanza Books, 1952.

Gosselin, Auguste. *Jean Nicolet et Le Canada de son temps, (1618–1642).* Quebec: J. A. K. LaFlamme, 1905.

Gough, Barry. *First Across the Continent: Sir Alexander Mackenzie.* Norman: University of Oklahoma Press, 1997.

Green, L. C., and Olive P. Dickason. *The Law of Nations and the New World.* Edmonton: University of Alberta Press, 1989.

Greer, Allan, ed. *The Jesuit Relations: Natives and Missionaries in Seventeenth-Century North America.* Boston: Bedford/St. Martin's, 2000.

———. "National, Transnational, and Hypernational Historiographies: New France Meets Early American History." *Canadian Historical Review* 91 (December 2010): 695–742.

Griffin, James B. "A Hypothesis for the Prehistory of the Winnebago." In *Culture in History: Essays in Honor of Paul Radin,* pp 809–863. Stanley Diamond, ed. New York: Columbia University Press, 1960.

Grignon, Augustin. "Seventy-Two Years' Recollections of Wisconsin." In *Collections of the State Historical Society of Wisconsin.* Vol. 3, pp 197–296. Lyman C. Draper, ed. Madison: State Historical Society of Wisconsin, 1857.

Hadlock, Wendell S. "War among the Northeastern Woodland Indians." *American Anthropologist* 49 (April–June 1947): 204–221.

Haefeli, Evan. "On First Contact and Apotheosis: Manitou and Men in North America." *Ethnohistory* 54 (Summer 2007): 407–443.

Hakluyt, Richard. *The Principal Navigations, Voyages, Traffiques and Discoveries of the English Nation.* Vol. 2. London: George Bishop, Ralph Newberie, and Robert Parker, 1599.

———. *The Principal Navigations Voyages, Traffiques & Discoveries of the English Nation.* Vol. 1. Glasgow: James MacLehose and Sons, 1903.

Hall, Robert L. *The Archaeology of Carcajou Point.* 2 Vols. Madison: University of Wisconsin Press, 1962.

——. "Red Banks, Oneota, and the Winnebago: Views from a Distant Rock." *Wisconsin Archeologist* 74 (March–December 1993): 10–79.

——. "Relating the Big Fish and the Big Stone: Reconsidering the Archaeological Identity and Habitat of the Winnebago in 1634." In *Oneota Archaeology, Past, Present, and Future*, pp 19–30. Office of the State Archaeologist, Report 20. William Green, ed. Iowa City: University of Iowa Press, 1995.

——. "Rethinking Jean Nicolet's Route to the Ho-Chunks in 1634." In *Theory, Method, and Practice in Modern Archaeology*, pp 238–251. Robert J. Jeske and Douglas K. Charles, eds. Westport, CN: Praeger, 2003.

Hamelin, Jean. "Nicollet de Belleborne, Jean." In *Dictionary of Canadian Biography.* Vol. 1, pp 516–518. George W. Brown, ed. Toronto: University of Toronto Press, 1966.

Hauser, Raymond E. "The Illinois Indian Tribe: From Autonomy and Self-Sufficiency to Dependency and Depopulation." *Journal of the Illinois State Historical Society* 69 (May 1976): 127–138.

Hayes, Derek. *Historical Atlas of Canada: Canada's History Illustrated with Original Maps.* Vancouver: Douglas & McIntyre, 2002.

Heidenreich, Conrad E. "Analysis of the 17th-Century Map 'Nouvelle France.'" *Cartographica* 25 (Winter 1988): 67–111.

——. "The Beginning of French Exploration out of the St. Lawrence Valley: Motives, Methods, and Changing Attitudes towards Native Peoples." In *Decentering the Renaissance: Canada and Europe in Multidisciplinary Perspective, 1500–1700*, pp 236–251. Germaine Warkentin and Carolyn Podruchny, eds. Toronto: University of Toronto Press, 2001.

——. "The Changing Role of Natives in the Exploration of Canada: Cartier (1534) to Mackenzie (1793)." *Terrae Incognitae* 37 (2005): 28–40.

——. "Early French Exploration in the North American Interior." In *North American Exploration.* Vol. 2, *A Continent Defined*, pp 65–148. John Logan Allen, ed. Lincoln: University of Nebraska Press, 1997.

——. *Explorations and Mapping of Samuel de Champlain.* Monograph No. 17, Cartographica. Toronto: University of Toronto Press, 1976.

——. "History of the St. Lawrence-Great Lakes Area to A.D. 1650." In *The Archaeology of Southern Ontario to A.D. 1650*, pp 475–492. Occasional Publications of the London Chapter, Ontario Archaeological Society, Publication 5. Chris J. Ellis and Neal Ferris, eds. London, Ontario: London Chapter, Ontario Archaeological Society, 1990.

——. "Huron." In *Handbook of North American Indians.* Vol. 15, *Northeast*, pp 368–388. Bruce G. Trigger, ed. Washington, DC: Smithsonian Institution, 1978.

——. *Huronia: A History and Geography of the Huron Indians, 1600–1650.* Toronto: McClelland and Steward Limited, 1971.

Heidenreich, Conrad E., and Edward H. Dahl. "Samuel de Champlain's Cartography, 1603–32." In *Champlain: The Birth of French America*, pp 312–333. Raymonde Litalien and Denis Vaugeois, eds., Käthe Roth, trans. Toronto: McGill-Queens University Press, 2004.

Heidenreich, Conrad E., and K. Janet Ritch. "Champlain and His Times to 1604: An Interpretive Essay." In *Samuel de Champlain before 1604: Des Sauvages and Other Documents Related to the Period*, pp 3–82. Conrad E. Heidenreich and K. Janet Ritch, eds. Toronto: The Champlain Society, 2010.

——. "Champlain's *Des Sauvages* and Edward Hayes's Treatise." In *Samuel de Champlain before 1604: Des Sauvages and Other Documents Related to the Period*, pp 457–461. Conrad E. Heidenreich and K. Janet Ritch, eds. Toronto: The Champlain Society, 2010.

——. "Champlain's Signature and Titles: A Discussion." In *Samuel de Champlain before 1604: Des Sauvages and Other Documents Related to the Period*, pp 436–446. Conrad E. Heidenreich and K. Janet Ritch, eds. Toronto: The Champlain Society, 2010.

——. "Of the French Who Have Become Accustomed to Being in Canada. Summary of *Des Sauvages* by Pierre-Victor Cayet, 1605 / *Des François qui se sont habituez en Canada. Sommaire de* Des Sauvages *par Pierre-Victor Cayet, 1605.*" In *Samuel de Champlain before 1604*: Des Sauvages *and Other Documents Related to the Period*, pp 367–370. Conrad E. Heidenreich and K. Janet Ritch, eds. Toronto: The Champlain Society, 2010.

——. "Preface." In *Samuel de Champlain before 1604*: Des Sauvages *and Other Documents Related to the Period*, pp xi–xxii. Conrad E. Heidenreich and K. Janet Ritch, eds. Toronto: The Champlain Society, 2010.

——, eds. *Samuel de Champlain before 1604*: Des Sauvages *and Other Documents Related to the Period*. Toronto: The Champlain Society, 2010.

——. "Textual Introduction to *Des Sauvages*." In *Samuel de Champlain before 1604*: Des Sauvages *and Other Documents Related to the Period*, pp 83–125. Conrad E. Heidenreich and K. Janet Ritch, eds. Toronto: The Champlain Society, 2010.

Hennepin, Louis de. *Nouveau voyage d'un pais plus grand que l'Europe*. Utrecht, the Netherlands: Chez Antoine Schouten, 1698.

Heos, Bridget. *Wisconsin: Past and Present*. New York: Rosen Publishing Group, 2010.

Hickerson, Harold. "The Sociohistorical Significance of Two Chippewa Ceremonials." *American Anthropologist* 65 (February 1963): 67–85.

Hill, Margot H., and Peter A. Bucknell. *The Evolution of Fashion: Pattern and Cut from 1066 to 1930*. London: B. T. Batsford, 1967.

Hintz, Martin. *Wisconsin Portraits: 55 People Who Made a Difference*. Black Earth, WI: Trails Publishing, 2005.

Hodge, Frederick W., ed. *Handbook of American Indians North of Mexico*. 2 Vols. Washington, DC: Government Printing Office, 1907–1910.

Hoffman, W. J. "The Menomini Indians." In *Fourteenth Annual Report of the Bureau of Ethnology, 1892–1893*. Part I, pp 3–328. Washington, DC: Government Printing Office, 1896.

——. "Mythology of the Menomoni Indians." *American Anthropologist* 3 (July 1890): 243–258.

Hunt, George T. *The Wars of the Iroquois: A Study in Intertribal Relations*. Madison: University of Wisconsin Press, 1940.

Hunter, Douglas. "Was New France Born in England?" *The Beaver* 86 (December 2006–January 2007): 39–44.

Iriye, Akira. "Transnational History." *Contemporary European History* 13 (May 2004): 211–222.

Jaenen, Cornelius J. "Amerindian Views of French Culture in the Seventeenth Century." *Canadian Historical Review* 55 (September 1974): 261–291.

——. *Friend and Foe: Aspects of French-Amerindian Cultural Contact in the Sixteenth and Seventeenth Centuries*. New York: Columbia University Press, 1976.

——. "The Problems of Assimilation in New France, 1603–1645." *French Historical Studies* 4 (Spring 1966): 265–289.

——. "The Role of Presents in French-Amerindian Trade." In *Explorations in Canadian Economic History: Essays in Honour of Irene Spry*, pp 231–250. Duncan Cameron, ed. Ottawa: University of Ottawa Press, 1985.

Jennings, Francis. *The Ambiguous Iroquois Empire: The Covenant Chain Confederation of Indian Tribes with the English Colonies from Its Beginnings to the Lancaster Treaty of 1744*. New York: W. W. Norton, 1984.

Jouan, Henri. "Jean Nicolet (de Cherbourg), interprète-voyageur au Canada, 1618–1642." *Revue canadienne* 22 (1886): 67–83.

——. "Jean Nicolet, Interpreter and Voyageur in Canada, 1618–1642." In *Collections of the State Historical Society of Wisconsin*. Vol. 11, pp 1–22. Reuben G. Thwaites, ed. Madison: State Historical Society of Wisconsin, 1888.

Jung, Patrick J. "Forge, Destroy, and Preserve the Bond of Empire: Euro-Americans, Native Americans, and Métis on the Wisconsin Frontier, 1634–1856." Ph.D. diss., Marquette University, 1997.

Jurgens, Olga. "Brûlé, Étienne." In *Dictionary of Canadian Biography*. Vol. 1, pp 130–133. George W. Brown, ed. Toronto: University of Toronto Press, 1966.

Kamen, Henry. *Early Modern European Society*. London: Routledge 2000.

Kay, Jeanne. "The Fur Trade and Native American Population Growth." *Ethnohistory* 31 (1984): 265–287.

Keener, Craig S. "Ethnohistorical Analysis of Iroquois Assault Tactics Used against Fortified Settlements of the Northeast in the Seventeenth Century." *Ethnohistory* 46 (Autumn 1999): 777–807.

Keesing, Felix M. *The Menomini Indians of Wisconsin: A Study of Three Centuries of Cultural Contact and Change*. Philadelphia: American Philosophical Society, 1939.

Kellogg, Louise P. *The French Régime in Wisconsin and the Northwest*. Madison: State Historical Society of Wisconsin, 1925.

Kelly, Francis M., and Randolph Schwabe. *Historic Costume: A Chronicle of Fashion in Western Europe, 1490–1790*. New York: Charles Scribner's Sons, 1925.

Kenyon, W. A., and J. R. Turnbull. *The Battle for James Bay, 1686*. Toronto: Macmillan of Canada, 1971.

Knowles, Nathaniel. "The Torture of Captives by the Indians of Eastern North America." *Proceedings of the American Philosophical Society* 82 (March 1940): 151–225.

Kuhn, Robert D., and Martha L. Sempowski. "A New Approach to Dating the League of the Iroquois." *American Antiquity* 66 (April 2001): 301–314.

La Blant, Robert, ed. "Le Testament de Samuel de Champlain: 17 novembre 1635." *Revue d'histoire de l'Amerique française* 17 (September 1963): 269–286.

Lanctôt, Gustave. *A History of Canada*. Vol. 1, *From Its Origins to the Royal Régime, 1663*. Cambridge, MA: Harvard University Press, 1963.

———. "La Roche de Mesgouez, Troilus de." In *Dictionary of Canadian Biography*. Vol. 1, pp 421–422. George W. Brown, ed. Toronto: University of Toronto Press, 1966.

La Potherie, Claude Charles Le Roy, Bacqueville de. "History of the Savage Peoples Who Are Allies of New France." In *The Indian Tribes of the Upper Mississippi Valley and Region of the Great Lakes*. 2 Vols. Emma H. Blair, ed., Vol. 1, pp 273–372; Vol. 2, pp 13–136. Cleveland: Arthur H. Clark, 1911–1912.

Lawson, Publius V. "Habitat of the Winnebago, 1632–1832." In *Proceedings of the State Historical Society of Wisconsin, 1906*, pp 144–166. Madison: State Historical Society of Wisconsin, 1907.

———. "The Outagamie Village at West Menasha." In *Proceedings of the State Historical Society of Wisconsin, 1899*, pp 204–211. Madison: State Historical Society of Wisconsin, 1900.

———. "The Winnebago Tribe." *Wisconsin Archeologist* 6 (July 1907): 78–162.

———. *Winnebago Village on Doty Island*. Menasha, WI: n.p., 1900.

Le Clercq, Christian. *The First Establishment of the Faith in New France*. 2 Vols. John Gilmary Shea, trans. New York: John Gilmary Shea, 1881.

Leggett, William F. *The Story of Silk*. New York: Little Ives & Co., 1949.

Le Goff, Jacques. *History and Memory*. Steven Rendall and Elizabeth Claman, trans. New York: Columbia University Press, 1992.

Lescarbot, Marc. *The History of New France*. 3 Vols. W. L. Grant and H. P. Biggar, ed. and trans. Toronto: The Champlain Society, 1907–1914.

L'Incarnation, Marie de. *Word from New France: The Selected Letters of Marie de l'Incarnation*. Joyce Marshall, ed. and trans. Toronto: Oxford University Press, 1967.

Little, Elizabeth A. "Inland Waterways in the Northeast." *Midcontinental Journal of Archaeology* 12 (1987): 55–76.

Lurie, Nancy Oestreich. "An Aztalan-Winnebago Hypothesis." Unpublished paper, Milwaukee Public Museum, 1973.

———. "Winnebago." In *Handbook of North American Indians*. Vol. 15, *Northeast*, pp 690–707. Bruce G. Trigger, ed. Washington, DC: Smithsonian Institution, 1978.

———. "Winnebago Protohistory." In *Culture in History: Essays in Honor of Paul Radin*, pp 790–808. Stanley Diamond, ed. New York: Columbia University Press, 1960.

Lurie, Nancy Oestreich, and Patrick J. Jung. "Jean Nicolet (Again): Comment on Ronald J. Mason's 'Where Nicolet and the Winnebagoes First Met.'" *Wisconsin Archeologist* 95 (July–December 2014): 303–307.

———. *The Nicolet Corrigenda: New France Revisited*. Long Grove, IL: Waveland Press, 2009.

Mancall, Peter. *Fatal Journey: The Final Journey of Henry Hudson: A Tale of Mutiny and Murder in the Arctic*. New York: Basic Books, 2009.

Marchand, Philip. *Ghost Empire: How the French Almost Conquered North America*. Toronto: McClelland & Steward, 2005.

Martin, Deborah B. *History of Brown County Wisconsin: Past and Present*. Vol. 1. Chicago: S. J. Clarke Publishing Company, 1913.

Mason, Carol I. "Historic Identification and Lake Winnebago Focus Oneota." In *Cultural Change and Continuity: Essays in Honor of James Bennett Griffin*, pp 335–348. Charles E. Cleland, ed. New York: Academic Press, 1976.

Mason, Carol L. "Where Did Nicolet Land?" *Fox Valley Archaeology* 23 (April 1994): 38–45.

Mason, Richard P. and Carol L. Mason. "The Doty Island Village Site (47 WN 30) Winnebago County, Wisconsin." *Wisconsin Archeologist* 74 (March–December 1993): 197–257.

Mason, Ronald J. "Archaeoethnicity and the Elusive Menominis." *Midcontinental Journal of Archaeology* 22 (Spring 1997): 69–94.

———. "Ethnicity and Archaeology in the Upper Great Lakes." In *Cultural Change and Continuity: Essays in Honor of James Bennett Griffin*, pp 349–361. Charles E. Cleland, ed. New York: Academic Press, 1976.

———. "Oneota and Winnebago Ethnogenesis: An Overview." *Wisconsin Archeologist* 74 (March–December 1993): 400–421.

———. "Where Nicolet and the Winnebagoes First Met." *Wisconsin Archeologist* 95 (January–June 2014): 65–74.

Maurer, Noel, and Carlos Yu. *The Big Ditch: How America Took, Built, Ran, and Ultimately Gave Away the Panama Canal*. Princeton, NJ: Princeton University Press, 2011.

Maza, Sarah. "Bourgeoisie." In *The Oxford Handbook of the Ancien Régime*, pp 127–140. William Doyle, ed. New York: Oxford University Press, 2012.

Mazrim, Robert F., ed. *Protohistory at the Grand Village of the Kaskaskia: The Illinois Country on the Eve of Colony*. Illinois State Archaeological Survey, Studies in Archaeology No. 10. Urbana: University of Illinois, 2015.

Mazrim, Robert F., and Duane Esarey. "Rethinking the Dawn of History: The Schedule, Signature, and Agency of European Goods in Protohistoric Illinois." *Midcontinental Journal of Archaeology* 32 (Fall 2007): 145–200.

McCafferty, Michael. "Where did Jean Nicollet Meet the Winnebago in 1634?: A Critique of Robert Hall's 'Rethinking Jean Nicollet's Route to the Ho-Chunks in 1634.'" *Ontario History* 96 (Autumn 2004): 170–182.

McKern, Will C. "Preliminary Report on the Upper Mississippi Phase in Wisconsin." *Bulletin of the Public Museum of the City of Milwaukee* 16 (December 1945): 109–285.

McLaird, James D. "The Welsh, the Vikings, and the Lost Tribes of Israel on the Northern Plains: The Legend of the White Mandan." *South Dakota History* 18 (Winter 1988): 245–273.

Mercator, Gerard. *L'atlas meditations cosmographique de monde et figure diceluy*. Amsterdam: Ioudoci Honij, 1613.

Michigan Historical Commission. *John Nicolet: Exercises at the Unveiling of the Tablet Commemorating the Discovery and Exploration of the Northwest*. Lansing: Michigan Historical Commission, 1915.

"Michigan Historical Commission Places Tablet to the Memory of Jean Nicolet." *Journal of the Illinois State Historical Society* 8 (July 1915): 346–348.

Moir, John S. "Kirke, Sir David." In *Dictionary of Canadian Biography*. Vol. 1, pp 404–406. George W. Brown, ed. Toronto: University of Toronto Press, 1966.

Morely, William F. E. "Chauvin de Tonnetuit, Pierre de." In *Dictionary of Canadian Biography*. Vol. 1, pp 209–210. George W. Brown, ed. Toronto: University of Toronto Press, 1966.

Morison, Samuel Eliot. *The European Discovery of America: The Northern Voyages, A.D. 500–1600.* New York: Oxford University Press, 1971.

———. *Samuel de Champlain: Father of New France.* Boston: Little, Brown, and Company, 1972.

Morissonneau, Christian. "Champlain's Dream." In *Champlain: The Birth of French America*, pp 258–265. Raymonde Litalien and Denis Vaugeois, eds., Käthe Roth, trans. Toronto: McGill-Queens University Press, 2004.

———. *Le rêve américain de Champlain.* Montreal: Les Éditions Hurtubise, 2009.

Moulton, Gary E., ed. *The Journals of the Lewis & Clark Expedition.* Vol. 5. Lincoln: University of Nebraska Press, 1988.

Neville, Arthur C. "Some Historic Sites About Green Bay." In *Proceedings of the State Historical Society of Wisconsin, 1905*, pp 143–156. Madison: State Historical Society of Wisconsin, 1906.

Newbigging, William J. "History of the French-Ottawa Alliance, 1613–1763." Ph.D. diss., University of Toronto, 1995.

Newman, Marshall T. "The Blond Mandan: A Critical Review of an Old Problem." *Southwestern Journal of Anthropology* 6 (Autumn 1950): 255–272.

Nicandri, David L. "Lewis and Clark: Exploring under the Influence of Alexander Mackenzie." *Pacific Northwest Quarterly* 95 (Fall 2004): 171–181.

Nora, Pierre. *Realms of Memory: The Construction of the French Past.* Vol. 1, *Conflicts and Divisions.* New York: Columbia University Press, 1996.

Nordenskiöld, A. E. *Facsimile-Atlas to the History of the Early Cartography.* Johan A. Ekelöf and Clements R. Markham, trans. Stockholm: P. A. Norstedt & Söner, 1889.

O'Gorman, Jodie A., and William A. Lovis. "Before Removal: An Archaeological Perspective on the Southern Lake Michigan Basin." *Midcontinental Journal of Archaeology* 31 (Spring 2006): 21–56.

O'Sullivan, P. S., and C. S. Reynolds, eds. *The Lakes Handbook.* Vol. 2, *Lake Restoration and Rehabilitation.* Maiden, MA: Blackwell Publishing, 2005.

Overstreet, David F. "The Elusive Menominee: Protohistoric Potentials at Peshtigo Point." *Wisconsin Archeologist* 95 (January–June 2014): 50–64.

———. "The Lake Winnebago Phase of Eastern Wisconsin." In *Archaeology at Lac des Puans, The Lake Winnebago Phase: A Classical Horizon Expression of the Oneota Tradition in East-Central Wisconsin*, pp 128–199. David F. Overstreet and Patricia B. Richards, eds. Milwaukee: Great Lakes Archaeological Press, 1992.

———. "McCauley, Astor, and Hanson: Candidates for the Provisional Dandy Phase." *Wisconsin Archeologist* 74 (March–December 1993): 120–196.

———. "The Mero Complex and the Menominee Tribe: Prospects for a Territorial Ethnicity." *Wisconsin Archeologist* 90 (January–December 2009): 179–224.

———. "Oneota Prehistory and History." *Wisconsin Archeologist* 78 (January–December 1997): 251–296.

———. "Overview of Theoretical Frameworks Addressing Models and Probable Correlates of Menominee Protohistory and Prehistory." Great Lakes Archaeological Research Center, Inc., Report of Investigations No. 398. Milwaukee: Great Lakes Archaeological Research Center, 1996.

Parkman, Francis. *La Salle and the Discovery of the Great West.* Boston: Little, Brown, and Company, 1879.

Parmenter, Jon. *The Edge of the Woods: Iroquoia, 1534–1701.* East Lansing: Michigan State University Press, 2010.

Payne, Blanche. *History of Costume: From Ancient Egyptians to the Twentieth Century.* New York: Harper and Row, 1965.

Pendergast, James F. "The Identity of Stadacona and Hochelaga: Comprehension and Conflict." In *Interpretations of Native North American Life: Material Contributions to Ethnohistory*, pp 53–87. Michael S. Nassaney and Eric S. Johnson, eds. Gainesville: University of Florida Press, 2000.

Peterson, Jacqueline. "Prelude to Red River: A Social Portrait of the Great Lakes Métis." *Ethnohistory* 25 (Winter 1978): 41–67.

Peterson, Jacqueline, and Jennifer S. H. Brown, eds. *The New People: Being and Becoming Métis in North America*. Lincoln: University of Nebraska Press, 1985.

Peterson, William J. "Nicolet and the Winnebagos." *Palimpsest* 41 (July 1960): 325–356.

Peyser, Joseph L., ed. and trans. *Jacques Legardeur de Saint-Pierre: Officer, Gentleman, Entrepreneur*. East Lansing: Michigan State University Press and Mackinac State Historical Parks, 1996.

Pluvinel, Antoine de. *L'instruction du roy en l'exercice de monter à cheval*. Paris: Chez Michel Nivelle, 1625.

Poetker, Albert H. "Jean Nicolet." *Michigan Historical Magazine* 18 (Summer–Autumn 1934): 305–315.

Purchas, Samuel, comp. and ed. *Hakluytus Posthumus, or, Purchas His Pilgrimes in Five Bookes*. 4 Vols. London: William Stansby, 1625.

Quaife, Milton M. "The Discovery of Lake Superior." *Wisconsin Magazine of History* 1 (December 1917): 197–199.

———. "The Landing Place of Jean Nicolet." *Wisconsin Magazine of History* 5 (December 1921): 201–202.

Quimby, George I. *Indian Life in the Upper Great Lakes, 11,000 B.C. to A.D. 1800*. Chicago: University of Chicago Press, 1960.

Quinn, David B. "Bellenger, Etienne." In *Dictionary of Canadian Biography*. Vol. 1, pp 87–89. George W. Brown, ed. Toronto: University of Toronto Press, 1966.

Quinn, David B., and Alison M. Quinn. *The English New England Voyages, 1602–1608*. London: Hakluyt Society, 1983.

Radin, Paul. *The Social Organization of the Winnebago Indians, An Interpretation*. Canada Department of Mines, Museum Bulletin No. 10. Ottawa: Government Printing Bureau, 1915.

———. "Winnebago Tales." *Journal of American Folklore* 22 (July–September 1909): 288–313.

———. "The Winnebago Tribe." In *Thirty-Seventh Annual Report of the Bureau of American Ethnology, 1915–1916*, pp 33–560. Washington, DC: Government Printing Office, 1923.

Radisson, Pierre-Esprit. *The Collected Writings*. Vol. 1. Germaine Warkentin, ed. Montreal: McGill-Queens University Press, 2012.

———. *The Explorations of Pierre-Esprit Radisson*. Arthur T. Adams, ed. Minneapolis, MN: Ross and Haines, 1961.

Radstone, Susannah, and Katharine Hodgkin, eds. *Regimes of Memory*. London: Routledge, 2003.

Ray, Arthur J. "The Northern Interior, 1600 to Modern Times." In *The Cambridge History of the Native Peoples of the Americas*. Vol. 1, *North America*, Part 2, pp 259–327. Bruce G. Trigger and Wilcomb E. Washburn, eds. New York: Cambridge University Press, 1996.

———. "Reflections on Fur Trade Social History and Métis History in Canada." *American Indian Culture and Research Journal* 6 (1982): 91–107.

Richards, Patricia B. "I Should Have Dug Red Banks: Winnebago and Menominee Ethnicity, Identity, and Homelands." *Wisconsin Archeologist* 84 (January–December 2003): 243–249.

———. "Winnebago Subsistence: Change and Continuity." *Wisconsin Archeologist* 74 (March–December 1993): 272–289.

Richter, Daniel K. *Ordeal of the Longhouse: The People of the Iroquois League in the Era of European Colonization*. Chapel Hill: University of North Carolina Press, 1992.

———. "War and Culture: The Iroquois Experience." *William and Mary Quarterly* 40 (October 1983): 528–559.

Rioux, Jean de la Croix. "Sagard, Gabriel." In *Dictionary of Canadian Biography*. Vol. 1, pp 590–592. George W. Brown, ed. Toronto: University of Toronto Press, 1966.

Risjord, Norman K. "Jean Nicolet's Search for the South Sea." *Wisconsin Magazine of History* 84 (Spring 2001): 34–43.

Ritch, K. Janet. "Discovery of the Baptismal Certificate of Samuel du Champlain." The Champlain Society. http://champlainsociety.utpjournals.press/findings-trouvailles/discovery-of-the-baptismal-certificate-of-samuel-de-champlain.

Robinson, Charles D. "Legend of the Red Banks." In *Collections of the State Historical Society of Wisconsin*. Vol. 2, pp 491–494. Lyman C. Draper and Reuben G. Thwaites, eds. Madison: State Historical Society of Wisconsin, 1903.

Rodesch, Jerrold C. "Jean Nicolet." *Voyageur: Northeast Wisconsin's Historical Review* 1 (Spring 1984): 4–8.

Romano, Louis G., and Nicholas P. Georgiady. *Exploring Wisconsin*. Chicago: Follett Publishing, 1957.

Ronda, James P. "The Sillery Experiment: A Jesuit-Indian Village in New France, 1637–1663." *American Indian Culture and Research Journal* 3 (1979): 1–18.

Roquebrune, Robert La Roque de. "La Rocque de Roberval, Jean-François de." In *Dictionary of Canadian Biography*. Vol. 1, pp 422–425. George W. Brown, ed. Toronto: University of Toronto Press, 1966.

Rosebrough, Amy L., John Broihahn, Leslie Eisenberg, and Heather Walder. "On the Edge of History: The Hanson Site (47-DR-0185), Town of Clay Banks, Door County, Wisconsin." Unpublished paper, Division of Historic Preservation-Public History, Wisconsin Historical Society, 2012.

Rule, John C. "The Old Regime in America: A Review of Recent Interpretations of France in America." *William and Mary Quarterly* 10 (October 1962): 575–600.

Sagard, Gabriel. *Le Grand Voyage du Pays des Hurons*. Paris: Denys Moreau, 1632.

———. *Histoire du Canada*. Paris: Claude Sonnius, 1636.

———. *The Long Journey to the Country of the Hurons*. George M. Wrong and H. H. Langton, ed. and trans. Toronto: The Champlain Society, 1939.

Sanson, Nicolas. *Amerique Septentrionale*. Paris: Chez l'Auteur et Chez Pierre Mariette, 1650.

Savours, Ann. *The Search for the North West Passage*. New York: St. Martin's Press, 1999.

Schenck, Theresa M. *"The Voice of the Crane Echoes Afar": The Sociopolitical Organization of the Lake Superior Ojibwa, 1640–1855*. New York: Garland, 1997.

Schlesier, Karl H. "Epidemics and Indian Middlemen: Rethinking the Wars of the Iroquois, 1609–1653." *Ethnohistory* 23 (Spring 1976): 129–145.

Schmalz, Peter S. "The Role of the Ojibwa in the Conquest of Southern Ontario, 1650–1701." *Ontario History* 76 (December 1984): 326–351.

Schneider, Seth A. "Oneota Ceramic Production and Exchange: Social, Economic, and Political Interactions in Eastern Wisconsin between A.D. 1050–1400." Ph.D. diss., University of Wisconsin–Milwaukee, 2015.

Schoolcraft, Henry Rowe. *Information Respecting the History, Condition and Prospects of the Indian Tribes of the United States*. Vol. 4. Philadelphia: Lippincott, Grambo and Company, 1854.

———. *Narrative Journal of Travels through the Northwestern Regions of the United States Extending from Detroit Northwest through the Great Chain of American Lakes to the Sources of the Mississippi River in the Year 1820*. Albany: E. E. Hosford, 1821.

Seaver, Kirsten A. "Norumbega and 'Harmonia Mundi' in Sixteenth-Century Cartography." *Imago Mundi* 50 (1998): 34–58.

Seed, Patricia. "Taking Possession and Reading Texts: Establishing the Authority of Overseas Empires." *William and Mary Quarterly* 49 (April 1992): 183–209.

Shannon, Harold T. I. "Green Bay Homecoming." *Wisconsin Magazine of History* 26 (December 1942): 144–152.

Shea, John Gilmary. *Discovery and Exploration of the Mississippi Valley*. New York: Redfield, 1852.

Skinner, Alanson. *Social Life and Ceremonial Bundles of the Menomini Indians*. Anthropological Papers of the American Museum of Natural History. Vol. 13, Part I. New York: American Museum of Natural History, 1915.

Slattery, Brian. "French Claims in North America, 1500–59." *Canadian Historical Review* 59 (June 1978): 139–169.

Smith, Beverley Ann. "Systems of Subsistence and Networks of Exchange in the Terminal Woodland and Early Historic Periods in the Upper Great Lakes." Ph.D. diss., Michigan State University, 1996.

Smith, G. Hubert. *The Explorations of the La Vérendryes in the Northern Plains, 1738–43*. W. Raymond Wood, ed. Lincoln: University of Nebraska Press, 1980.

Spector, Janet D. "Winnebago Indians, 1634–1829: An Archeological and Ethnohistoric Investigation." Ph.D. diss., University of Wisconsin–Madison, 1974.

Speth, Janet M. "The Site Complex at Red Banks (47-BR-4/BR-31), Brown County, Wisconsin, As Seen Through the Collections at the Neville Public Museum." Unpublished Archaeological Reports, Series 2834, File 99-6601, Box 114, Wisconsin Historical Society. Madison, Wisconsin, 2000.

Springer, James W., and Stanley R. Witkowski. "Siouan Historical Linguistics and Oneota Archaeology." In *Oneota Studies*, pp 69–83. Guy E. Gibbon, ed. University of Minnesota Publications in Anthropology No. 1. Minneapolis: University of Minnesota, 1982.

Starkey, Armstrong. *European and Native American Warfare, 1675–1815*. Norman: University of Oklahoma Press, 1998.

Starna, William A., and José A. Brandão. "From the Mohawk-Mahican War to the Beaver Wars: Questioning the Pattern." *Ethnohistory* 51 (Fall 2004): 725–750.

Steckley, John. "The Early Map 'Novvelle France': A Linguistic Analysis." *Ontario Archaeology* 51 (1990): 17–29.

Stevenson, Katherine. "Chronological and Settlement Aspects of the Valley View Site (47 LC 34)." *Wisconsin Archeologist* 75 (September–December 1994): 237–294.

Stiebe, Ronald. *Mystery People of the Cove: A History of the Lake Superior Ouinipegou*. Marquette, MI: Lake Superior Press, 1999.

Sulte, Benjamin. "Etienne Brûlé." In *Proceedings and Transactions of the Royal Society of Canada*, 3rd ser., vol. 1 (1907): 97–126.

———. "Jean Nicolet et la decouverte du Wisconsin, 1634." *Revue Canadienne* 6 (1910): 148–155, 331–342, 409–420.

———. *Mélanges D'Histoire et de Littérature*. Ottawa: Imprimerie Joseph Bureau, 1876.

———. "Le nom de Nicolet." *Bulletin des Recherches Historiques* 7 (January 1901): 21–23.

———. "Notes on Jean Nicolet." *Canadian Antiquarian and Numismatic Journal* 8 (April 1880): 157–164.

———. "Notes on Jean Nicolet." In *Collections of the State Historical Society of Wisconsin*. Vol. 8, pp 188–194. Lyman C. Draper, ed. Madison: David Atwood, 1879.

Tanner, Helen H., ed. *Atlas of Great Lakes Indian History*. Norman: University of Oklahoma Press, 1987.

Tapié, Victor L. *France in the Age of Louis XIII and Richelieu*. D. McN. Lockie, trans. New York: Praeger Publishers, 1975.

Tessier, Albert. "Boullé, Eustache." In *Dictionary of Canadian Biography*. Vol. 1, pp 109–110. George W. Brown, ed. Toronto: University of Toronto Press, 1966.

Theler, James L., and Robert F. Boszhardt. *Twelve Millennia: Archaeology of the Upper Mississippi River Valley*. Iowa City: University of Iowa Press, 2003.

Thwaites, Reuben G., ed., *The Jesuit Relations and Allied Documents*. 73 Vols. Cleveland: Burrows Brothers, 1896–1901.

———. *Wisconsin: The Americanization of a French Settlement*. Boston: Houghton Mifflin Company, 1908.

Tooker, Elisabeth. *An Ethnography of the Huron Indians, 1615–1649*. Syracuse, NY: Syracuse University Press, 1991.

Tortora, Phyllis G., ed. *Fairchild Dictionary of Textiles*. 7th ed. New York: Fairchild Publications, 1996.

Treasure, Geoffrey R. R. *Cardinal Richelieu and the Development of Absolutism*. London: Adam & Charles Black, 1972.

Trigger, Bruce G. *The Children of Aataentsic: A History of the Huron People to 1660*. 2 Vols. Montreal: McGill-Queens University Press, 1976.

———. "The French Presence in Huronia: The Structure of Franco-Huron Relations in the First Half of the Seventeenth Century." *Canadian Historical Review* 49 (June 1968): 107–141.

———. *Natives and Newcomers: Canada's "Heroic Age" Reconsidered.* Kingston: McGill-Queens University Press, 1985.

———. "The Original Iroquoians: Huron, Petun, and Neutral." In *Aboriginal Ontario: Historical Perspectives on the First Nations.* Edward S. Rogers and Donald B. Smith, eds., pp 41–63. Toronto: Dundurn Press, 1994.

Trigger, Bruce G., and James F. Pendergast. "Saint Lawrence Iroquoians." In *Handbook of North American Indians.* Vol. 15, *Northeast,* pp 357–361. Bruce G. Trigger, ed. Washington, DC: Smithsonian Institution, 1978.

Trigger, Bruce G., and William R. Swagerty. "Entertaining Strangers: North America in the Sixteenth Century." In *The Cambridge History of the Native Peoples of the Americas.* Vol. 1. *North America,* Part 1, pp 325–398. Bruce G. Trigger and Wilcomb E. Washburn, eds. New York: Cambridge University Press, 1996.

Trouillot, Michel-Rolph. *Silencing the Past: Power and the Production of History.* Boston: Beacon Press, 1995.

Trudel, Marcel. *An Atlas of New France.* Quebec: Les Presses l'université Laval, 1968.

———. *The Beginnings of New France, 1524–1663.* Patricia Claxton, trans. Toronto: McClelland and Stewart Limited, 1973.

———. "Caën, Emery de." In *Dictionary of Canadian Biography.* Vol. 1, pp 165–172. George W. Brown, ed. Toronto: University of Toronto Press, 1966.

———. "Caën, Guillaume de." In *Dictionary of Canadian Biography.* Vol. 1, pp 159–162. George W. Brown, ed. Toronto: University of Toronto Press, 1966.

———. "Cartier, Jacques." In *Dictionary of Canadian Biography.* Vol. 1, pp 165–172. George W. Brown, ed. Toronto: University of Toronto Press, 1966.

———. "Champlain, Samuel de." In *Dictionary of Canadian Biography.* Vol. 1, pp 186–199. George W. Brown, ed. Toronto: University of Toronto Press, 1966.

———. "The Continent on which Champlain Set Foot in 1603." In *Champlain: The Birth of French America.* Raymonde Litalien and Denis Vaugeois, eds., Käthe Roth, trans., pp 61–62. Toronto: McGill-Queens University Press, 2004.

———. "Jean Nicollet dans le lac Supérieur et non dans le lac Michigan." *Revue d'histoire de l'Amerique française* 34 (September 1980): 183–196.

———. "Letardif, Oliver." In *Dictionary of Canadian Biography.* Vol. 1, p. 473. George W. Brown, ed. Toronto: University of Toronto Press, 1966.

———. "New France, 1524–1713." In *Dictionary of Canadian Biography.* Vol. 1, pp 26–37. George W. Brown, ed. Toronto: University of Toronto Press, 1966.

———. "Noël (Nouel), Jacques." In *Dictionary of Canadian Biography.* Vol. 1, p. 520. George W. Brown, ed. Toronto: University of Toronto Press, 1966.

———. *La Population de Canada en 1666: Recensement reconstitué.* Sillery, Quebec: Septentrion, 1995.

———. "Vignau, Nicolas de." In *Dictionary of Canadian Biography.* Vol. 1, pp 662–663. George W. Brown, ed. Toronto: University of Toronto Press, 1966.

Turgeon, Laurier. "The French in New England before Champlain." In *Champlain: The Birth of French America,* pp 98–112. Raymonde Litalien and Denis Vaugeois, eds., Käthe Roth, trans. Toronto: McGill-Queens University Press, 2004.

Twitchett Denis, and Frederick W. Mote, eds. *The Cambridge History of China.* Vol. 8, Part 2, *The Ming Dynasty, 1368–1644.* Cambridge: Cambridge University Press, 1998.

Vachon, André. "Jolliet, Louis." In *Dictionary of Canadian Biography.* Vol. 1, pp 392–398. George W. Brown, ed. Toronto: University of Toronto Press, 1966.

———. "Marsolet, de Saint-Aignan, Nicolas." In *Dictionary of Canadian Biography.* Vol. 1, pp 493–495. George W. Brown, ed. Toronto: University of Toronto Press, 1966.

Vancouver, George. *A Voyage of Discovery to the North Pacific Ocean and Round the World*. Vol. 3. London: G. G. and J. Robinson, 1798.

Varron, A. "The Origins and Rise of Silk." *Ciba Review* (Basel, Switzerland) 11 (July 1938): 350–353.

Vaugeois, Denis. "Seeking Champlain." *The Beaver* 88 (February–March 2008): 22–35.

Vimont, Barthélemy. *Relation de ce qui s'est passé en la Nouvelle France, en l'année M. DC. XL.* Paris: Sebastian Cramoisy, 1641.

———. *Relation de ce qui s'est passé en la Nouvelle France, en l'année 1642 & 1643.* Paris: Sebastian Cramoisy, 1644.

Waugh, North. *The Cut of Men's Clothes, 1600–1900*. New York: Theater Arts Books, 1964.

Wallace, Anthony F. C. *The Death and Rebirth of the Seneca*. New York: Vintage Books, 1972.

Weibel, Adele C. *Two Thousand Years of Textiles*. New York: Hacker Art Books, 1972.

White, Richard. *The Middle Ground: Indians, Empires, and Republics in the Great Lakes Region, 1650–1815.* Cambridge, United Kingdom: Cambridge University Press, 1991.

Whiteley, Peter M. "Archaeology and Oral Tradition: The Scientific Importance of Dialogue." *American Antiquity* 67 (July 2002): 405–415.

Williams, Glyn. *Voyages of Delusion: The Quest for the Northwest Passage*. New Haven, CN: Yale University Press, 2003.

Williamson, Ron. "'Otinontsiskiaj ondaon' ('The House of Cut-Off Heads'): The History and Archaeology of Northern Iroquoian Trophy Taking." In *The Taking and Displaying of Human Body Parts as Trophies by Amerindians*, pp 190–221. Richard J. Chacon and David H. Dye, eds. New York: Springer, 2007.

Wilson Clifford. "Étienne Brulé and the Great Lakes." *Canadian Geographical Journal* 66 (February 1963): 38–43.

———. "Where Did Nicolet Go?" *Minnesota History* 27 (September 1946): 216–220.

Wilson, Joseph. *French and English Dictionary*. London: Joseph Ogle Robinson, 1833.

Winsor, Justin. *Cartier to Frontenac: Geographical Discovery in the Interior of North America in Its Historical Relations, 1534–1700.* Boston: Houghton, Mifflin and Company, 1894.

Wisconsin Cartographers' Guild. *Wisconsin's Past and Present: A Historical Atlas*. Madison: University of Wisconsin Press, 1998.

Wonderley, Anthony. "Effigy Pipes, Diplomacy, and Myth: Exploring Interaction between St. Lawrence Iroquoians and Eastern Iroquois in New York State." *American Antiquity* 70 (April 2005): 211–240.

Worcester, Donald E., and Thomas F. Schilz. "The Spread of Firearms among the Indians on the Anglo-French Frontiers." *American Indian Quarterly* 8 (Spring 1984): 103–115.

Wrong, George M. *The Conquest of New France: A Chronicle of the Colonial Wars*. New Haven, CT: Yale University Press, 1920.

Wroth, Lawrence C. "An Unknown Champlain Map of 1616." *Imago Mundi* 11 (1954): 85–94.

Wykoff, Larry M. "The Physical Anthropology of the Sand Point Site (20 BG 14)." *Michigan Archaeologist* 27 (January–June 1981): 5–30.

Wyman, Mark. *The Wisconsin Frontier*. Bloomington: Indiana University Press, 1998.

Zeisberger, David. *Zeisberger's Indian Dictionary*. Cambridge, MA: John Wilson and Son, 1887.

Index

Page numbers in *italics* refer to illustrations.